BECOMING DYNAMIC

BECOMING DYNAMIC

Creating and sustaining dynamic organisations

David Jackson

© David Jackson 2000

All rights reserved. No reproduction, copy or transmission of this publication may be made without written permission.

No paragraph of this publication may be reproduced, copied or transmitted save with written permission or in accordance with the provisions of the Copyright, Designs and Patents Act 1988, or under the terms of any licence permitting limited copying issued by the Copyright Licensing Agency, 90 Tottenham Court Road, London W1P 0LP.

Any person who does any unauthorized act in relation to this publication may be liable to criminal prosecution and civil claims for damages.

The author has asserted his right to be identified as the author of this work in accordance with the Copyright, Designs and Patents Act 1988.

First published 2000 by
MACMILLAN PRESS LTD
Houndmills, Basingstoke, Hampshire RG21 6XS
and London
Companies and representatives
throughout the world

ISBN 0–333–73541–2

A catalogue record for this book is available from the British Library.

This book is printed on paper suitable for recycling and made from fully managed and sustained forest sources.

10 9 8 7 6 5 4 3 2 1
09 08 07 06 05 04 03 02 01 00

Designed and formatted by
The Ascenders Partnership, Basingstoke
Illustrations by *Ascenders* and David Woodroffe

Printed and bound in Great Britain by
Creative Print and Design (Wales),
Ebbw Vale

Published in the United States of America by
ST. MARTIN'S PRESS, INC.,
Scholarly and Reference Division,
175 Fifth Avenue, New York, N.Y. 10010

ISBN 0–312–23779–0

To my Chris, Andrew and Claire – my future.
To Janet – my support and inspiration.

Contents

Foreword	ix
Acknowledgements	xi

PART I THE LEARNING JOURNEY — 1

1 The Changing World — 3
- Economic growth — 3
- The shifting economy — 5
- The knowledge era — 9
- Organisation design redefined — 13

2 Dynamic Organisations – The Core Competencies — 16
- Understanding customers — 17
- Excellence in products and processes — 21
- Enabling people — 24
- Leadership, vision and values — 28
- Information plus passion — 30

3 Learning about Dynamic Organisations — 39
- What is organisation design? — 44
- Lessons from other sources — 49

4 It all Begins with Human Nature — 62
- The brain — 63
- Organisational values vs personal values — 65
- Characteristics of human nature — 68

PART II DYNAMIC CHANGE — 81

5 Bounded vs Dynamic Change — 83
- Navigating bounded change — 84
- Bounded change process — 87
- Dynamic change — 93

6	**Building Dynamic Organisations**	98
	Dynamic organisations	98
	Building dynamic organisations – a roadmap	101
7	**Preparing For Change**	104
	Assess the need to change	105
	Capability to change	106
	Building the change team	109
8	**Creating the Framework for Change**	112
	What is vision?	113
	The organisational framework	116
	Organisational processes	124
	Communicating the vision	140
9	**Communiaction**	146
	Change exhibitions	149
	Education and learning	150
	Access to business information	153
	Change projects	154
	Managing connections	155
	Removing barriers	156
10	**Embedding Change**	160
	Business first	163
	Enhance feedback mechanisms	163
	Business modelling	168
	Developing teams	170
	Clarifying purpose and values	172
11	**Values Based Leadership**	173
	Activity not role	174
	Leadership activities	175
12	**Case Study**	187
	Background	187
	A new structure?	190
	The change process	192
13	**Dynamic Organisations**	210
	The primacy of values	211
	Dialogue: The primary process	212
Appendix – Selected Value Statements		216
Notes		224
Index		228

List of Figures

Figure

1.1 World economic growth
1.2 The changing economy
1.3 Rate of adoption of technology
1.4 Economic growth in OECD countries
1.5 Growth of knowledge based industries
1.6 Change in employment by occupation 1996–2006
2.1 Four capabilities of dynamic organisations
2.2 The dimensions of quality
2.3 The butterfly model of listening
2.4 The vicious circle of low pay
3.1 Business and organisation development
3.2 The brain
4.1 Values and the thinking process
4.2 TNT's recognition process
4.3 Layers of cultural complexity
5.1 Bounded vs dynamic change
5.2 Bounded change process
5.3 Pizza Hut (UK) accountability triangle
6.1 The dynamic organisation roadmap
7.1 The causes of change
8.1 Cendant Membership Services Vision
8.2 Two types of vision
8.3 Organisational framework components
8.4 Hoshin Kanri Planning Matrix
8.5 Mitsubishi Heavy Industries – Pentagon campaign
8.6 Linking values and measures
8.7 Values fit matrix

Figure

9.1 Behaviours that block change
10.1 Development parallels
10.2 The impact of perceived fall in quality
10.4 Data and intuition
10.5 The interconnected organisation
10.6 Team alignment process
11.1 Leadership as role and activity
11.2 Enrolling people into a vision
11.3 The Doing–Being link
11.4 Development needs
12.1 Dynamic organisation assessment
12.2 Change map
12.3 Organisational principles
12.4 Change exhibition storyboard
12.5 Change investments
12.6 Alignment of initiatives and staff priorities
12.7 Balanced scorecard
13.1 Human processes of organisation
13.2 Dynamic vs traditional organisations

Foreword

As I was writing *Dynamic Organisations* I was being asked 'But how do you go about building a dynamic organisation?'. The seeds for this book were sown.

In the last five years I have become more convinced that we pay too little attention to the capabilities and needs of the people working in organisations. I dislike intensely the term 'human resources'. Who gets up in the morning and sees a resource staring back in the mirror? The term, used by many as a label of enlightenment, reflects the lack of basic values behind much of the thinking that underpins modern management theory. Yet, behind every great organisation, there are these so called 'human resources' doing great things. They do so because they want to do a good job. Because they value the challenge and association that great organisations provide them. Above all, they do great things because they are trusted and valued.

As an eclectic reader, I was developing a deeper interest in the human brain and how it operates. I began to see parallels between the structure and function of the brain and the workings of organisations. The more I read, the more the associations between nature and organisations became clear. Nature is a wonderful and hugely complex organisation. Rather than mechanics and engineering, why not study what the natural sciences can teach us about organisation? After all, there is a track record of change stretching back millions of years to study. No one knows what nature will throw at us next, despite spending millions on technology. Business is no more predictable than nature so why not use some of her ideas and concepts? That is what this book is about.

In Part I, I will share with you some of the key lessons I have learned about the natural world and change. I do this so that the reader can better understand the simple but powerful concepts that underpin fundamental organisational change. In Part II, I have set out a process of change that translates these ideas into practice, a process that I have used successfully in my consulting work.

One of the keys to nature's success is her ability to learn. I would welcome the opportunity to exchange views and experiences. If you would like to discuss either the ideas or the practice, please contact me via my web site: www.davjac.demon.co.uk

Dave Jackson

Acknowledgements

This book is about my learning. My ability to learn is dependent on the willingness of others to share ideas, argue about concepts and work together. Without their participation, my understanding of organisations would be impoverished.

First thanks go the team behind the Management Today/Unisys Service Excellence Awards. I was involved in setting up the awards in 1994 and have remained an active member of the team ever since. The staff at Unisys who administer the scheme, notably Christine Carroll, Tony Locke, Tony Harrington, and Andrew Fincham have provided me with many challenges. A big thank you must also go to the numerous participants of the awards whose efforts to build great organisations provide many examples and inspiration. These include Triple A Animal Hotel and Care Centre, First Direct, Pizza Hut, Birmingham Midshires Building Society, Bromley Environmental Health and Trading Standards, TNT Express Parcels and Cendant Membership Services.

Whenever I have been pondering over an idea for the book, my first call has been to Lesley Colyer of Avis Europe. Lesley and Avis have given me support, ideas and inspiration beyond the call of duty for which I am very grateful.

Thanks also to the team at Macmillan, notably Stephen Rutt who has cajoled and encouraged, but never threatened me despite missed deadlines. They have worked hard to bring this book to life.

Finally, I must thank my family. Writing a book takes time and I have spent many evenings locked in my study when my three children and my wife have also had calls on my time. On winning Olympic Gold, oarsman Stephen Redgrave instructed people to shoot him if he ever went near a boat again. That is how I feel about starting another book. Good luck to Stephen and his crew at the 2000 Olympic Games!

Part I
The Learning Journey

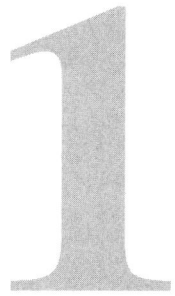

The Changing World

*He that will not apply new remedies must expect new evils:
for time is the greatest innovator.*
FRANCIS BACON

Change is the battlecry for today's managers. Wherever you turn, people are advocating the birth of a new era – the knowledge era. We are assailed on all fronts with views of how the Internet's rapid growth will, according to many, change every aspect of life. Companies are merging and acquiring to gain an advantage as globalisation of markets increases. And as companies grow ever larger and more powerful, governments seek greater power of regulation in the name of consumer protection. At the same time, governments around the world are merging their powers. In all this, one thing that has always been true will continue to be true. The world that we face in the future will be different. It is therefore striking that with all this change, most organisations are still built with stability in mind. They are built on an assumption that tomorrow will be very much like today; that what has worked in the past will continue to work in the future. This complacency lies behind the failure of many organisations. In a dynamic world, organisations need to be dynamic – active partners of change, not just pawns reacting to its turns and twists. This book will examine what I believe is needed to build a successful organisation but I want to begin by looking at some of the changes that are shaping the world we face.

Economic growth

Economic growth continues apace. There are a few blips along the way. The so-called Asian crisis of 1998 created a domino effect around the world. Asia sneezed and the world caught a cold. Or did it? Despite the stock market devaluation, the US economy continued to grow, as did much of Western Europe. The US economy grew by 3.6 per cent, Ireland by a whopping 9.1 per cent. The UK managed to achieve 1.5 per cent growth. The Asia crisis did not affect the whole of Asia. China grew by 7.8 per cent in 1998 and Taiwan by 4.5 per cent. It is true that other countries took a beating. Korea's economy shrank by 8.2 per cent, Thailand by 8.2 per cent and Indonesia by a massive 15.9 per cent. But by 1999, all these economies were beginning to recover.

The short-term tribulations of different countries and regions and our reaction to them hides an important point. The world economy continues to grow inexorably. The long view paints a different picture. Figure 1.1 from the Royal Institute of International Affairs, a UK based think tank suggests that in the next 15 years, world economic output will grow by the same amount that has been achieved in the last 150 years.

Economic growth only comes about as the result of increased demand, greater productivity and continuing innovation. Consider for a moment the changes the world has experienced over the last 150 years; the changes that lie behind that growth. People who are reaching middle age today could not imagine what life was like 150 years ago. What we take for granted was not even dreamt of. Domestic appliances consisted of a broom and wash tub and dolly. Toilets were, for the vast majority, outside. It is the period before the Victorians had built the vast water and sewerage systems upon which today's sanitary arrangements are built. Cars were nowhere to be seen and home entertainment had nothing to do with television or the radio. Communication had just been revolutionised by

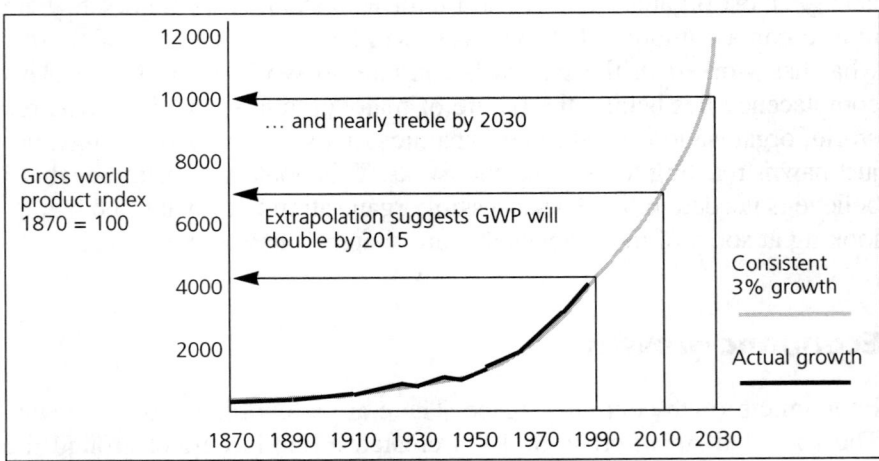

Fig. 1.1 World economic growth[1]

the postal system and the recent introduction of the postage stamp. Life expectancy for the masses was some 20 years less than it is now and healthcare was crude to say the least.

In the subsequent 150 years, change has made enormous differences to our daily lives. How can we begin to envisage what life will be like in 15 years, given the changes that we have experienced over the past 150 years. Now imagine twice that amount of change happening not in two lifetimes but in the period a child takes to reach middle age. That is what is implied in the chart above. Economic growth comes from selling more and selling higher value products and services. Technological innovation and population growth will fuel much of that growth. But this will bring with it changes not just in scale, but in the structure of the economies around the world and the societies in which we live and work. Change of this scale and type cannot be achieved without concomitant change in the nature of the organisations in which we work.

These changes are not something that is going to happen in the future; they have started now. The growth of the so called knowledge economy is here and now. Furthermore, change is about what we do differently today. Organisations that sit idly by will not be passive observers of the changes, they will be annihilated by them. There is no opt-out option for any organisation that wants to be around in the future.

The shifting economy

We are in the midst of a significant shift in the structure of economies and that change is happening faster than previous changes of this magnitude occurred.

Before looking forward it is interesting to look back over the past few hundred years at the different stages of economic development in Europe. Change is not a new phenomenon. We have faced similar situations in the past. Whilst the solutions will undoubtedly be different, history can cast some light on the types of things that may have to change.

In medieval times (1300–1700) economies were dominated by agriculture. Land ownership was the source of economic wealth and power. Applying more labour and rudimentary machines led to increased output. Labour was cheap, expendable and in no position to argue back. Labour was purely a resource that rich landowners exploited, often ruthlessly. The limiting factor to production was land ownership. There was little or no opportunity to climb the social ladder to greater prosperity save the luck of being born into a land owning family. The system of patronage slowly spread land ownership more widely, but it remained the privilege of a tiny minority.

The early industrial era began around 1750 in England. Wealthy men applied their education and capital to the new technology of iron. The factory was founded. The labour mix changed. Much more skilled labour was needed, although the majority of labour was still unskilled or semi-skilled. Some landowners used the wealth they earned from the land to invest in the new technologies and became factory owners. A small number of skilled craftsmen acquired wealth. This 'new money' was still a small minority. Capital to build and equip factories was the limiting factor to production. Organisations were places characterised by bosses who did the thinking issuing orders to workers who worked. This was a reflection of the social structure of the time and a necessary response to dealing with an uneducated workforce. Bosses determined the what, who and how of work to the smallest detail. This period extended up to the last World War. The focus of management was on securing capital and structuring jobs to maximise productivity.

The industrial era continued into the 1950s with basically the same model of operation. There were some changes in its application. Technological developments increased the proportion of skilled labour required and some skilled men invested their earnings in new business ventures and joined the 'new money' set. Some organisations recognised the growing importance of people. Others adapted to the growing concern for social justice, becoming paternalistic in their relationships with employees. There was little or no shift in the distribution of control and work design, which remained firmly in the hands of the managers.

Towards the latter quarter of the twentieth century, commentators were beginning to talk about the information age. The computer formalised the discipline of information management in business. The information spewed out by ever increasing numbers of computers created new opportunities to cut costs and manage the business. As computers were applied to control machines, the nature of work changed. Machine operators no longer needed the physical skills of turning; now they worked with information. The integration of 'islands of automation' both within an organisation and across value chains saw computers replace the people that had acted as links and co-ordinators. The 1980s was the decade of delayering, down sizing and outsourcing. The ability to generate and move information rapidly and accurately was a prerequisite to these trends. Information and the technology that went with it removed much of the traditional work of middle managers. No longer were they needed to collate, interpret and report on performance of their subordinates.

Computers – some said – had the potential to provide senior managers with all the data they needed. Some senior managers failed to grasp the importance of computer technology. Even today, some senior managers have no real understanding of what technology means for the businesses they run. Many of those that adopted the technology overlooked the gap between data and understanding, which cannot be found in computers.

The information age was an intermediate step between the industrial era and the knowledge era. In the knowledge era the primary generator of wealth is the intellectual capability of people. Their ideas, application and commitment are what count. The constraint on production is the ability of an organisation to get people to participate in the generation, sharing and application of what they know. The constraint is management. There are almost no barriers to entry for new competitors other than knowledge and courage. The investments needed to start a business based on what someone knows are small. Capital availability exceeds the flow of ideas. Many new knowledge based businesses are created when people in large organisations recognise that they can do what they currently do without the support and constraints that employment entails.

The changes involved in each shift are additive, not replacement.

Era	Source of Wealth	Constraint on Production	Role of People	Management Focus
Agricultural	Land ownership	Land	Unskilled workhorse	None
Industrial	Factory	Capital	Skilled and unskilled labour	Productivity of capital
Knowledge	Ideas	Creativity and innovation	Co-producers	Maximising people's contribution

Figure 1.2 The changing economy

Agriculture remained throughout the industrial era, and will continue to remain active and vital into the foreseeable future. What changes in the economy is the mix: the proportion of time and effort applied to each element of the economy. Each shift is accompanied by an increase in productivity of the previously dominant activity. As the knowledge era develops and matures there will be an ongoing need for industry and agriculture. Companies operating in these areas will have to continue to improve quality and productivity to remain competitive. Old techniques and equipment give way to new ideas and technology, but the essential elements of the activity still have to be carried out. The birth of the knowledge era does not spell the death of industry, merely a shift in its relative importance.

Those that succeed as the shift from one era to the next is acted out are those that invest in the new sources of wealth and find ways of managing the constraining factor most effectively. They embrace the new ideas and technologies and seek ways to exploit them. These changes often require the slaughter of sacred cows. New business opportunities and ways of doing things often involve threats to existing products and ways of doing business that have formed the basis of past success. Failing to recognise the need to change however is often a greater source of danger. It requires courage and close attention to the outside world; a point I will address in greater detail later.

These changes are being driven by ever more sophisticated technologies. Information technology has driven much of the change of the past thirty years. Developments continually emerge. Key has been the development of the Internet. Whilst this is a relatively young technology, the speed with which it has been adopted is staggering. It was over 70 years between the invention of the telephone and the landmark of 50 million users. The Internet reached the same landmark in a mere four years.

The Internet provides a global reach for any organisation and a global market for those dealing in information or knowledge based products and services. The changes do not end here.

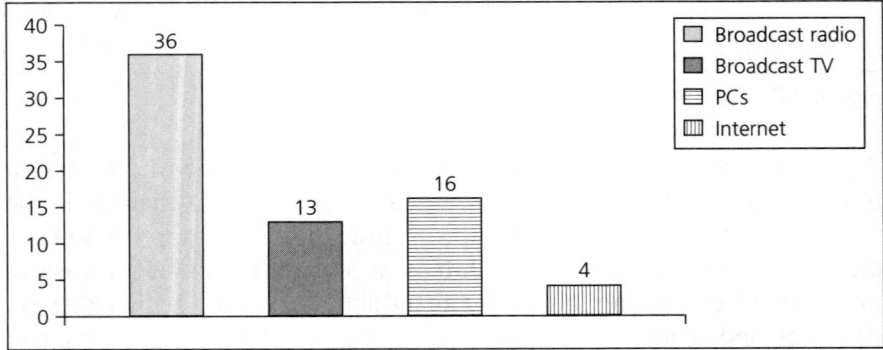

Fig. 1.3 Rate of adoption of technology

The knowledge era

The shift to the knowledge economy is well under way. More and more people are employed in work that has little or nothing to do with manufacture. Be it people working in pure service businesses like retail, leisure and financial services or those involved in the non-manufacturing aspects of manufacturing companies, fewer people make things. There are two important trends in operation. First, the world economy continues to grow. Figures produced by the Organisation for Economic Co-operation and Development (OECD) show that the major economies of the world grew by an average of 2.3 per cent in the 1990s, slightly weaker than the 3.8 per cent growth experienced in the 1970s and 3.0 per cent in the 1980s.[2] Despite the blip in the Asian economies, the trend is inexorably upwards, pushing us along the curve shown in Figure 1.1.

In this growing economy, there is a second important trend. The rate of growth of knowledge based industries outstrips that of the total business sector.

Some countries are moving faster towards a knowledge based economy than others as the Figure 1.5 shows.

The DTI calculate that the knowledge based industries' share of UK output has grown from 18 per cent in 1980 to 23 per cent in 1996.[5] The

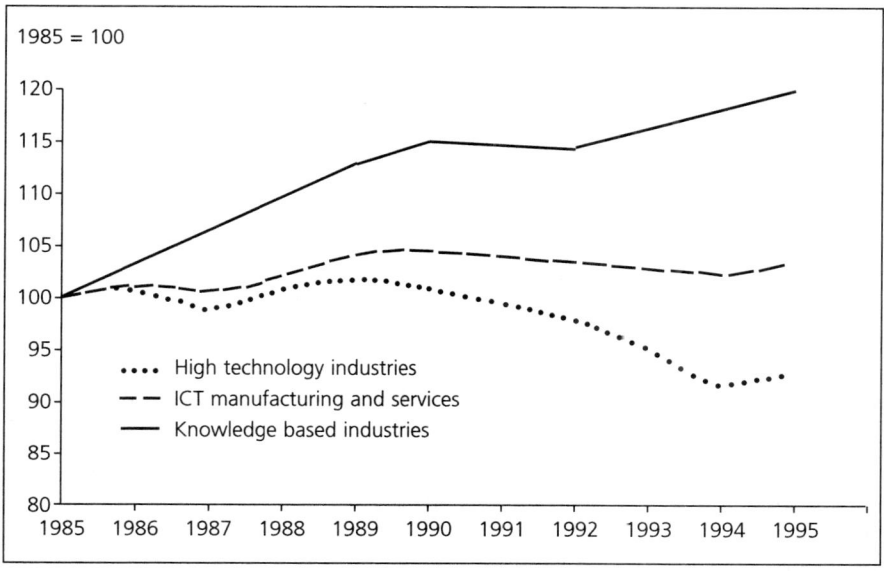

Figure 1.4 Economic growth in OECD countries[3]

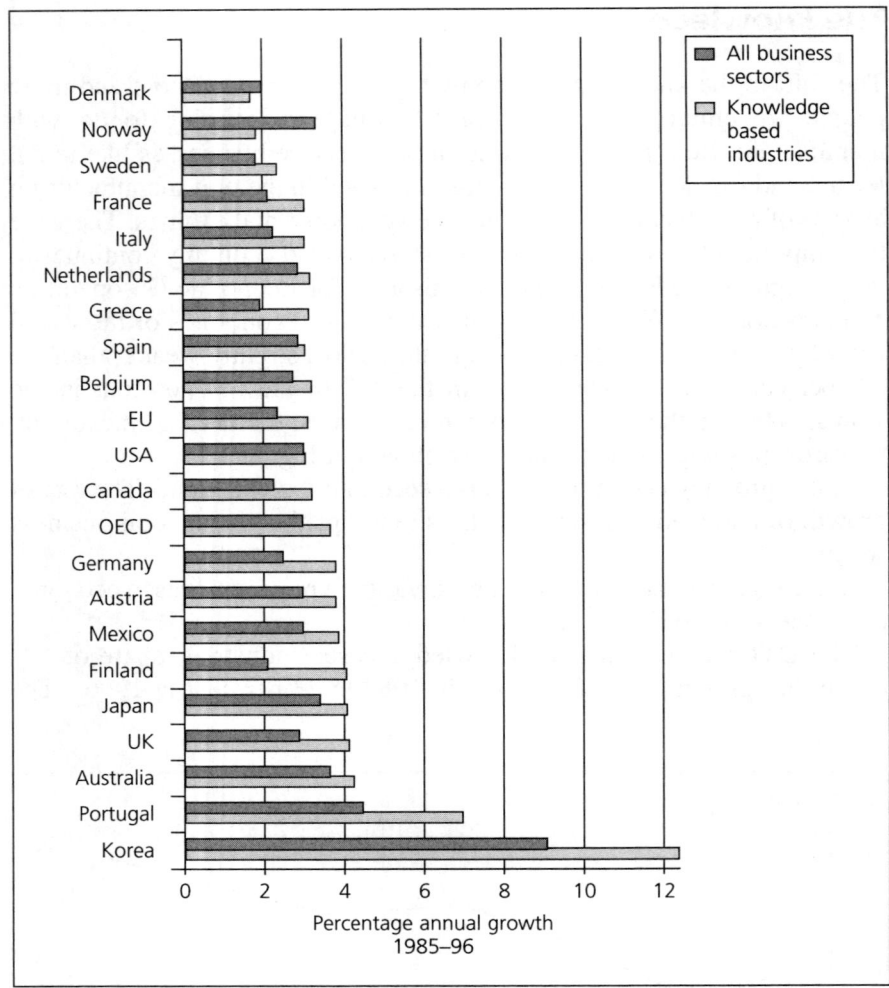

Fig. 1.5 Growth of knowledge based industries[4]

US is an even more knowledge intense economy. This economic shift is reflected in a change in the mix of investment between manufacturing and service related activity. Service R&D has risen dramatically in the last 20 years. In the UK in 1980, service related R&D accounted for 5.5 per cent of the total. By 1997, that had grown to 19.1 per cent. The largest shifts have been experienced by Canada (15.2 per cent to 37.4 per cent), Norway (15.5 per cent to 32.4 per cent) and Australia (11.1 per cent to 28.5 per cent).

Despite this extensive growth in service based R&D, it still takes up a smaller percentage of GDP than manufacturing R&D. This is essentially because most service-based innovations are not R&D driven but driven by the ideas and actions of people at work. New products are subject to extensive product development processes, many of which begin in a science laboratory several steps removed from the consumer. As the product idea develops further research and development investment is expended to refine, test and bring the product to market. There have been significant efforts to shorten this process, but the major stages often apply. Additionally, new products are more complex and require greater levels of investment in R&D to bring them to market. The improvement in the price/performance of computer processor chips is well known. Each improvement requires an ever-greater investment in R&D to deliver the increase in performance. Early developments were impressive but today higher performance is only achieved by pushing the boundaries of physical science towards its molecular limit. That needs more brainpower, equipment that is more sophisticated and therefore more money. Despite the enormous developments to date computing technology will continue to move along the price/performance curve; we are still some distance from the absolute limits of physics as applied to IT. And already people are begin to conceive of entirely new paradigms of computing using biotechnologies.

Service and knowledge based industries present a different picture. New services are developed much more rapidly based on the needs and expectations of customers. Product and process innovations are much less likely to involve formal R&D. They are more typically the result of teams of people close to the customer working together. New ideas are tested in the market, not in the lab. There is a cost associated with this type of development, but it is much more difficult to identify the boundary between delivery and development when the roles and activities merge.

The changing employment pattern clearly shows a shift to knowledge based work as figures from the UK's Department of Trade and Industry show (Figure 1.6).

We can also see the growth of the knowledge era reflected in infrastructure investments. In OECD countries in 1995, investment in the physical infrastructure, including machinery and equipment represented 20.1 per cent of GDP compared with 7.9 per cent in knowledge based infrastructure. Between 1985 and 1995, both grew at about the same rate, 2.7 per cent for physical infrastructure and 2.8 per cent for knowledge infrastructure investments. These figures however hide a variety of

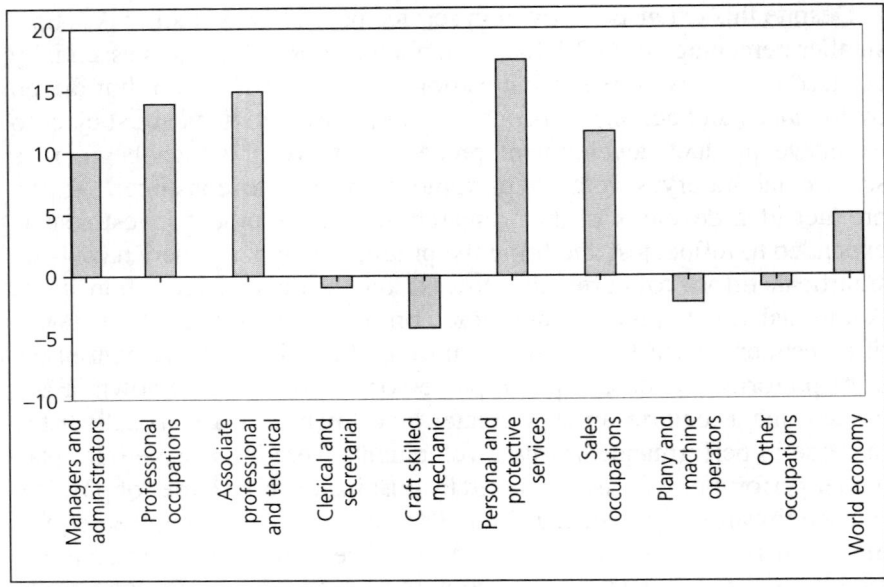

Fig. 1.6 Change in employment by occupation 1996–2006[5]

national results. In Japan, Germany, The Netherlands, Belgium and the UK the average annual growth in physical infrastructure investments exceeded that of knowledge infrastructure. In the US, France, Norway, Sweden and Finland however the reverse was true. These countries have shifted the emphasis to favouring investments in their knowledge infrastructures. Whilst government spending is an important aspect of this, the actions of private companies accounts for much. Are some countries and companies positioning themselves to better exploit the knowledge economy? Time alone will tell. It is no coincidence that the countries where the growth of knowledge infrastructure investment has exceeded investment in physical infrastructure include those recognised for their manufacturing prowess. In the information technology industry it is said that companies that lead in the exploitation of one form of computing rarely go on to lead the field in the next. IBM led the mainframe market, but fell behind in the race for personal computers. Can the same be true of countries? There is evidence that companies can 'reinvent' themselves but it is a difficult task requiring strong, clear leadership. How many countries are blessed with the necessary politicians?

Organisation design redefined

The shift to the knowledge era differs from other shifts in one important way. When we moved from the agricultural to the industrial era, machines became the locus of activity. Information processing machines were involved in the shift to the information age; computers had to be mastered. The shift into the knowledge era requires a mastery of the organisation of people, and that is not new. Relationships between people have been the subject of study for hundreds of years, and everybody has a lifetime of experience of it. It is however a subject that too many companies have neglected.

As service industries become a larger and therefore more important part of the economy, the ability of organisations to generate and exploit ideas will grow. Successful economies will require successful leadership of their organisations. This is why the most important 'technology' of the knowledge era is organisation design. Leadership and its role in the creation of organisations designed for people is an issue of national importance.

Changes will be needed in the skills we will need to apply. The knowledge era requires a rethink of our management concepts and ideas and we will need to develop new approaches and technologies to improve the new constraint on performance – people's involvement and ability. The danger is that we forget that we also have to manage the other aspects of business. Productivity, cost, marketing and distribution will still have to be done, and done well to survive. The single most important message in this book is that organisations have to design their activities in these different areas to work together. Far too many companies have struggled because what they do in one activity compromises what they do elsewhere.

It is a truism that organisations are perfectly designed to achieve the results they do. With the previous focus on production and operations and the heritage of scientific management, it is not surprising that the mechanistic aspects of business have taken precedence in our thinking. Companies have learned how to design and optimise value chains. Strategies have been designed, planned and implemented, just like we build new products. Financial management systems have been improved and new approaches to marketing products introduced.

Many organisations, though perhaps not enough, have worked hard to improve the motivation and skills of the people they employ. They have invested in training and development and sought ways to help people take greater responsibility for aspects of their working life. Some organisations have expressed the values that they want to see their organisations reflect. For some, this has been another activity to tick off the checklist of management fads tried. Some have driven this beyond the poster on the wall and sought to change the attitudes and behaviour of their people. A small percentage have invested in the development of the leadership capacity of their organisations.

All of these approaches have value; they are necessary activities. But alone they fail to realise the potential of the organisation and its people. They are not wrong but they are incomplete answers, none of which will work if they are implemented in isolation. They may deliver short-term benefits, but they cannot deliver the sustainable advantage that organisations seek. What is at fault is our belief of what organisation design is about. If it is true that organisations are perfectly designed to achieve the results they do, then it is also true to say that to achieve different results, organisations have to be designed differently. The knowledge era will require different results.

Organisation design is not about changing structures, or redesigning processes, although these are parts of it. Nor is it about changing cultures, although that is a much more fundamental part of the real work of organisation design. The real of work of organisation design is about creating an organisation around a strong sense of shared purpose and values that guide all the organisation's activities thus creating a cohesion and consistency without excessive bureaucracy. It requires that purpose and values be reflected in all the organisation's activities and people. As such, purpose and values are not some statement of a future desire, but a living reflection of the organisation. It is about creating an organisation (and not just a business) that works by design.

The concept of holistic organisation design sounds simple and as a concept it is simple. In practice however it is highly complex for two reasons. First, the sheer number of components that make up an organisation and their interrelationships are immense. Managing this complexity is a logistical nightmare beyond the wit of any one person.

Secondly, the central element in any organisation is people and they defy logic and common sense. We are all individuals and want to be treated as such; we bring to work our aspirations, our problems and our opinions. We want to have our say. Now overlay the unpredictable and irrational nature of people with the complexity involved in the number of components in an organisation and you are presented with a task that seems impossible. As the needs of the individual take on greater importance in the knowledge era the difficulty of the task increases requiring a fundamentally different approach to organisation design and change.

I believe that organisation design is to the knowledge era what the steam engine was to the industrial revolution and the computer was to the information age. Excellence in organisation design, in the full sense of the phrase, is the essential skill for success in the knowledge era. Recognising organisation design as a process, not an outcome shifts our perspective. There will never be one form of organisation that is right for all situations. The key is not to find the right organisation but rather to master the art of organisation design. This is an essential competence in an era where change is a part of everyday life.

2 Dynamic Organisations – the Core Competencies

*Business is a lot like tennis –
those who don't serve end up losing.*
ANONYMOUS

Since writing *Dynamic Organisations* I have had much time to reflect on whether the basic premise that an organisation needs to succeed at four capabilities (understanding customers, product and process excellence, enabling people and leadership, vision and values) was right or wrong. I have continued to observe successful organisations and have met a great many more that do not make the grade. I have looked at other research in this area. All of this leads me to believe that these four interconnected capabilities are still valid. For those who have not read *Dynamic Organisations*, this chapter will review the important points in each area and examine some of the changes that I perceive are taking place.

Fig. 2.1 Four capabilities of dynamic organisations

Understanding customers

Understanding customers is a simple concept that is enormously difficult to do well. Each customer is an individual, and as such is a collection of experiences, moods, prejudices, aspirations and expectations. Unfortunately, these characteristics change according to what side of bed we got out of, the phase of the moon or what our best friend said to us an hour ago. As customers, we are unpredictable, irrational and emotional. Having said that, there is no choice but to actively build both a more complete understanding of our customers and an organisation that can deal with their individual needs and aspirations.

Understanding customers is simply about constantly seeking the answers to three questions:

1. Who are our customers?
2. What are the needs and aspirations of these customers?
3. How are we doing in meeting those needs?

Many organisations occasionally seek answers to at least two of these questions through the annual 'do you love us survey'. In an environment where needs and choice are changing so quickly, can you really afford to wait a year before you get to know about what your customers want, or how your competitors are outperforming you? A dynamic organisation is one where listening to customers is a continuous, not a discontinuous activity.

Who are our customers?

Many businesses have failed by trying to be all things to all people. The corollary of this, is that organisations choose what products and services to offer and which customers to serve. Whilst there is plenty of evidence of the former, there are fewer examples of the latter. Most organisations' customer bases are an accident of history, not a result of intellectual thought. Choosing customers is a complex decision that interacts with decisions about the products and services that the organisation offers. Often, these two are in conflict, hence the popularity of the discussion about being product focused versus customer focused. But the act of choosing which customers to serve is not a one way street. Customers also exercise the choice of which suppliers to buy from.

What do customers want?

The second question is the one that any organisation has to answer. Many businesses start when entrepreneurs spot a need that is not being addressed, or is being badly addressed. Many come from within the industry and have often tried to get their existing organisation to adopt the new product or approach.

Quality from the customer's perspective has two dimensions, as shown in Figure 2.2.

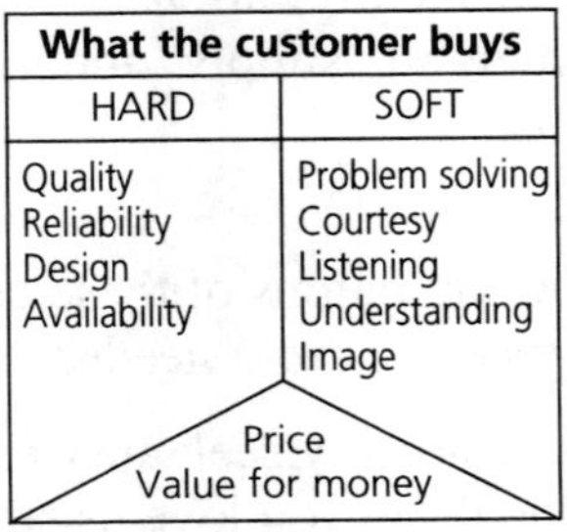

What the customer buys	
HARD	SOFT
Quality Reliability Design Availability	Problem solving Courtesy Listening Understanding Image
Price	
Value for money	

Fig. 2.2 The dimensions of quality

Much emphasis has been placed on developing the hard aspects of quality, which relate to aspects of the product or service. Indeed it is in this area that TQM has its roots. Led by the Japanese, who themselves were taught by Americans, the world as a whole has made significant strides in designing and building quality products. But in a competitive market, quality of the core product or service is nothing more than table stakes. When a product can be studied and copied in months, the sustainability of product based advantage is usually limited. That is not to imply that organisations should not seek to develop their products; they must. They must not assume that is all they need. Customers demand more than products. We want to be recognised as individuals. If we have a problem, we want to be listened to, to have our problem recognised and solved. We assume a level of knowledge exists in the organisation at least equal to what we have told any part of it.

For organisations that offer complex products or services, the implications of the above model are greater. Let me illustrate by way of an example. If you hire a lawyer for advice (the core product), you have no way of really assessing the quality of that advice unless you are trained in law yourself or if something goes dramatically wrong. You can however assess the soft aspects of quality. You will have a perception of the effort the lawyer has put into understanding your problem, and the degree with which she has empathised with you. You can assess how friendly she has been, the quality of the facilities and the way she has explained the bill. These experiences, and here logic flies right out of the window, will significantly influence your assessment of the total experience. You will perceive her as a good lawyer not because of the quality of the advice, but due to the care she has taken with her customer. And of course you will go and tell people of your experience and recommend your lawyer to others.

There is another important point to be drawn from that simple diagram. Excelling at the hard aspects of quality, with the exception of design, is effected essentially through processes. Product quality, reliability and availability are process-based attributes. The soft aspects of quality however all rely on people. They are about relationships, respect for the individual, and shared learning. They are rooted in the values and culture of the organisation. It is one of the main reasons that customer focus is an organisation wide issue, with people, culture, values, vision, and leadership at its core. It is why this book focuses on organisation design as the route to success.

How are we doing?

The third question in understanding customers is all about performance – from the customer's perspective. The dynamic organisation uses a range of techniques to constantly test how it is doing in meeting customers needs. No one technique is right. Surveys, comment cards, focus groups and customer panels all have their role to play. There are however two golden rules. The first is that whatever research is undertaken, it is linked to action in some way. The second is that listening to customers, monitoring performance, has to be a continuous activity that spans the organisation.

Figure 2.3 is useful for understanding the range of opportunities for listening to customers. The three areas of measurement relate to three areas for action.

Every organisation has a number of events: the delivery of a product, dealing with a telephone enquiry, serving a meal. A sample of these are monitored against the factors customers have determined to be important. The results of this listening is fed to the functions responsible for the event. It is important that the data fed back is complete and rapid. This allows the function or team to do two things. First, they can contact the customer with an appropriate message. Birmingham Midshires Building Society

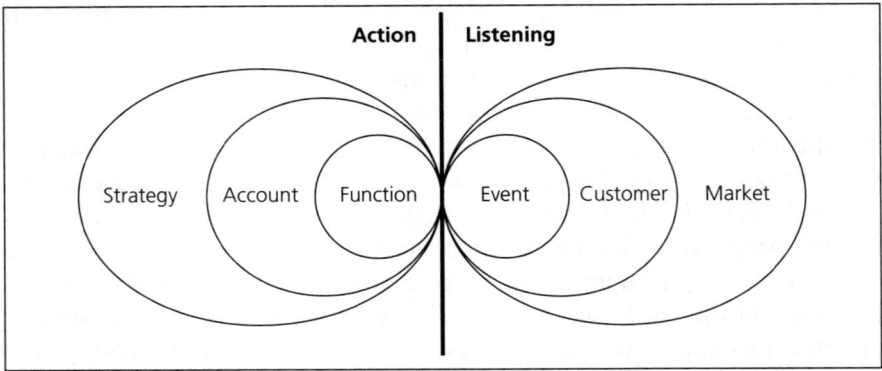

Fig. 2.3 The butterfly model of listening

issues an apology or a thank you for every survey or comment card returned by customers. Secondly, the data give the organisation information on which further improvements can be built. Teaching people the statistical tools of quality can improve their ability to understand and exploit this data. Using event driven mechanisms for tracking satisfaction is one of the reasons Avis Europe improved productivity for 15 consecutive years.

The customer element of the model refers to the collective perceptions of an individual customer. This is of course more relevant to organisations where the overall relationship between customer and supplier is important. The customer's perception of a supplier is of course more than the sum of the events, although these will influence the overall perception. Other factors like word of mouth, press coverage, sponsorship and key individuals will impact this. For large business to business relationships, this image is multi-faceted due to the myriad of contacts.

The final element of the butterfly model links the perceptions of the marketplace with direction. In my opinion, marketplace has to extend beyond the customer base. It should address lost customers, customers of competitors and people who do not buy that type of product or service. This mechanism seeks to tap into the trends of the market; what's new, what's loosing popularity, what are the new issues out there? This element of listening should also identify what the key buying criteria are and how the organisation is performing against its competitors using these criteria. The information gathered in this element of the model is used to inform product development, basic research, and improvements in the effectiveness of the organisation.

The cycles of three elements should be tied into the rhythm of the organisation. Event sensing will have a much faster cycle than the marketplace sensing. Whilst some of the mechanisms will be structured, planned events, it is important not to constrain the ongoing collection of data.

The emphasis on the soft aspects of quality is growing.

Relationships are important in marketing because they are the basis of retention. They are founded in satisfaction that has both hard and soft elements. The latter group is people related, and strongly influenced by a person's values and beliefs. Our values and beliefs frame our thoughts and actions, often subconsciously. People and organisations with similar values and beliefs place importance on similar things; they think the same way. Understanding these values and beliefs is therefore important when considering long-term relationships. The likelihood is that two organisations sharing similar values will be better able to sustain a relationship.

The relationship between culture and success has been extensively studied, notably by Professors Kotter and Heskett at Harvard Business School. In a long-term study they have proved a link between culture and financial performance. They identified that those organisations with a culture that is strongly shared across the organisation AND is in line with the needs and expectations of the market generate superior financial returns. The 'right' culture is profitable. These organisations, often subconsciously, have built a culture that suits the way customers want to do business. They project in their brand and corporate identity, in the products and services they offer, and in the way the world perceives them. This requires a greater emphasis on the role of values when building a dynamic organisation.

Excellence in products and processes

Organisations are also collections of processes. The effectiveness with which they turn their understanding of customers into new products, and improvements in the way the organisation conducts its business is critical to the dynamic organisation. As already pointed out, having the right products is the foundation of quality, and being easy to do business with is also a significant factor in a customer's perception of satisfaction. Both are factors underpinned by the quality of processes and systems.

Continuously adapting to the changing needs of customers underpins the dynamic organisation. But customers do not always know what they want because they do not know what is possible. Improvement, be it of products or processes is therefore a constant balancing of innovation and customer understanding. There is of course a connection between the two. The more points of data available, the better able one is to spot patterns. There is a biological equivalent. A neurone in the brain can receive inputs from between 10000 and 100000 other neurones, building a complex pattern of activity. Alzheimer's disease restricts this connectivity, with devastating effects. What is key to organisations therefore is how they can tap into the rich vein of information and foster the connectivity of ideas that is so essential for innovation.

Having the whole organisation working on improvements brings its own difficulties. There is a real danger that improvements in one area might actually be detrimental to other activities in the organisation. Being able to see the big picture is therefore invaluable. Equally, sharing improvements saves time and effort. Improvements in a process designed for budgeting purchase spending might be equally valid for budgeting in other aspects of the business.

We all need to operate processes that focus on serving customers. We all need levels of productivity that match or better our competitors. We need to be innovative in how we conceive, sell, deliver, and account for the products and services we offer. I strongly advocate efforts to simplify, speed up, remove, and most of all humanise the processes we work with. Bureaucracy is any activity that does not add value to the customer or is not required law. Included in the first element are those essential support activities, notably those about leading and developing people and partners. Too few organisations actively consider what they can stop doing. This is particularly important as we change the nature of managing organisations. What we have done in the past is not always an accurate pointer to what we should do now. Much of what we do is rooted in custom and practice and old rulebooks, rather than in the needs of customers.

Process improvement should be a continuous, not a discontinuous activity. An activity carried out by everybody, everyday; not a special programme. Re-engineering therefore is a fundamental and everyday tool of performance improvement not an expensive, consultant led exercise. This is the approach adopted by Avis Europe. Their People's Ideas, Profitable Solutions process is embedded as part of their organisation. Everyone participates, anyone can initiate a PIPS, and the learning they generate is shared across the organisation. Using such simple mechanisms, Avis Europe have experienced 16 years of productivity growth, far exceeding the results of any BPR project. Like the Japanese, they have learned that cost reduction is not about dieting, it is about healthy eating. It is something that is done all of the time.

Dynamic Organisations – The Core Competencies

The need to improve processes has always existed. For many organisations, the need is more urgent now as they try to operate in a modern, competitive environment using processes, tools and beliefs designed for the 1930s. This is as much a reflection of the lost opportunity of continuous improvement as it is a case for the discontinuous business process re-engineering some advocate. If organisations had not rested on their laurels, few would need revolutionary change.

Let me give you an example of the type of process improvement we need more of. In an IT organisation customers and staff were dissatisfied and unhappy with the way they handled administration in the UK. The company's management held back from the normal 'we think and decide you do' approach to change. Instead they gave responsibility for improvement to the people themselves.

The people started the task of changing their work by looking at why they existed. They talked to customers, to the sales people, to finance; indeed to anyone who had an interest in what they did. From this understanding they developed a simple statement of purpose: *'To turn orders into payable invoices'*. By doing this well, customer administration contributes to customer satisfaction, reduces arrears and makes other people's jobs easier. Now that may seem very simple, but try the exercise for yourself. Think of a short, simple statement that sums up why you and your group do the work you do. Now try and get common agreement to it.

This simple statement of purpose was more than a slogan. It was the focal point for everything they did. Around that single statement, the staff identified the work that was core to fulfilling that purpose. This was where the key process changes happened. As a result, five disparate administration groups combined into one, with each administrator responsible for all activities of a customer, or group of customers. The changes delivered the sought for improvement in customer satisfaction. In addition, the number of staff reduced from 86 to 53, managers cut from 12 to four and office space reduced by 600m^2. The key thing to remember is that the people themselves did all the design. Managers gave them their head and they delivered.

They succeeded not only because of the new-found freedom to express their creativity and intelligence, but because they could design the process they needed. With a common goal and the motivation that comes from trust and responsibility, people usually exceed your expectations of them. People really do it all.

Training people in the techniques and tools of improvement is therefore essential. If people do not have the skills to carry out the research, analysis and design, and implement the solutions, continuous improvement just will not happen. The seven basic quality tools, process mapping and competence mapping form the core of the curriculum. As important however is to coach people in how to deal with the dynamics and conflict that team working inevitably brings.

With the emphasis on the quality of the overall experience growing, it is easy to forget that product and process excellence remain as the foundations of customer satisfaction. As soon as their integrity is compromised, customers will leave. There is a great danger that in their quest to improve the soft aspects of quality, organisations will take their eye off the product and process ball. They do so at their peril. Dynamic organisations also recognise the importance of providing product and process excellence at the lowest cost. They place a much greater emphasis on continuous improvement led by staff rather than management led re-engineering initiatives. This focus on involving everybody in improving quality and reducing cost is one of the reasons that Avis Europe has been the most profitable car rental company in Europe for the past 30 years. Their corporate beliefs and values include the following statement: *'We regard efficiency as central to our whole business philosophy and we continuously search for means to reduce the cost of delivering a better product to the customer.'* Like Avis' other values, continuous improvement is translated into organisational processes and leadership activities.[6]

Enabling people

Most organisations profess that 'in our business, the customer is king' and 'people are our greatest asset'. In many organisations, however, the propaganda does not stand up to scrutiny. The dynamic organisation derives its impetus from the outside world, notably its customers. Personal relationships are all important. I may transact with an organisation, or even a machine, but I build relationships with people. Personal relationships are not an option in most businesses. One study into buying behaviours and drivers of customer satisfaction I was involved with unearthed the following comment from a person who spent a six figure sum annually with a particular supplier: *'The reason I buy from a supplier probably boils down to my perception of one or two people'*.

Customers are people, not statistics in a market survey. We demand quality, we appreciate courtesy, we feel better when people are nice to us and we like to feel recognised, if not important. We are fed up with being treated like a number or just another body on the conveyor belt of business. We are also irrational. We will choose to buy elsewhere because people are nice to us; indeed we will often pay for the privilege. Even in the hard-nosed world of big business, we will find reasons to buy from people we like. We might justify our decisions logically, but emotions guide the logic we apply. Try factoring that into a business model; you can't. People who like people however can. Their empathy, tact, intuition and patience can resolve most awkward situations; if they are allowed to.

Our ability to both deliver the improved value customers will demand from us and increase productivity to meet global competition cannot be done without the active support of our people. This will require us to ditch the Taylorist basis on which people have been managed for most of this century. We have to start now to build organisations where satisfied people work together to satisfy customers. Fine words, but what do they really mean.

In January 1996, Adair Turner, then Chairman of the Confederation of British Industry, hit headline news by claiming that economic growth was only sustainable if workers (his term, not mine) were given a fair reward for their efforts. That such an idea should be newsworthy in the first place says something about the political and economic environment of the UK in the last decade of the twentieth century. It certainly is not a new idea. Indeed, there is much to suggest that leading companies already put this idea into practice. Many organisations claim they cannot afford high pay, but fail to see the correlation between higher pay, satisfied customers and greater volumes of business. But whilst the evidence may point that way, few seem able to break the vicious circle which begins and ends with low pay. Low pay leads to discontent, which in turn increases staff turnover. This turnover depletes the skillbase of the organisation, which impacts customer satisfaction and profitability. Low profits squeezes the cash available for pay increases, and the cycle begins again.

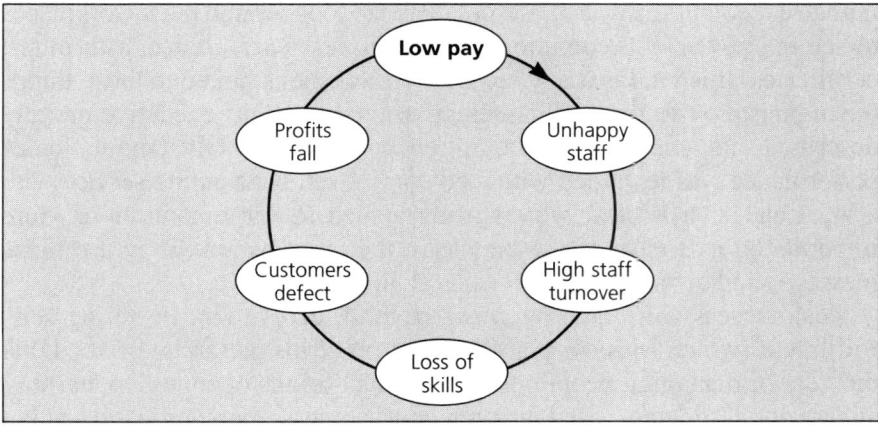

Fig. 2.4 The vicious circle of low pay

Turnover of people inflicts a much more infectious, gnawing damage on an organisation than simply losing skills. Regaining those skills incurs a cost of recruitment, training costs and a cost associated with the effect of the learning curve. But in many roles, there is a more subtle cost: the cost of the lost customer relationship. I recall a conversation with a customer of a computer supplier. He was truly annoyed at yet another change of his account manager, the result of the latest of a seemingly continuous cycle of reorganisations. He made two points. The first was the cost to him of a change of account manager. He believed it took at least four months to get the new person to meet the key individuals in his organisation and to get up to speed with their issues, culture and practices. Secondly, a truly productive relationship required a degree of trust, something that is personal and cannot be built instantly. Customer focus means just that and it starts with designing the organisation with the customer's perspective at the fore.

Recognition is a greatly underused tool in the armoury of motivation. Recognition is simply the act of publicly highlighting, and therefore encouraging, the skills, knowledge and behaviours that make a difference. All organisations have their heroes and role models; the people others in the organisation look up to and seek to emulate. Unfortunately, many of these are operating in the old paradigm. Managers have to determine the new behaviours they want to foster and, through visible praise, sponsorship and promotion, build a new cadre of heroes.

This does not have to be a high powered, bureaucratic process, indeed that suggests a level of management involvement that is unhealthy.

To be effective, recognition has to be visible, quick, sincere and earned. Everyone in the organisation should have the opportunity, and power, to initiate a recognition award. You only have to look around most workplaces to see the power of recognition. Walls and desks are littered with mugs, certificates. It is vital that any recognition scheme is linked to those things the organisation values and is seeking to promote. One executive proudly described his company's recognition programme. Outstanding sales performance was rewarded with a colour TV set, outstanding service with a lapel badge. It is clear what is truly valued in that organisation. More importantly, it is clear to the people in the organisation. They see those messages and act accordingly – sales at any cost.

Real success will come by going beyond recognition. Fostering self-fulfilment (which Maslow placed at the top of his hierarchy of needs) is the goal of managing people. Self-fulfilment brings openness to learning and an outward focus based on inner confidence – a personification of the organisations we all seek. Recognition becomes more important in a world where front-line people have greater responsibilities. The 'E' word – empowerment – is increasingly popular in business circles and for organisations seeking to improve customer satisfaction, the rewards are significant. The bottom line of empowerment is just that – the bottom line. Lesley Colyer of Avis Europe explains why: '... customer satisfaction and retention is maximised when we do the job right first time and when we effectively resolve complaints. So the business case for implementing employee empowerment was very clear. It was one of the key processes to increasing customer satisfaction'. It is of course obvious. If you have a problem, you want it resolved there and then. At that point in time, your focus is on getting the problem fixed – for your own convenience. The longer the problem goes unresolved, the more it festers. An irritating delay becomes a major organisational failure. Problems grow with time and the threshold for a satisfactory solution also increases. It is not too long before all hope is lost. You vow never to be a customer of theirs again, and take any opportunity to explain your experience. Any process of handling complaints has a cost associated with it. The longer the process goes on, the greater the cost.

Empowerment removes the need for much of the control element performed by middle managers. It minimises the need for costly and constraining procedure manuals and demands the simplification of the rules, which of itself removes swathes of costly bureaucracy. Image and loyalty also improve. An employee who has all the answers and the freedom to do what is needed to satisfy the customer is more likely to make a favourable impact than one who is constrained from doing anything but following the rules.

Whilst empowerment may be financially sound, it is not easy to accomplish. It requires certain foundations. Empowerment can only be done by people able to do the work – competent people. Access to information is also important. Empowerment without information is like sex on your own; it's possible, but not the real thing. The third foundation stone of empowerment is a supportive culture. People will not take on responsibility if doing so leaves them open to criticism, or worse still, threat. It also requires a management willing to let go. Empowerment often fails in practice because executives pay too little attention to the important shifts of power and culture that are needed to make it happen. As Machiavelli noted, the best way to keep your reputation has always been to let someone do your dirty work for you. Empowerment and abdication are two different things.

Empowerment cannot be given, although it can be withheld. It is taken by people confident in their abilities and the support of people around them. A culture where mistakes are allowed, but people work together to avoid failure is needed. Discipline is also needed. The freedom to act has to be balanced with recognition of the needs of the rest of the organisation and a sense of purpose. A strong sense of purpose – 'Why am I here?' – guides what has to be done. Clear values guide the behaviours that are acceptable in fulfilling the purpose.

Exploiting the opportunities presented by customers' changing needs demands teams. Indeed in a fast changing world, people increasingly spend their working day in a variety of teams: new product development teams, customer project teams, improvement teams. They might go under a different title – working party, steering group, or task force – but they're all teams.

An increasing number of organisations will find that forming, operating and dissolving teams is a core competence. Traditional organisation models of hierarchy and matrix constrain the development of a flexible, team-based organisation. They confuse ownership of task with ownership of resources. We need a new paradigm of organisation, which I liken to clouds. A cloud forms, performs it work and evaporates. Its resources are not lost; they eventually become clouds again, but in a different place and at a different time. Whilst seemingly operating independently, clouds are governed by the laws of nature. Purpose and values are an organisation's equivalent to the laws of nature.

To perform well people need four things: competence, information, confidence and opportunity. Competence is about skills, knowledge and behaviour. It is about having the wherewithal to do the job properly.

Leadership, vision and values

Gerard Langler, President of Mentor Graphics Corporation says 'Followers want their leaders to take them on increasingly inspirational journeys. In fact they judge leaders on the basis of this ability ...'. But he warns of grand visions which may become masterpieces of poetry but not of profit. The most powerful visions are not those which are handed down from above, but those which come from inside. Helping people develop their own dreams for their work and personal lives is the major task facing leaders today.

Control will however remain important to an organisation's success, but not in the way we currently envisage it. We will need new ways to communicate direction to replace the hierarchical baton passing. In his excellent article[7], John Kotter said,'... leadership and management are two distinct and complementary systems of action. Each has its own function and characteristic activities. Both are necessary for success in an increasingly volatile business environment'. He went on to add that most [US corporations] are over-managed and underled. With leadership strengthening the sense of values and purpose within the organisation, more control will come from people exercising self-control.

Much is written about the role of CEO as a leader. Whilst this is vitally important, leadership is not a role exclusive to top management. In the dynamic organisation, change will be initiated throughout the organisation and leadership is required wherever change is needed. Indeed, with the wind of change becoming a constant hurricane, the skills described are as important to people on the shop floor as they are to the boardroom. Only through their widespread adoption can an organisation hope to keep pace.

Bill Gore (of GoreTex fame) summed up the leader's problem in one of the company's four core values – the waterline. A hole above a ship's waterline won't sink it, but one below it will. Certain decisions, say like building a plant demand consultation and agreement. Others, like launching a new product don't.[8] Gore used this value as a substitute for budgets in what he called his 'unmanaged' company. Helping people know where the waterline is, is the leader's job. It is not a fixed line. As people develop more skill in testing their ideas, the waterline can be lowered. Different people will see the waterline at different levels. The most common mistake of leaders is shifting the waterline arbitrarily. It is all too common (though perfectly understandable) for leaders to rein back power when things are going wrong. This not only destroys confidence and breeds cynicism, it stops people developing the real skills of developing ideas and exploiting opportunities. The real leader will hold his nerve, knowing he has created the environment where self-discipline guides those with their finger poised on the drill.

Actions speak louder than words, and top management actions scream. Talking about visions and values is not enough. Leaders live them. They never miss an opportunity to relate their decisions to the visions and values. Decisions are then made consistent with those guiding ideals.

Leadership focuses on behaviour as much as performance, knowing that the values have been selected to enhance business performance rather than constrain it. Like other skills and behaviour, self-discipline can be coached. Knowing the values and being personally committed to them is only part of the picture. Frank, open and honest communication is needed to provide regular feedback. Feedback, often criticism, focuses too much on performance of the task and not enough on behaviour, the stuff that makes values come to life.

We need leadership that reflects an understanding of human nature. We need leadership that develops a deep understanding of the organisation's values and through constant challenge and activity tests and reinforces those values. We have to develop a greater understanding of the powerful role values can play as guiding and controlling mechanisms in organisations. These are points I will return to in the book.

Information plus passion

For several years now I have been actively involved with the Management Today/Unisys Service Excellence Awards. The awards were built around my four factors model developed initially in the late 1980s. Following the 1998 awards, I took some time to reflect on what made the difference between the winners, all of which are truly excellent companies and the others. The winning formula is that service excellence = information plus passion.

We have all been faced with someone who has provided the product or service we requested, but with an attitude that makes Attilla the Hun seem friendly. It's the person who tells you what you want to know or delivers the service correctly but with a brusqueness or total disinterest in you. This sort of service failure is annoying. It leaves you with a bad taste in your mouth, like you have been an unwelcome intrusion into their angst. It leaves you feeling cross that you chose to spend your money to be treated like dirt. Now consider how you feel when you come across the really nice, friendly and effusive member of staff who cannot do too much to help you, but is unable to because they don't have the right information. They are apologetic and clearly want to help but can't. A sense of frustration overwhelms you.

They may be for very different reasons, but both are service failures. And if they are regular events, they share one other characteristic. They are a failure of management to create the sort of organisation winning companies enjoy. Winning companies do suffer such failures, but not as often; their leaders build organisations where such failures are definitely the exception.

What is needed to succeed in business is well understood. It is not rocket science. A clear and regularly updated picture of customer needs is coupled to a mechanism for continuous improvement of products and processes. People are trained and motivated to perform and guided by a clear sense of purpose and values. Winners are different because they have translated that understanding into approaches that work in the context of their own organisations. They have built an organisation where everything is focused on profitably winning, satisfying and keeping customers better than the competition. They recognise that service excellence involves the whole organisation in a complex web of interconnected activities. They have purposefully built their organisations around the customer and put in place mechanisms that continually fine-tunes their ability to understand and deliver what the customer needs. Above all, they have recognised that service excellence is a strategy for growth and profit that demands the involvement of the whole organisation.

Within this fundamental premise, two factors, information and passion, separate the good from the great.

The best organisations aggressively manage information. This has several different perspectives.

Information about the customer

Firstly, the best organisations collect far more information about their chosen customers than others believe is necessary. They build a rich picture of customers' needs and expectations and how well they are performing in meeting those needs. Lloyds/TSB issues $2\frac{1}{2}$ million customer surveys each year, with one in five being returned. This mass of information provides staff at all levels of the bank with insights into the whole range of interactions between the bank and the customer. Information is available to managers showing performance at branch, region and group level across all products and services. The information is supplied to branches, allowing local teams to identify local needs. This rich flow of information generates a whole range of improvement activities that contributes to the bank's growth and profitability.

Size is not important. Triple A Animal Hotel and Care Centre in the north-east of England employs only 21 people and has 11 000 customers on its books. Every customer is asked to give their views about the service that they have received. A paper-based survey is issued when the pet is collected from the centre. This is backed up by a telephone survey after a couple of weeks to any customer who has not submitted their survey. This survey-based information is in addition to the complaints, compliments and comments also collected from customers. Staff themselves enrich this picture by recording any failures of the processes. The result is a flow of information that is used at weekly meetings to identify service failures and plan improvements.

In collecting this information, it is important to recognise the importance of qualitative feedback. Knowing that 95 per cent of customers were satisfied is less important than knowing why they were satisfied and why the other five per cent were dissatisfied. It is in these comments and suggestions that organisations find the real nuggets that drive them onwards and upwards. Spending time with customers in their day to day environment is therefore important for managers that want to really understand the customer. This hands-on approach maintains the closeness to the customer that is an everyday part of a senior manager in a small business. It is also one source of information that is often lost to managers in big organisations that rely exclusively on market research and survey data to tell them what life is like for customers. There is no substitute for the real thing.

It is why Avis Europe Chairman Alun Cathcart and his senior managers spend at least three consecutive days each year doing a frontline job. And yes, it does really mean serving at reservation counter for a full shift, or driving the bus between the terminal and the rental station. During this time, they are in touch with real customers in real situations. An injection of reality is only painful for managers who live in dream worlds. It is here that the small business organisations in the awards have an edge over their bigger brothers. The senior managers at organisations like Triple A and public relations company Firefly Communications are an active part of the cutting edge where the organisation meets the customer. And their belief in the importance of the customer means that as they grow (and they surely will) they will maintain that all important reality fix.

Information at the point of service

In serving customers, how well an organisation is able to make information available at the point of service counts for much. Many organisations have sought to give frontline staff greater responsibility and authority in an effort to improve service. These efforts are futile if the staff cannot access the information they need to provide the service customers demand. In this arena, it is the financial service companies that lead the field. They have invested heavily in systems that provide frontline staff with access to information about the customer's complete relationship with the bank. First Direct and Lloyds/TSB both use systems that enable staff to call up a complete history of the customer's transactions, requests and complaints.

It is this information that enables the organisation to offer a single point of contact that is able to deal with the vast majority of a customer's needs; essential to delivering satisfaction. Research, and our own personal experiences, show that satisfaction falls as the points of contact required to fulfil a need increases. We all get intensely frustrated when we have to tell the same organisation, sometimes the same person, the same information time and time again. We get annoyed when we are passed to another part of the organisation and have to retell the story or have to wait again because they too don't have all the information they need to carry out seemingly simple tasks. For too many organisations, the most significant investment in systems integration is still a pack of Post-It notes. They simply fail to see the world as customers see it.

Sharing performance information

It is not just in the area of collecting, sharing and acting on customer needs and aspirations that winners are better in their management of information. We found that the leading exponents of service excellence are much better at sharing information about their performance with staff and in some cases, with customers. At Triple A, each month's service performance results are circulated to all staff and posted in the reception area, a clear indicator to both staff and customers of the importance the organisation places on meeting customers' needs. Indeed staff spend a great deal of time collecting, sharing and analysing a whole host of performance information about service, staff performance and costs.

People have an innate need to know where they stand; to understand how they are doing. How can people be expected to contribute to the development of the organisation if they do not know which areas are weak? I have already talked about the link between customer feedback and improvement action. Winning organisations extend this concept by ensuring people understand the bigger performance picture and the major issues and activities of their market generally. In effect, they develop the organisation's ability to think as business managers. It was precisely this type of information that kick started PHH into action. In the early 1990s, the chairman of their American parent asked if they had done any benchmarking. As a profitable market leader, PHH never considered the need for such an exercise. But to keep the chairman sweet, they did benchmark themselves and got a shock when the results came back. Any lead they had was slipping and competitors were introducing new services and approaches that were slowly winning customers. As a result, PHH instigated Driving for Excellence, a programme designed to ensure that PHH was the service company of choice. Each team has key performance indicators clearly displayed and alongside are details of the projects they are undertaking to fulfil the ambition. Regular discussion between directors and the teams helps facilitate a continuous and meaningful dialogue around direction, performance and change.

At Matra Bae Dynamics Customer Support Services, a company wide approach called value planning creates a framework for managing the informed dialogue about competitive performance. Value planning requires all levels of the business to develop competitive plans around a common vision and set of values. This common approach is used by individuals and teams right through to the BAe group executive team. The process includes competitive reviews and regular monitoring of progress towards goals. Financial services provider Halifax uses a PC based scorecard to share, at all levels, performance information about service, people satisfaction, costs and key processes.

Many organisations still operate with the belief that knowledge is power; that sharing information about strategy, performance and concerns will raise doubts and concerns in the minds of staff. It often does. But not sharing such information creates a climate of uncertainty and rumour, which is far more pernicious. Are senior managers really concerned for the psychological well being of their staff, or are they more worried about the penetrating questions and their lack of understanding that might result from the widespread sharing of information? Winning organisations respect, indeed rely on the ability of their staff to understand and act on the information. David Glass, CEO of the hugely successful American retailer Wal-Mart was asked for the key to future success. He had no answer, other than 'Wal-Mart's associates [employees] will find a way'.

Adding flame to the fuel

Information, in its various guises and contexts, provides the organisation with a source of energy, but that energy is of little value without a spark with which to ignite it. That spark – passion – is the second thing factor that I believe makes the difference.

TNT Express, the UK parcels carrier has captured the essence of this passion in a programme called Expressionism. The introduction to a staff communication video begins thus: 'You can't see it. You can't hear it. You can't touch it. But you can feel it. It is what makes a difference'. It is the passion for excellence and the intense desire to satisfy customers and to win. It is found in winning organisations, and if it could be bottled, would be a best seller.

Deep-seated beliefs

When talking about passion I am not talking about simple unbounded enthusiasm, although that is often present. What the winning organisations possess is a deep belief that life can be better for customers and for staff. It often begins with a deep dissatisfaction with the performance and attitudes of the industry as a whole. Anne Adlington, managing partner of Triple A Animal Hotel and Care Centre sees her role in life as bringing a new level of professionalism to an industry lacking common standards and qualifications. Claire Walker founded Firefly Communications because she believed that PR and communication agencies generally had a bad name. She built Firefly on a fundamental belief that customers deserved better from her industry. Both women play an active part in industry and professional bodies in an effort to raise standards across the board. Being the best of a bad bunch is not enough for these people. They care deeply about their industries and the customers served by them, even though they may be customers of the competition. This passion is not altruism. By raising the stakes, they make life more difficult for competitors. Such vision is underpinned by a deep understanding of how the industry works, and a desire to be an active partner in shaping its future.

Not all the leaders I describe are at the top of their organisations. Many of the people were not CEOs or Managing Directors. They often are heads of part of an organisation, but they still make their mark. Sometimes they lead their part of the organisation with the support of their bosses. In other cases, their bosses seem to have little interest, so long as the numbers stay right. No matter where they sit in the organisation, they are true leaders.

It is also important to differentiate between passion and enthusiasm or charisma. Not all people who have the type of passion I describe are charismatic. They are not always the archetypal gung-ho, bundle of fun fire and brimstone characters typified as passionate leaders; although they often have a certain 'joie de vivre'. Some are quietly spoken, almost reserved characters. The one thing they do have in common is the drive to convert their passion into something real; something that makes a difference. And for that they need other people.

Passion in people

Word and deed communicate the passion that these leaders exude, further enhancing the desire to build an organisation that excels at what it does.

It often begins by expressing that passion as a series of core values that underpin the organisation's activities. This is often not a conscious act, although many are now recognising the power of values as a mechanism for enacting change. For leaders with real passion, a poster of the organisation's values is not that important. What counts is that the organisation acts consistently with these inner beliefs. PHH is one organisation that has written their values down. In common with many organisations, each member of staff has a little yellow card with the values printed on them. What is different is the way PHH uses them. If someone believes a colleague is acting counter to the values, they will pull the yellow card out of their pocket, and just like a football referee, issue a caution. The Chief Executive has a red card. Through this simple idea, people are constantly reinforcing the link between the organisation's values and everyday work.

All of these leaders work endlessly with people. It begins by recruiting and developing people who can share those values. These organisations recruit first and foremost on behaviours. A manager of a previous year's service excellence winner, Birmingham Midshires Building Society once commented: 'We don't hire people if they don't smile sometime during the interview'. Wirral Alcohol Service test potential recruits attitudes with a game that identifies how judgemental a person is, weeding out those who do not genuinely believe in the dignity of the individual and the work the centre is doing.

Having recruited people, winning organisations foster the passion and values by recognising individuals and teams for exemplary actions. Such schemes were found in many of the winners. PHH recognise achievement by an invitation to join the Service Quality Club. First Direct have two schemes, Dream Ticket and Going for Gold and TNT Express UK recognises outstanding staff in their very own the Hall of Fame. The recognition usually carries a monetary award, which is important as it shows the organisation attaches real value to the achievers. But never underestimate the immense pride that this recognition generates. Chris Atkinson, Sales Director of TNT Express UK, himself a former driver, tells the story of a driver he met on one of his depot visits. The driver received a recognition award from Chris many years ago. During the visit Chris was introduced to the driver who said he had met him previously. When asked when, the driver pulled out of his top pocket a tattered piece of paper – the recognition letter Chris had presented to him many years earlier.

Recognition is also provided through promotion. Candidates for senior management appointments at PHH are assessed as against the company's values. These organisations also ensure that promoting from within does not dilute the passion. The Managing Director and Sales Director of TNT Express UK both started life as drivers. Over 90 per cent of Avis Europe's senior managers started with the company working on the frontline. The cultures that these organisations have crafted are the real source of their advantage. Through careful recruitment, constant recognition of excellence and the continuing development of people, they have built an organisation designed to win.

This is how the organisation's leaders guide people as to what is acceptable and unacceptable and thus encourage the kind of attitude we all appreciate when we experience it.

Passion in processes

Whilst people are the undoubted source of advantage, organisations comprise more than people. Processes are essential to the delivery of the products and services that customers want. But even here, there is a clear link between the passion that winners possess and the way they do things. Just as the leaders I described imbue their people with their passion, so do they design processes that enact that passion. If they say customer satisfaction counts, then they build processes that deliver satisfaction. If they believe people are their greatest assets then they build processes that develop and value people. In the application of values to the everyday work and activities, winning organisations are boringly consistent.

PHH values include quality, efficiency, initiative and team spirit. Their continuous improvement process, 'Driving for Excellence' therefore is team based, seeks to improve both quality and costs and encourages people to try new things. TNT Express UK print their customer care logo on all their stationery, so they devised the concept of a 'perfect transaction' to try to ensure that at all stages of the collection, delivery and payment process, the customer gets what is promised. Within 12 months of introducing the scheme, 94 per cent of transactions were flawless. Cendant Membership say they respect the quality, trust and integrity of their people, so they are introducing Manager Free Zones; activities that are run solely by the staff with no management involvement.

Many organisations have at some time in their lives created organisations that have served customers with excellent products/services and excellent processes. They have captured the imagination of their people and had inspiring visions and values. And yet they have gone from success to failure, sometimes absolute failure. Since Arie de Geus and his team of planners at Shell studied long lived companies, there has been much interest in the characteristics of long-term success. In 'The Living Company' De Geus suggests there are four characteristics vital to longevity: sensitivity and an ability to adapt to the outside world, a sense of cohesion and identity, tolerance to experimentation and change and a conservative approach to financing. In their US study 'Built to Last', Collins and Porras suggest that visionary companies focus on building organisations that continuously manage the dynamic tension between preserving a set of core values and stimulating progress. Both provide important evidence of what makes for success and provide rich examples of these characteristics in action in a range of companies. Neither however suggests how an organisation might go about building these characteristics and thus setting them on the path to longevity.

3
Learning about Dynamic Organisations

The beginning of knowledge is the discovery of something we do not understand.
FRANK HERBERT

I am a great advocate of learning. I have constantly sought new experiences and viewpoints. I have always been fascinated to look at different organisations and how they work. I have also found it invaluable to look outside the usual boundaries of management for new lessons and insights. In this chapter I want to set out some of the lessons I have learned from traditional and other sources in my quest to better understand dynamic organisations. I share these ideas because they have been so useful in helping me think about organisations in new ways; I hope they have the same value to you.

For five years now the dynamic organisation model has been used as the basis for a national award for service excellence in the UK. Sponsored by Unisys and Management Today the awards recognise those organisations which deliver excellent service to their customers. In the five years that I have been judging the awards, I have examined entries from hundreds of organisations and visited over 80. From this rich source of organisational practice and other research, I have identified five important points.

1. **Singular excellence is important but not enough**
   Introducing the organisational capabilities model in *Dynamic Organisations* I wrote, 'It is not enough to be good at any one of them. An organisation succeeds because of the sum of what it does, not because it does one thing particularly well'. The fact that all four capabilities are necessary hides another important point. An organisation that has only one or two capabilities developed has taken

a piecemeal approach to building its organisation. This is typical of organisations that jump from one fad to the next. Understanding customers without having excellent products and processes cannot succeed. And even if these two factors exist, it is unlikely that they can be sustained without the commitment to develop and enable the people in the organisation, which in turn is unlikely to happen without the commitment of leadership that value people.

To be truly dynamic it is not enough to excel in one capability alone. Other commentators have stated that to be successful an organisation must focus on one capability such as customer intimacy or product excellence making it the central theme of the organisation. I believe that this is wrong. Excellence and the success it delivers require a contribution from the whole organisation. The winners of the Service Excellence Awards are excellent in all areas. They use a deep understanding of customers to build products and services that meet their needs and expectations. They constantly use feedback from customers and their tracking of competition and innovation to improve the way they deliver to customers. They know the importance of, and therefore invest in, the development of people's skills. They reward and recognise people's contributions and motivate them to greater performance. Leadership is widely practised and based on clear, well understood values that are used as the touchstone to guide decisions.

In all these areas, excellent organisations find new ways of doing things. These are often simple, but highly effective ideas generated by people across the organisation. The culture of the organisation is such that new ideas are tried and the good ones spread. This learning and improvement is the result of a culture that is open to other people's ideas and suggestions, willing to try new things and encouraging to those who contribute. This culture is reinforced by leaders who act as conduits for new ideas and is institutionalised by forums and systems that encourage and enable the sharing of good ideas. In this way improvements spread quickly. A good idea generated in one small part of the organisation gets adopted in other parts. Rapidly, a small contribution to service and profit makes a noticeable difference.

2. Fit is as important as excellence

Excellence in all the four capabilities is a big step forward but not the total answer. To achieve success, the organisation has to be designed as a whole. An excellent car, whether it is a sports convertible or a town run-around, has a good engine and transmission on a responsive chassis with a sound body with the right equipment. Whilst different people may lead the detailed design of the components, they understand they are part of a car design team. They understand that changing the engine performance might require different gear ratios. Each team understands the linkages between its components and the whole car. They also understand the design concept – the particular characteristics and ethos of the car they are designing. They may be specialists in a particular field, but they understand the whole thing. The same is true of dynamic organisations

In the very best organisations, the four capabilities are fully integrated. By ensuring fit between the different parts of the organisation, a seamless view is presented to customers, costs are reduced by minimising duplication and waste (mainly of people's time) and new ideas and innovations generated through the constant interactions between people in the organisation and with customers and other external constituencies. This fit reaches the point where much of what happens seems to occur intuitively. Actions become part of the fabric of the organisation. When researching Avis for the case study in *Dynamic Organisations*, I was constantly struck by how little of what the organisation does was overt – recorded in process and rules. So much of what makes them excellent is done because it is 'the Avis way', a natural result of the culture that is so carefully cherished and developed. This does not happen by accident. What is now second nature is the result of a constant stream of improvements and a focus on what is right for the whole organisation, or more typically for the customers.

Fit between the different processes that deliver products and service to the customer is a vital first step. It is the basis for service and competitiveness. TNT Express Parcel's thrust to define and deliver the prefect transaction is an excellent example of achieving fit in the core processes of delivering service. Excellent organisations go beyond the processes of delivering to customers. They also seek fit between these processes and the processes that they use to manage the organisation. These organisational processes (a subject I will address in greater detail in Chapter 8) are important because they institutionalise the organisation's culture. They are one of the most powerful ways that leadership is translated into the everyday activity of the organisation. The concept of fit is therefore one that embraces leadership, work and organisational processes.

3. Values are the basis of fit

Fit is not just about integrating the process of delivering service and managing the organisation. It is fundamentally about the coherence of the activities of the organisation with the values to which the organisation aspires. Speaking and acting in accordance with values is my definition of integrity.

Values have received much attention in recent years and deservedly so. Many organisations have however missed the point. The values that I am interested in are the values that are evident in the practices and activities of the organisation and less so the words that adorn corporate posters. Bringing values to life involves dialogue and leadership. Dialogue across the organisation is essential if the meaning of what are often simple words is to be fully grasped. This does not mean a one-off series of workshops where people debate the meaning of words and then decide upon a few actions. Values can only be fully understood in the context of a situation. Dialogue is therefore a continuing activity where values are brought into the debate about what actions are required in a given situation. This dialogue generates a deeper understanding of the situation. It is the activity of leadership that translates the understanding generated by dialogue into decisions and action. Hence leadership is not reserved to a few senior managers but open to all who have both an understanding of the values and the courage to act.

This interplay of conversation between values and context is a creative act. Many of the changes that organisations face do not have prescribed responses or answers. Values, unlike rules and processes, can bring forth many actions. Values that are deeply understood allow people to act in a way that is coherent but at the same time unique. Coherence comes at the level of the values with everyone in the organisation being guided by them. Uniqueness is provided by intelligent individuals acting to address the situation they face. It is an approach that allows a great deal of creativity yet provides a focus and a reference point that is essential if people are to feel the sense of commitment that comes from belonging to something worthy.

4. Leadership and people make the difference

Every winner in the Unisys/Management Today Service Excellence Awards has recognised that it is people that make the difference. They select people that have empathy with the organisation's values. They train, coach, encourage and give them the opportunity to perform. They do this by building the organisation's leadership capacity. They focus leadership development not just on those in managerial positions but on those who show the potential and willingness to lead. As people develop they are given greater responsibilities and challenges and further training and coaching. An important part of this development is to help people develop their understanding of the organisation's values. Because this relies on context, much of this development is coaching orientated.

This focus on people reflects an element of the values held by all winning organisations. Respect for people is a value they universally express and practise. This does not mean they are a soft touch. They place high demands on people and expect them to deliver, but they do not set them up to fail.

I will return to the issue of leadership in Chapter 11.

5. **Winners build winning organisations**
The final and most important observation is that winners build winning organisations. I have met many organisations over the years that have developed an excellent business. They have great products or have exploited a new idea to create new and different propositions for the customer. This is the core of any business success. In many organisations however this capability is not fully exploited because the organisation does not work properly. People trying to implement strategy and build business are constrained by policies and process. Sometimes it is lack of process; more often, they are overburdened with out of date or unsuitable management processes that do not reflect the values of the organisation. In many cases, the processes simply do not complement each other. In some instances, it is worse; processes that have been developed piecemeal contradict or counteract others. In the worst cases, processes retain or reinforce elements of the culture that are undesirable. Kevin Kelly of Wired magazine says[9] 'Organisations by their design are not made to adapt ... beyond a certain point. Beyond that point, it's much easier to kill them off and start a new one than it is to change'. Kelly is right, most organisations are not designed to adapt but that does not mean that they cannot be designed to adapt. My central point is that organisations can be designed not just to cope with change, but to thrive on change. They may look very different to what we think of as organisations today, indeed they will have to. The old models and concepts are now over 100 years old and ill-suited to constant adaptation and change. The challenge is to design organisations for change. That begs the question 'What is organisation design?'.

What is organisation design?

The experience of the past few years led me to the simple conclusion *that every organisation is perfectly designed to achieve the results it does*. If an organisation is to deliver different results, the organisation has to change. For many the changes have focused on two factors – the cost base represented in people and organisation structure. Organisations have downsized, rightsized and restructured. The lines and boxes have been drawn and redrawn countless times.

To emphasise the importance of structure is one of the biggest mistakes managers make when considering organisation design. An organisation is a collection of people working together to achieve a common purpose. The role of organisation design is to facilitate the relationships between people so that purpose can be achieved. To focus on structure is akin to saying that the skeleton is the only important part of the human body. Few illnesses of the skeleton are life threatening. We are more likely to die because of failures of the soft tissues of our body – the heart, the brain and the liver. The same is true of organisations. Organisation design therefore has to focus on the soft processes and relationships. If these don't operate properly and in concert, organisations are more likely to suffer sickness and death.

Fig. 3.1 Business and organisation development

It is also wrong to believe that good organisation design is sufficient. Success requires both a good business strategy and an excellent organisation. Much has been written about strategy and that is not an area I intend to address in this book although I will comment on the strategy process in Chapter 8. To maximise and sustain success managers must pay more than cursory attention to the development of their organisations. It is essential to look beyond redrawing the lines and boxes of an organisation chart. If the organisation is struggling, changing the structure alone is unlikely to help.

Consider the following story.[10] It is my interpretation of the decline of a once great company. Whilst it is only my opinion and is recounted with some licence it does reflect the events that took place.

> Once upon a time, the results did not go as planned. We would be reorganised. We changed some of the senior management team and put in place a new organisation. We actually did this several times and each new organisation and management team was introduced with the same message. 'The new organisation is designed to get us closer to the customer and make us more efficient. The new team is the right team to make things happen. Come-on folks, let's all get behind this new team and make things work.' So we all went away and tried to do our best while the new organisation was put in place. What most people did was wonder what their job would be and who their new boss was. Everybody seemed to be in meetings working feverishly to get the new organisation in place, and boy were they working hard. Sales people who had just got the customer to understand one organisation and team went forth to spread the new gospel. They also told their friends and the customers what they really thought about the changes.
>
> The new organisation would settle down, usually after about three to six months of activity. But strangely enough, the results did not change. So the bosses hit upon an idea. 'I know, let's reorganise' one manager would say. 'What we need is a new team and a more customer focused organisation'. And hey presto out of the bag would come another organisation and another team that was the answer to the still falling numbers. The new organisation would be put in place. We were told that the decline in profits was because the new organisation had not bedded in. Then other things began to happen. A hiring freeze was introduced to control costs. That didn't work because the organisation was actually very short of the skills that it had deemed essential to its success. So then we had the 'intelligent hiring freeze': hiring was allowed provided someone could show how it contributed to second-quarter revenues. Well was that intelligent! But it didn't seem to have the right effect. Other things happened. Some of my best colleagues left; I left. Senior managers

started talking about how customers would be wowed by the new products. And when they saw the benefits of the new organisation they would return to buy more. I guess it was at that point that most people realised management had lost the plot.

Revenues continue to fall so we tightened up on costs. Away days were cancelled so people did exactly the same things but in-house – with catering. This probably cut costs less than 0.001 per cent but it was visible action from the senior management team. Air travel was stopped, until managers recognised the people needed to travel to meet global customers, the servicing of which was a central tenet of the last organisational change, or was it the one before that. So then a manger hit on the bright idea of getting people to submit a justification identifying how the travel impacted their quarterly revenue goals and getting it signed off by the senior management team. Of course, they knew insufficient about the detail of each account to make an intelligent decision, so they signed 99 per cent of them anyway. By the way, senior managers seem to be exempt from this rule. I guess that's what senior means.

Now was the time for strong management. We imported these are from a competitor who was making bigger losses than us. With each announcement of the quarterly results, the managers announced another number, the redundancy number. The incoming managers were very experienced at this. Off-course to make the figures look good, redundancies had to be made quickly so we took out huge swathes of people with only cursory regard to what they were doing. At this time, the number of consultants employed rose dramatically. These were the people made redundant that we now paid as consultants to do the same work because no one had associated people with necessary work. These consultants were very happy. They had a healthy redundancy payment and were now being paid consultancy rates to do essentially the same things in half the time. Whoever said redundancy always make people unhappy!

At the beginning of each quarter, you went to work wondering if you were going to get the invitation to meet your manager to discuss your future. The better people welcomed it with glee. They had lined up another job with a competitor and were waiting for the redundancy payment to feather their nests. Less capable people worried greatly, and consequently did less work, less well. Fear does that to people.

But you know, in all the time I worked at this company I can't recall a senior manager inspiring me with a view of the future. Those guys had their heads so far up their accountant's backsides they could not see where the sun shone. Every reorganisation was to get us closer to the customer but management had no regular or reliable data about customer satisfaction other than a once a year survey, which they buried because they did not like the results. I never did figure out how we could design organisational changes that would bring us closer to customers without real customer data. Of course, I forget that senior managers used to be salesmen and engineers when they talked to customers, so they would know all that stuff. They still did talk to customers – occasionally.

If you asked a senior manager what the strategy was you got an answer, but it was a different answer from each manager. The strategy was supposed to focus on product and service sales to major accounts, developing third party distribution, improving customer satisfaction and developing cost leadership. There was no consistent interpretation of what that meant. Consequently, there was no co-ordinated operational plan. Middle managers tried to fill the gaps between a clear and consistent message from above and the demands from below for a strategy by making up their own. The board watched the numbers like a hawk. Weekly and even daily figure were called forth from an already over stretched organisation. But strangely enough, the board only looked at the overall numbers. No one told us, regularly and convincingly, how we were really doing. It was impossible for anyone to get meaningful numbers about how our business unit was doing. Revenue was counted and allocated to several different groups; costs were often lost. Simple administrative tasks consumed inordinate time and effort.

I cannot think of a senior manager at this company I would want to work for again. I think of several for whom I will never work again, even if they paid me a fortune. There are only two managers I remember with any respect. One was my manager. She was ineffective as a business manager, but looked after her team as best she could. She had little idea about running a business but knew how to manage people. The other was a more senior manager. He insisted on maintaining his training budget, collected monthly customer satisfaction data and ensured that people across his organisation knew chapter and verse about the state of the market. Teams would meet regularly to identify weaknesses and implement small improvement projects. He ran one of the few profitable pieces of the business.

You must understand that this was all happening whilst the closest competitor with a similar background and product line was growing like Topsy. They had a similar product line although our products performed better and were more innovative, or so we were told. They were not complaining about the changing nature of the industry. Their management reports made fewer references to economic downturns and restructuring costs. I wonder if it is any coincidence that this company is recognised as having one of the best cultures and leadership teams in the industry, indeed anywhere.

The style of the story reflects the unreal nature of the events as they were experienced. It was, quite literally, unreal to live through, like watching a film rather than real life. People would comment that it would make a great story if only it wasn't true. But it was true.

The story is perhaps an extreme example of an organisation that does not work and of how futile it is to focus just on structure. Real change demands more than that. The story is not however unique. Other companies have gone the same way. I have recently experienced another great organisation fall from grace and the story is even more unbelievable. Incompetent management, extreme arrogance and a total inability to see the changes around them are killing the organisation. The management undoubtedly deserve the failure that is so inevitable but the thousands of people who are also affected do not.

Examples such as these graphically illustrate the fact that shuffling boxes is not the same as organisational change. This is not a new issue. Consider the following lesson from history.

> 'We trained hard and it seemed every time we were beginning to form into teams we would be reorganised. I was to learn later in life that we tend to meet every new situation by reorganising. And a wonderful method it can be for creating the illusion of progress while producing confusion, inefficiency and demoralisation.

The Roman Gaius Petronius uttered these words in the first century AD. As we begin the next millennium these words still resonate with people in organisations around the world who have become cynical of the constant reshuffles and restructuring. And rightly so. They are often the actions of ill-informed and desperate senior managers who believe that redrawing lines and boxes and shuffling the pack will radically change fortunes. It is true that great leaders make a difference, but giving people new responsibilities is not enough. The seeds of failure for the company described in the story above and the many like them were lodged in a culture that believed it knew best, that building the best mousetrap would have customers queuing at the door, and that fobbing people off with second rate managers was winning business practice. Failure stemmed from the lack of any reliable process for gathering and acting on data about customers, the lack of a coherent approach for communicating and enacting strategy and the lack of real involvement of the people on the ground in change. The company's previous success had blinded it to the realities of life in a competitive market. The blinkers were self-imposed.

Another organisation I know had a number of highly successful businesses in high growth markets. The growth of competitors suggested a strong market. The introduction of e-commerce presented new opportunities for the organisation to become an essential part of the information flows of customers in all aspects of trade – commercial and retail. The business however was outstripped by competitors who brought new ideas to market quickly. Staff turnover was high with many of its best people leaving. Strategies were devised, but there was no effective way of translating strategy into the work of the organisation. Measurement of performance was purely financial with no real data on issues such as productivity, customer satisfaction and customer retention. The organisation was incapable of delivering real service to customers because almost all decisions were the preserve of the executive team. Here was a classic case of a great business and a poor organisation. At the heart of the problems was a highly authoritarian chief executive who did not believe in people at all. In his mind, the staff were there to unquestioningly carry out the orders of the senior management team. In a discussion about organisation culture, he once told me: 'Culture change here is not difficult. I decide what culture we want and tell people. If they don't like it they leave.' People did leave. They left not because of poor pay but because there was no development and no opportunity to make a significant contribution. People did not feel they belonged. To cap it all, the posters proclaimed 'people' as one of the organisation's four values. The fastest growth area in that company was cynicism.

There are other examples where a poor organisation has held back a good business. One reason for this is that the art of organisation design is not well understood and badly practised by many. Many senior managers fail to see beyond structure. Building a business cannot be done effectively unless attention is also paid to building the organisation that sustains it. Indeed, it can be argued that building the organisation is more important as one organisation may, over time, serve several businesses. In the words of one commentator: 'In the last analysis, Walt Disney's greatest creation was Walt Disney (the company).'[11]

Lessons from other sources

Reviewing my experiences and thoughts about successful organisations was a useful exercise that caused me to ponder about what else I could learn about organisations and how they work. My thoughts about organisation design being about relationships between people were reinforced at a recent conference by Tony Buzan. Buzan, renowned for his Mind Mapping™ technique, showed a short video of a single brain cell at work – an opportunity to observe thinking. Anchored at one end of a container filled with fluid and hundreds of microscopic beads, the brain cell set about its work. The cell's finger-like arms were constantly searching the surrounds looking to make new connections. Here were relationships being formed at the cellular level. The cell continued, constantly seeking and testing new connections. Its one goal in life is to make connections and thereby contribute to a much greater scheme of things.

That short video spawned more questions. What else can nature and science teach us about organisations? My research, patchy as it is, has generated more insights. I would like to share some of the learnings with you and how they have shaped my thinking about organisation design and change.

The brain

Our brain is perhaps the most complex natural structure known to man. Comprising a trillion (100 000 000 000) individual cells, each constantly seeking connections, the brain works without creating any permanent physical connections. Cells communicate with each other by exchanging chemical messages. As we repeat an activity or thought, these chemical pathways become more established and easier to use. Memory is formed enabling us to recall distant events, facts and skills. This ability extends to the control of physical activity. Athletes learn how muscles feel when they perform well and can recall and repeat this performance. Like a muscle, the more we use our brains, the better they become. We can learn to have a better memory, to be more effective at mental arithmetic and even to think ourselves to be healthier. Like driving a car, repetition leads to a skill becoming implicit, it becomes second nature. That applies to bad practices as well as good ones. Because there are no physical connections, we also have the capacity to unlearn. We can, under the right conditions, lay new paths that become more accessible than the old ones. This is the cellular basis for change. We can create conditions where it is easier and more advantageous for people to do the things that are needed to help build and maintain a dynamic organisation. This ability to unlearn is not lost as we get older. The existing pathways may be particularly well formed, but given the right stimulus, an old dog can learn new tricks. What we often lose as we get older is the access to or willingness to seek out new stimuli. As organisations age, typically when they get to 35–40 years old, they lose the willingness to face up to new stimuli – to changes in the outside world. They become comfortable. That is the path to failure.

The number of possible combinations of connections between brain cells is immense. Each of the one million billion cells is capable of making up to 15 000 connections. One smart egg worked out that the number of possible combinations was one followed by ten and a half kilometres of typewritten zeroes. These combinations are the source of new ideas. As the tendrils of our brain cells wander around our heads making new connections, we conceive new things. Most of them are no more than passing thoughts. Occasionally someone makes a connection and acts on it. Much of this idle wandering is incidental, a by-product of some other activity. Daydreaming can be a highly valuable activity. One German researcher found that most work related ideas came when walking in the outdoors thinking of nothing in particular. The largest source of ideas when at work was while people were bored in meetings. It is then that we have our brainwaves – our bright ideas. Eureka recognised the key to mass when he climbed in the bath, not hard at work at some laboratory bench or desk. Much work was needed 'at the office' to turn the brainwave into a coherent body of usable knowledge but that would not have been possible without the initial brainwave which he might never have had if he had restricted his thinking to the office.

We make the same mistake at work. We confuse activity and work. We build organisations that require people to look busy even if they know they are not doing something of real value. We do not allow people time to think. I remember as a student laughing at one manager who came to talk to us when he advised all of us to close the office door for twenty minutes each day and just think. No specific agenda or subject, but just let the mind wander. The brain needs time to reflect and we might all be more successful if we did less and thought more. Real thinking (as against simply recalling known facts) is a process that needs time. It is hard work.

The brain is also reconfigureable. Stroke victims can, to a certain degree, recover from the damage inflicted on their brains. People who have had sections of brain removed due to cancer have shown that the brain can rewire itself to cope with a degree of damage. The lack of hard-wiring is the reason that the brain's recovery powers are so great. When centres of the brain known to be responsible for certain functions are damaged, function can often be relocated. The one essential component in all these situations is the strength of the patient's desire to succeed and live as normal a life as possible. The brain is not a passive slate onto which we write things. The actions we take, the senses we experience and the relationships we build are each a function of our brain. But these actions also shape the way our brains develop. No two people are alike because their brains experience different things.

Organisations can also be reconfigureable. People can, within limits, take on new and different tasks if they are given the right support and training. Organisations can be designed to be flexible. That requires much less emphasis on structure and much more on process.

> **Organisational redundancy at 3M[12]**
>
> 3M, the inventors of the Post-It Note set themselves a target of generating 25 per cent of annual revenues from products that are less than three years old. They argue that if they do not constantly renew their product lines, competitors will and 3M will thereby lose out. This requires a constant stream of new ideas and innovations. 3M design their organisation to meet this challenge.
>
> Those responsible for product innovation and development take advantage of two elements of what 3M call organisational redundancy. The first is that all staff working on product development are given two weeks to work on an idea of their choosing. There is no restriction on their choice. The topic does not have to fit within 3M's existing product lines. It is selected simply on the interest of the individual.
>
> A second mechanism used by 3M is to cross-fertilise people from different disciplines. A scientist or engineer from say the abrasives division has to spend part of his/her time working with a team from another division, perhaps adhesives. There is no specific objective to deliver certain learnings or benefits associated with the secondment. What does happen however is that through a process akin to diffusion, good ideas and working practices spread across the organisation. This mechanism also helps build networks across the organisation. People increase their stock of useful contacts. When they come across a problem, they often refer to one of their contacts who faced a similar problem. No one dictates that these learnings are transferred, they just happen.

Finally, the thinking process reflects our development, both in the womb and our evolution. How often have you been surprised at the response you have received when you have told people news, even what you think was good news? They respond to a perfectly reasoned argument with irrational concerns and emotions. This seemingly irrational response is wired into our brains; we cannot escape it. How people think underpins what they do and our thinking process has been established over millions of years of evolution.

The brain has three major elements that reflect our evolution and still today determine the order of our thinking.

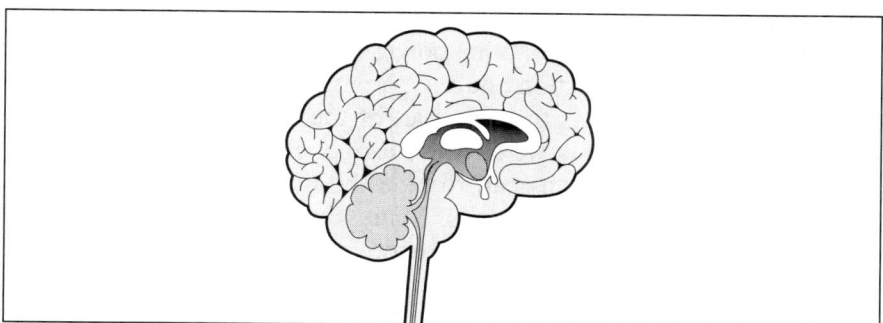

Figure 3.2 The brain

The reptilian brain is the part of the brain we share with all animals and birds. This part of the brain is responsible for our basic life systems – the autonomic systems that control our basic functions. Aggression and reflex behaviours are developed here. It is also thought that instincts are controlled by this part of the brain. The reptilian brain ensures our survival.

The limbic system developed as mammals evolved. This part of the brain helps us distinguish between that which is agreeable and disagreeable. The limbic system also controls our emotions such as love, hate, sadness and for some aspects of personal identity. Emotional instincts such as mothering are controlled by the limbic system. Unlike the reptilian brain, the limbic system has the ability to think and learn. We learn our values and emotions and can therefore unlearn them. Values are not fixed in perpetuity.

The final part of the brain, which in humans comprises the bulk of its mass is the neo-cortex – the rational brain. Here sits our centres of intellect. The ability to read, write and perform mathematical calculations are down to neo-cortex (literally meaning 'new cortex'). The size and power of this piece of the brain is what separates us from beasts. Only the higher primates, dolphins and whales have a significant neo-cortex and homo sapiens has, by far, the largest.

The evolutionary development of the brain is matched by the development of the brain in a foetus and early life. The first part of the brain to develop is the brain stem and the other structures of the reptilian brain, followed by the limbic system and finally the neo-cortex.

When faced with a decision, it is believed that the brain follows a particular process. The most basic thinking process goes back to our basic need for survival. When faced with a threat, the brain has to decide what action to take. The first thing the brain does is assess whether the decision is a life threatening situation. If it is then the structures of the reptilian brain trigger a release of adrenaline to deal with the danger. Our decision to stand our ground or run away to fight another day, the fight or flight response, is our most basic thinking process. It is believed that other basic instincts such as reproduction and the parenting instinct are also part of the reptilian brain. This is the only part of the brain that does not have learning capabilities. What we have we cannot change through learning.

Non-threatening decisions call first on the limbic system. This is the source of our emotions and values. Many situations have such a large number of responses that it would take too much time and effort for even a device as remarkable as the brain to process. The limbic system therefore uses our beliefs and emotions to limit our choices. It filters possible decisions, highlighting those options that are consistent with our values and emotions. We are therefore literally blinded by our emotions. It is why we believe some things to be right, even when the facts do not support that point of view. It is why a sports fan believes his/her team can do no wrong. The limbic system has the capability to learn.

Only when the limbic system has had its say does the neo-cortex, the conscious, rational thinking part of the brain, get a look in. It weighs up the options and possible outcomes before making the final selection. Here we apply logic and reason. We seek the data that throws light on the situation. The neo-cortex was the last part of the brain to develop in our evolution and is only found in the higher mammals. Homo sapiens has the most highly developed neo cortex of all beings on earth. The neo-cortex comprises 80 per cent of our brain's mass.

Decisions always therefore involve some emotional response. There is probably no such thing as pure logic in humans. Yet we often design organisations as if logic were the only thinking tool people use. They are structured, with clear boundaries. Information is circulated on a 'need to know' basis. People are recruited based on their skills. But the growing field of emotional intelligence shows us that logic and intelligence, our rational selves, are poor indicators of success. What counts is our emotional intelligence rather than our rational intelligence. Whilst this is being recognised at the level of the individual, it is not yet fully understood at the level of the organisation. We do not build organisations that release and develop emotional intelligence. To do so we need to break away from structure and process and focus more on values. We need emotionally intelligent people working in emotionally aware organisations. We need leaders who understand and enact human nature and processes for guidance and measurement, who operate at the emotional and individual level as well as the intellectual and rational level.

Robins and blue tits

Arie de Geus who was formerly the Head of Strategic Planning at Royal Dutch Shell. de Geus gave a talk about the research he and his colleagues had undertaken into the characteristics of long-lived companies. One of the things common with companies that had survived for more than 100 years was an ability to innovate. de Geus' team wondered what might be learned from the animal world and consulted Professor Wilson, a specialist in the way animals learn.[13]

Wilson told de Geus and his colleagues the story of the robins and blue tits in the UK. The UK has distributed milk to homes in bottles for many years. In the early days, the bottles had no caps. Both robins and blue tits learned to drink the cream off the top of the milk. The rich cream required a small adaptation of the animal's digestive system – a trait that was passed on in both species through natural selection. In the 1920s foil caps were placed on the bottle to prevent the birds getting to the cream and thus limit any threat of contamination and disease. By the early 1950s, the entire UK population of blue tits – about a million birds – had learned how to pierce the caps. Only a few robins matched this development.

Songs explain how blue tits were so successful in spreading the learning about pecking through milk bottle tops. A blue tit spends much of its time in flocks and uses songs to communicate with others in the flock. A robin however uses its song to announce and protect its territory.

Wilson has concluded that for a species to sustain learning and thereby accelerate its evolution, three conditions must be present:

1. Innovation: Either an individual or a community has to innovate.
2. Social Propagation: There has to be a social process for transmission of the new skill.
3. Mobility: Individuals can and do move around the community rather than sit in isolated territories.

The lessons for organisations are clear. Organisations are collections of people and Wilson's three conditions apply. Knowledge management is a popular theme of the moment. To capture and share what different parts of the organisation knows is recognised as vital to success. Wilson's characteristics of animal learning point to the fact that knowledge management has to be built into the organisation. Systems may be effective at sharing information but getting people to recognise and use that information is a social process.

Following the talk, I chatted briefly with de Geus. His description of Wilson's work on animal learning fascinated me. It also prompted a question. In a flock of blue tits, which bird is the leader? de Geus had not considered this. My own thoughts are that leadership arises out of the situation; that we are mistaken when we vest leadership into a predetermined position in a group or hierarchy. It is much better to think of leadership as a set of activities that anyone has the potential to carry out. Some people do all these activities well; others may be good at some, but less able at the rest. What is important is not the number of leaders, but the leadership capacity of the organisation. We have self-managed teams. Why not self-led organisations? Self-managed teams still carry out management tasks, it is just that no one person has that role or responsibility. In the same way organisations can have leadership without having people who are called leaders. This route towards building organisational leadership will be examined in Chapter 11.

Termite nest

A termite nest is recognised as one of the most amazing structures created by a species other than man. These highly complex mounds, often rising to 6m comprise tunnels and chambers of different types. There are structures that encourage airflow to cool the nest, others provide drainage. Special galleries for hatching eggs are heated by the fermentation of organic matter. Networks of interconnecting tunnels provide access to these various structures. All this is built by a vast horde of termites operating without a project plan or a project manager. There is no blueprint for the nest. There is no design authority that says what is required where. The structure evolves and changes as the needs of the colony change. The co-operation that is required to build nature's equivalent of the Petronas Towers is achieved by the interactions of the termites as they, collectively, respond to the colony and its environment. No single termite has overall responsibility. Each insect plays its part in concert with the others. It is this process of interaction that determines the structure. As conditions change and the colony grows, so the nest changes and develops. There is no end point to the nest; no point at which the structure is finished, because there is no end to the interaction between the termites and their environment. The process is the design.

Structures need to serve a purpose but do not need to be elegantly designed. What is important is that people are able to interact effectively to achieve the chosen purpose. Once the purpose is understood, able people who can effectively interact can achieve great things. What counts is the quality of the interaction. The termite organisation is one that is designed to facilitate relationships and interaction. In many companies however, structure is seen as the focus of organisation design. Fine blueprints might result, but relationships are social processes that cannot be defined in blueprints.

Shoals of fish

Ships are used as a common metaphor for organisations. People talk about the captain on the bridge and the delay between decision and visible result to describe the difficulties of managing an organisation. Organisations are compared to super-tankers and organisations without effective leadership are described as rudderless. These metaphors fit the mechanistic and hierarchical perceptions many have of organisations. A shoal of fish is another metaphor drawn from the sea. A shoal of fish can turn as a single organism in an instant. Like the termites, the shoal has no appointed leader. There is no one at the centre of the shoal issuing the orders to turn here and there. It is the fish on the outside that determine the direction of a shoal. Any fish on the edge of the shoal can signal to the shoal and cause a change of direction. They do this in response to a perceived threat or a source of food. As the shoal twists and turns, different fish find themselves on the edge. There is no special qualification for being an 'outside fish'.

Organisations on the other hand are not good at taking their lead from those closest to the market. Despite the claims of many to be market led, customer focused or highly responsive, most organisations are centrally directed and controlled. Not only is little attention paid to the people who deal with customers and meet competitors daily, many managers direct their organisation without regular and reliable customer and market data. When coupled with hierarchy and bureaucracy, the slow turning super-tanker metaphor is appropriate. It does not have to be that way.

Companies in the Virgin Group are always small – by design. In his autobiography[14], Richard Branson talks about his approach to business using the record company as an example:

> Because I believe small is beautiful, whenever the company got too big I would ask to see the deputy managing director, the deputy sales manager and the deputy marketing director and tell them they were now managing director, sales director and marketing director of a new company. They were given a stake in the company, so they too could become entrepreneurs. In quantitative terms, the job I was asking them to do was no more significant than that of the deputy in a fairly large company, but the zest, the enthusiasm and the tenacity with which it was performed were wholly different .... . The end result was that we had 50 small record companies around the world, with no more than 60 people working out of any one building.

He goes on to conclude:

> If instead of having one company rather than 50, I believe we would not only have not become the largest independent but I doubt we would have survived.

It is easy for a group of 60 people to know each other. Each member of the group is close to the edge. It is impossible to become buried at head office miles away from customers and the market. Relationships can be quickly formed and information is easily shared without the need for expensive IT systems. In a small group it is difficult to hide. This sort of environment demands high calibre people who are not afraid of taking a chance.

Nature has a version of Branson's rule of 60. It is called Haldene's Law which expresses a relationship between volume and surface area. A given volume requires a certain surface area to service that mass. Nature knows of no species that has exceeded that ratio and survived.

Fractal geometry

I have been aware of fractals – the brightly coloured computer generated patterns – for some time. Fractals are created by a small set of relatively simple non-linear equations. The vital features of a fractal equation are that they are iterated and that each iteration includes a feedback variable. In effect, the future shape of the fractal is dependent on the results of the previous step. What is happening now determines the future shape of a fractal. This feedback creates both variation and consistency. Look at any fractal (like the illustration on the jacket cover of the book) and you will see a pattern that is repeated at different places and at different levels of scale. Fractals are found across nature. Ferns, trees, snowflakes, lungs and the brain are all fractal. These non-linear equations seem to be at the heart of almost everything around us.

I chose fractals to illustrate the covers of my books because they symbolise the role values play in an organisation. Values are an organisation's fractals. They are simple rules that are interpreted through the organisation in a continuing iteration of action and feedback. What is important is that the organisation has the necessary mechanisms to communicate its values across the organisation. When presented with simple but clear values, people – the independent variable in our organisational equation- can generate creative ways of solving problems. Values bring a degree of coherence at a fundamental level; coherence about why things are being done. People may do things differently, they may even do different things but if that variety stems from a desire to enact like values then it is a source of strength, not a weakness. Organisations have sought consistency in what people do and how they do it. Fractals teach us that we should seek consistency in why we do something, leaving what and how to those that are better placed – those closest to and best equipped to deal with the problem. In this way, values are a powerful way of programming the organisation. They allow people to act in different and creative ways whilst still achieving the same purpose. What is important is that people understand why. In the same way that fractal equations lead to highly creative but self-repeating patterns of behaviour, leading with values will lead to highly creative and coherent organisations.

Criteria of living systems

The final lesson I discovered was also the most insightful on my journey to understanding organisations. In his book *The Web of Life*[15], Fritjof Capra examines the work of a number of leading scientists. Drawing together work of diverse backgrounds, Capra integrates these into three key criteria for living systems.

1. Pattern of Organisation: the configuration of relationships that determines the systems essential characteristics.
2. Structure: the physical embodiment of the system's pattern of organisation.
3. Life Processes: the activity involved in the continual embodiment of the system's pattern of organisation.

It is the role of life processes to translate the pattern of organisation into structure. By structure, Capra does not just mean skeleton; rather he describes the whole of a living system's structures.

It is a short step from Capra's view of living systems to my thoughts about organisation design. Companies have patterns of organisation. They are the values that live in the organisation. In excellent organisations, the values seen in the actions and decisions of people reflect those found on posters and in the words of the senior managers. Organisations seek to bring those values to life by implementing organisational processes. The result is an organisation that reflects, nay embodies its values. In the words of Arie de Geus, it is a living company.

Underpinning the view of life processes is autopoiesis. The concept was developed by two Chilean neuroscientists, Humberto Maturana and Francisco Varela in their efforts to understand the functioning of the nervous system. Literally translated, autopoiesis means self-making. They defined autopoiesis as 'a network of production processes in which the function of each component is to participate in the production or transformation of other components in the network'. The components of an autpoietic network are produced by processes operating within the network. It is self-perpetuating – the components are being constantly replaced by the system's own processes. Autopoiesis is an essential characteristic of any living system. This interaction of processes creates a system where actions and outcomes are not clearly linked but the result of a complex network of interactions. A specific outcome cannot therefore be planned as it is impossible to understand the complexity involved with any degree of confidence. It is why organisations have emergent properties where actions result from actions. All that we can really know is that action will have some result. We cannot know precisely what that result will be. That is a familiar story to anyone who has planned change only for the result to be quite different from that intended.

From nature to organisation

Translated into the field of organisational design and change, my learning journey can be summed up in the following six principles.

- Organisations need a focus. Purpose provides that by answering the question 'Why does the organisation exist?'.
- Values are the organisation's fractal equation. They are reflected in everything the organisation does and are a powerful and creative way of programming the organisation.

- There are two powerful vehicles for enacting values: leadership and organisational processes. Leadership is a series of activities not a role. Organisational processes define how the organisation carries out guidance and change.
- Real change is about changing the nature of the relationships both within the organisation and with its various customers, suppliers and other interested parties.
- Organisation design is about creating and maintaining a series of agendas and conversations across the whole organisation. The results of these conversations cannot be planned; to do so would constrain creativity and limit the potential of what might emerge.
- If you want to effect change focus more on organisational processes than structure.

In the rest of this book I will describe an approach to change that reflects these fundamental principles.

4 It all Begins with Human Nature

If you are planning for one year, grow rice,
If you are planning for 20 years, grow trees,
If you are planning for 100 years, grow people.
CHINESE PROVERB

The subheading of a short article discussing research into bullying at work read 'Workers should be treated like human beings'.[16] What a strange thought. Workers are human beings. How could they be treated as anything else? The article went on to describe the dichotomy between 'the type of boss employees want and the type needed to make companies successful'. This sums up many of the problems we face in organisations today. As the proportion of work that is reliant on the contribution of people increases, the ingrained attitudes that workers can be viewed as resources to be exploited will become a millstone around the necks of those who perpetuate such views. There is already a growing recognition of the link between employee satisfaction and productivity and customer satisfaction. Xerox's European services business headed by Olaf Odlind has shown this relationship. The maintenance teams with the highest productivity also have the highest customer and employee satisfaction.[17]

Organisations are essentially collections of people and it should be no surprise therefore that they reflect the way people think. This is not widely recognised in the actions and processes that many managers and organisations practice, although I do believe that this is the result of learned behaviour rather than an innate disbelief in people. The last 100 years of organisations have focused on structures and processes, often at the cost of people.

It is however people that make organisations and it is important therefore that those responsible for designing and leading organisations have a clear understanding of how people work. In this chapter, I will describe some of the more important aspects of how we as individuals think, the major characteristics of human nature and their implications for organisation design. I believe that without an understanding of human nature, leaders are unable to operate effectively. This is less a case of having to learn something new – we all understand human nature because we all contribute to and interrelate with the collective that is human nature. The greater task is to unlearn the behaviours that have accreted in the culture and traditions of management over the last 200 years. We have to remove the millstone that history has burdened us with.

The brain

In Chapter 3, I outlined some basic facts about the brain. I want to delve a little deeper into this wondrous organ.

In the previous chapter, I explained how the brain thinks emotionally before it does so logically. This 'beliefs before logic' structure for decision making is important for managers to understand. It explains why people often react in a seemingly irrational way to data that is presented: irrational that is in the view of the provider of that data. The implications of this are significant. It helps explain why values are an important element in recruitment and why communication is so difficult.

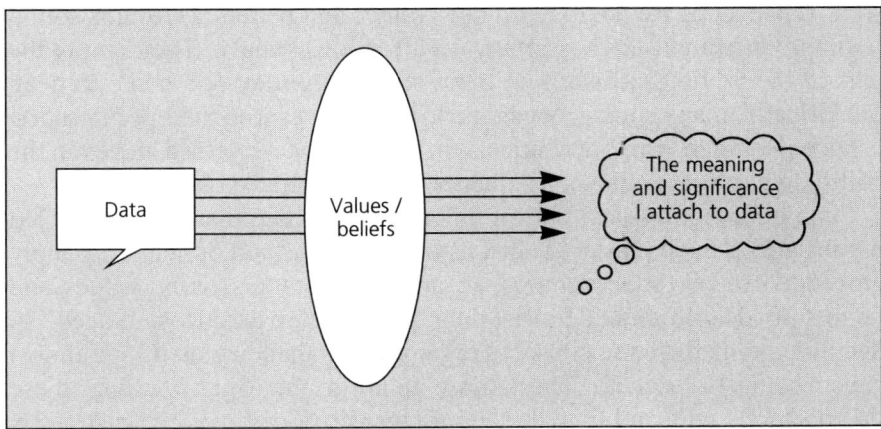

Fig. 4.1 Values and the thinking process

Remember that values are not the whole picture. Whilst values play an important role in our thinking, they do not dominate it. Where reason creates a compelling case, we will act against our values. Our ability to think and learn is what separates us from other species. We may do this for expediency or where we are forced to choose between two strongly held beliefs. This choice between right and right is much more difficult than the choice between right and wrong. It is also a choice that provides a much greater learning opportunity. We agonise over these choices. This soul searching causes us real difficulty and because of this, we may change our values, although the more strongly held the value, the less likely this becomes. This has significant implications for the development of leadership, a point I will return to later.

Our basic values are shaped early in life. Parents and others with whom we spend time in the formative years have a great influence on us. We are wired from our formative years to be beholden to the emotions and beliefs that we form as children. That does not mean we cannot change. Because the emotional centres of the brain have the ability to think and learn, we can change our beliefs and values. It is not an easy task and often requires the intervention of a very significant event such as a major illness, death of someone close, a change in life circumstances or a concerted effort to think through our beliefs. Part of the reason for this is that our true values are not conscious. We rarely bring our values into the open when we make a decision. Indeed we often search for the reasoned arguments that support our beliefs, further reinforcing them. We choose to ignore or ridicule reason and facts that suggest our values are inappropriate. We therefore do not present ourselves with the opportunity to question them and that is what is needed if we are to learn new values and beliefs. Does this sound familiar? It is precisely how many organisations behave. They ignore the part of the world that is telling them something they don't like to hear. Specifically, many senior managers do this. The cost to their organisation is huge: lost market opportunities, winning products rejected and even the ability to survive are the consequences of such blindspots.

Tapping the emotional pull of values is a practice that true values led organisations have mastered. Just as our emotions and beliefs are deeply embedded in our subconscious, so are some organisations' values and beliefs so deeply embedded in their psyche and practices. Indeed, so deeply ingrained are they in some organisations that they do things almost subconsciously because they know them to be right. Asking these organisations why and how they do things can sometimes be frustrating. They will often reply with confusion and comments like 'Well how else would you do it?' or 'It's just the right thing to do'. Whilst these organisations can draw great strength from such deeply held beliefs, they can also be damaging. I will return to this point later in the chapter.

Our reaction to the difficult task of managing people has all too often been to exclude emotions and beliefs and rely on rational decision making processes. A success model that has focused almost exclusively on financial performance as the sole measure of success has reinforced this rationality. When we are faced with emotionally charged situations our response is to try to convert the decision making process to one based on objectivity. But it can be argued that a rational response is itself irrational. Ignoring something because it is difficult to do does not make it go away. We have to face up to the reality of emotional, irrational people and find ways of building organisations that tap into the power of emotions and beliefs, not ignore them.

There is increasing evidence that sustainable success lies down this path. In their study of visionary companies, Collins and Porras[18] conclude that shared values coupled with a continuous restlessness with the status quo are the keys to long term success. In my first book[19] I identified leadership, vision and values as the driving force behind successful organisations. Kotter & Heskett[20] also point out the relationship between strong corporate cultures and successful financial performance. The success of companies like Avis Europe, Birmingham Midshires Building Society, First Direct and the US Army all show that building organisations around strong, shared values can and does lead to success.

Why are shared values so important? Shared values create an organisation where people can communicate better. If the filtering processes our brains automatically employ are working from similar shared values, there is less room for misunderstanding. Collaboration is easier to achieve between people who share the same values.

Organisational values vs personal values

We use the word 'values' in an organisational context to describe those vital few beliefs that underpin the organisation's way of doing things. The values of an individual are just that – individual. They guide the choices we make about our lifestyle, religion, politics and actions. Organisations have an interest in these but only if they are directly relevant to the work of the organisation. The church has little interest in people who want to be priests but who do not believe in God. Religious or political beliefs should be of little interest to organisations unless they are extreme and cause undue conflict. Tolerance of people with different values is a great strength. Companies that deal with customers and suppliers on a global scale need people who understand the values these groups operate with.

There is also great benefit in having people question and test the values. This is vital if the values are to be fully understood and remain relevant in a changing world. This latter point is particularly important and I will therefore return to it later in the chapter.

The process of building shared values in an organisation has to be embedded in every part of the organisation.

Starting with recruitment and with constant reinforcement through training, coaching and feedback and the very way they operate, companies like Avis Europe and TNT invest considerable money and effort in developing shared values. This investment is recouped through improved performance. They are able to form teams more quickly as people more readily build relationships with those who hold similar values. As the examples above show, Avis Europe has consistently been the most profitable rental car company in Europe. TNT Express Parcels has outperformed its competitors in growth and profitability.

There are two dangers to watch for when building shared values as a basis for organisation design.

The first is to recognise that shared values do not have to be altruistic to achieve performance. Hitler built a team around him that had a strong set of shared values, and performance against a chilling objective was high. The political landscape is peppered with groups that 'punch above their weight'. I am not placing commercial organisations in this category, although a number suggest through their actions that they have little regard for the people they employ. They will find it increasingly difficult to attract talented people to work for them and those that do will rarely perform at their best. Customers also are expressing concern about organisations that ruthlessly exploit people. The makers of soccer balls have come under great pressure to change their supply strategy to ensure that under age children in less well off countries are not unfairly exploited. Indeed a whole movement is growing to put pressure on large companies to employ ethical sourcing strategies. There is no evidence that successful organisations share the same values, but as I will explore later in this chapter, an understanding of human nature is a common thread.

The second, and more significant danger for organisations building shared values, is the danger of creating a culture that becomes disconnected from the larger world. To be successful the shared values of an organisation have to reflect the values and needs of the broader communities they serve. But values can blind individuals and organisations to the often subtle changes in their operating environment. As a result, some organisations become increasingly self-serving and generate false confidence. This is a reason behind many corporate failures.

Too many organisations believe that what has succeeded in the past will succeed in the future. They believe their own propaganda and ignore the signs of change in the outside world. Just as the brain's limbic system filters decisions and blinds people to certain pieces of information, values can filter information and decisions in organisations.

There are ways to avoid this values induced myopia. For the individual, it involves taking a second look at reality and being personally open to the possibility of being wrong. When considering important issues people should take alternative views to those held and test to see which fits the facts best.

For the organisation, there are two mechanisms that can limit the danger. The first is to include in the shared value set a curiosity for the world outside the organisation. A natural curiosity for how well the organisation is serving its customers, the changes that are happening in society as a whole, technology and the actions of competitors and other organisations undertaking similar activities is essential. This belief in the need to understand the outside world builds into the organisation's values a dynamic that constantly creates the need for change.

The second is strategic appointments, a concept used by Avis Europe to test its values. To ensure its values continue as a strong thread, around which the organisation weaves its activities, Avis Europe promotes from within. Eighty-eight per cent of its senior managers began life at the frontline. The remainder are recruited externally either to fill a skill gap created by rapidly changing technologies or as a way of bringing fresh blood into the organisation. This group is expected to test the culture for its relevance to the needs of a modern organisation. To date the values of Avis Europe have stood the test of time.

Shared values in the context of an organisation do not mean that everyone thinks the same. Whilst they may share the underlying beliefs, they have different ideas and opinions about how these values should be enacted and what decisions should be taken. They bring to the discussion their own ideas, experiences and skills. Paradoxically shared values encourage a difference of opinion and the discussion and dialogue associated with it. People who truly hold a value will argue their case with passion, putting forward their own ideas and thoughts. Through this process of dialogue, ideas and actions are refined and a sense of commitment is built. The dialogue also helps people to gain a deeper understanding of the real meaning of the values that underpin the decisions. This is in effect a virtuous circle of action and dialogue that continually tests and improves the values and people's understanding of them. The process also tests the values themselves. If they cannot stand up to the rigour of fundamental examination, they are weak values. It is this process that makes values implicit in an organisation. Organisations that have achieved this have an added competitive dimension.

Characteristics of human nature

The things that make people tick have not changed over thousands of years. There is evidence from the field of evolutionary psychology that human nature is innate.[21] We cannot escape it. Our implicit understanding of it shapes our actions and reactions. It is important therefore to recognise it and build organisations that work with the grain of human nature, not against it. Indeed, it is the key to creating successful organisations. Organisations that play to the strengths of human nature are more likely to succeed over the long term. In considering the factors that organisations have to consider, I have excluded some of the very basic characteristics and instincts such as physical survival, parenting and sex. This is not to say that these do not have a bearing on how people behave, but to address them lies outside the scope of a book on managing organisations.

It is also wrong to assume that everybody shares the same traits of human nature. Despots and dictators have always acquired and exploited power for evil means but they are a small, albeit high profile minority. The vast majority are decent human beings seeking a worthwhile and satisfying life for themselves and their families.

So, what are the characteristics that people leading organisations need to take cognisance of?

A desire to know the big picture

We all need to know where we fit into the grand scheme of things. People have an innate need to know what is happening around them. This search for a broad understanding is manifested in different ways: the search for the origin of the universe and research into the mechanisms of the creation of life. The desire to understand the big picture underpins our quest for learning. This knowledge gives people greater control and security. When people know how things fit together, they can make a more considered judgement of the actions and decisions of others. People can more clearly perceive and understand the context in which things around are happening. Without this rich contextual understanding people feel powerless because they can make no sense of the world around us. Decisions don't make sense. Actions seem unconnected and aimless, if not downright contradictory. Creativity is suppressed because the context which creativity needs to thrive is unclear or even worse, non-existent.

It is lack of this knowledge of the big picture that is behind the question 'why' – the most asked and least answered question in any organisation. People ask why because they do not understand the big picture and the reasons behind decisions. They can make no sense of things and are subsequently frustrated. Cascade mechanisms that are so popular in organisations reinforce a narrow view of the organisation. People are told in great detail about their part, their little box but lack the perspective that helps them understand how their activities fit into the big picture. They are doomed to be small cogs in a faceless machine.

Need for meaning

There is a second reason that people ask 'why?'. It is that everyone has to find meaning in their life. A life without meaning is not really living, it is merely existing. Community health studies have identified that three factors underpin a sense of well being in individuals: physical vitality, belonging to community and a sense of meaning or purpose.[22] I contend that the same is true of organisations. People who have a purpose in their lives enjoy life more and have a greater feeling of control over their own destiny. They exude drive and determination. Meaning provides a powerful raison d'être for our actions.

Meaning is that part of life where you give something to participate in activity that has higher ideals. It is the need to know that life is something other than merely existing. Maslow described it as self-actualisation, but believed it was a need that was only addressed when other, more basic needs were fulfilled. Meaning however is a basic tenet of human nature. It is a fundamental need. People will forgo other benefits in the quest to fulfil their need for meaning. Rather than the tip of a hierarchy, meaning is one of several needs that humans have, each of which dynamically interacts with the world around to shape our drive and motivation.

For most people work accounts for about one quarter of our time between the ages of twenty and sixty. If work has no meaning to people there is little wonder that we have problems with motivation. Action without meaning is merely toil. If we are to truly engage people, by which I mean tapping into their creativity and commitment, life in the organisation has to make some contribution to an individual's sense of meaning. Profit does not provide a sense of meaning, nor does an increasing share price. Meaning is of a higher order than survival and salary. Meaning involves relationships and aspiration to a more noble cause. This cause does not have to be a grand, world-changing cause. Charity work, school governorship and working with community groups are all noble causes that attract people who want to give something back.

More people are turning to such activities because work no longer contributes to meaning in their lives. Many of the generation coming into middle and senior management have different views. Helen Wilkinson, a member of the National Work/Life Forum spent four days discussing the future of work with peers from North America.

> For those four days we put aside the realities of our working lives – long hours, increasing job insecurity – and dared to imagine another future. We were all in our twenties and thirties and well educated, and had lived through a middle-class recession. We were all too aware that the old rules no longer applied, and we were there that weekend to brainstorm on what might take their place. In contrast to our parents' generation, we did not spend much time discussing job security. Instead we discussed employability. *But most of the time we talked about wanting interesting and varied work: work which gave our lives meaning as well as bringing us a pay cheque at the end of the month.*[23] [Author's emphasis]

Need for security

The most basic of human needs is a need for security; knowledge that next week and next month the individual will be able to fend for him/herself and the family. When a sense of security is removed or threatened people worry. As with many other things in organisations the feeling of insecurity may be unrealistic and entirely without foundation, but perceptions count. Many children need a security blanket, or favourite teddy, without which they are unable to sleep. Their physical and social conditions may be no different, but that one thing makes a difference. That thing is less the physical item but much more the state of the mind. This need for security and our irrational response to any threat to it – real or perceived – dogs many organisations.

Security in an organisational context has different perspectives, employment being the main one. Organisations are being exhorted to move towards more part-time and contract workers in an attempt to bring costs more in line with business volumes and activities. Charles Handy's shamrock model suggests that organisations will comprise a small, full time core supplemented by part-time and contract workers. This will undoubtedly provide organisations with the flexibility to balance the supply and demand of labour and to shift the skill set employed in a rapidly changing economy, but what will be lost? What happens to loyalty and commitment? How willingly will people bring forward creative new ideas when they have no guarantee of being able to share in the benefits of such ideas? I believe that the old fashioned values of loyalty and security of employment have life in them yet.

Natural curiosity

Every organisation has at least one very effective communication process – the rumour mill. This is a natural response to our curiosity. We have a desire to know about the world about us. It is the same reason that 'fly-on-the-wall' documentaries are so popular and why the tabloid press and the paparazzi are so insistent. We have a real interest in everything about us because we cannot help it, it is part of our make-up. This curiosity is what has fed our development for hundreds and thousands of years. It is an essential component of our ability to learn, our great capacity for which differentiates us from other species. Our natural curiosity provides the new stimuli on which learning is based.

Curiosity is one of the fundamental ways the brain works at the cellular level. Brain cells spend their lives looking for other cells to exchange impulses with. Until it has exhausted all possible connections, it continues searching, pushing out its tentacles looking for a connection. When it repeatedly fails to find a connection, it dies.

In organisations this is expressed as genuine interest in the health and direction of the company. We want to know how we are doing, individually and collectively. We want to know about new developments that will affect our lives, not just because they have a direct impact but because curiosity expands our understanding. The rumour mill is so successful and pervasive because our curiosity is starved of the information that our curiosity drives us to seek out. We are continually trying to add more reference points to the big picture.

Every time information is shared on a 'need to know' basis our curiosity is denied its sustenance. The implication of curiosity being ignored goes beyond the rumour mill. Creativity thrives best in an information rich environment that allows people to make connections, just like the cells in our brains.

Curiosity is also suppressed by fear. When people are afraid of the consequences, their natural curiosity is held in check. Unfortunately, we have structured this fear into many of our organisations. Autocratic management, systems that leave no space for learning and dole out reprisals for failure, work to suppress curiosity and the learning that is associated with it. Unfortunately, that curiosity might well be the key to survival.

Need for recognition

We know when we have done a good job but we still get an enormous sense of pride when that is recognised. We might not let on to our friends and colleagues, but inside we glow when our efforts are recognised. Recognition provides us with a sense of status that often exceeds our position in the pecking order. For a brief moment we are a star.

Recognition also helps us also build a view of what is important. When we see people recognised for their actions we will often infer that that behaviour or action is worthwhile. Recognition creates heroes and winners in our minds. It is a powerful way of sending a signal to the rest of the organisation about what counts.

In many organisations, recognition is a significantly under-utilised tool. Too few people understand the power of a simple thank you.

Recognition at TNT

This text is an extract from TNT's winning entry for the European Quality Award 1999. The names of customers and partners have been changed to protect confidentiality.

Recognition at TNT is one of the company's nine principles; it states:

> Recognising individual and team achievements, promoting from within wherever possible and encouraging everyone to enjoy rewarding careers which provide security and job satisfaction.

In their winning European Quality Award submission, the recognition process is described as follows:

> We incentivise staff by rewarding performance and recognising

exceptional achievements. Commendation of effort and achievement is a routine part and of our working practices.

There is a well developed structure of the Divisional recognition linked to KPIs. We measure the effectiveness of our approach to recognition by reference to our people surveys. As a result of review and refinement of the approach we have introduced a plan that divisional recognition schemes, for example, TNT Excellence Awards and a Group Driver of the Year awards to support existing divisional awards.

Our formal recognition process is set out in Figure 4.2.

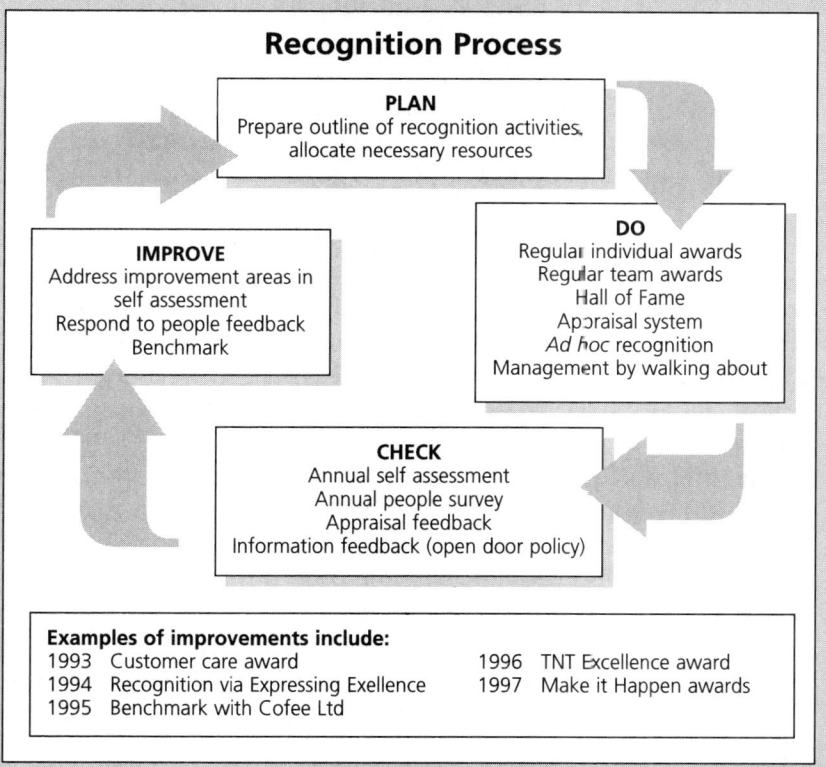

Fig 4.2 TNT's recognition process

Every piece of paper passed to our CEO showing good performance by any individual is sent immediately to that individual with a handwritten a note of thanks and a recognition. Dozens of such notes which include praise for individual performance on all league tables and newsletters are sent each week. When TNT won the UK Quality Award and each of our three European Quality Prizes letters of congratulation were sent to every employee.

Following the role model behaviour of the CEO all managers showed timely recognition and efforts and successors at local level. Recognition is often verbal rather than written because there is every day contact between local managers and members of the depot teams. Effectiveness of leaders' involvement in recognition is measured via the people survey.

The TNT Express operations director has identified five 'Best Ever' measures and targets. Performance charts are published weekly. Successful locations receive recognition and a financial incentive. In TNT Newsfast key performance indicators are load discrepancies and on-time delivery. Good performances are recognised in letters from the operations director and divisional managing director.

In TNT Logistics specific performance indicators are identified and mutually agreed with each customer during the contract development process which is controlled within the scope of our ISO9000 certification. The KPIs are monitored weekly and 20 standard KPIs are tracked across all contracts. Local managers recognise good performance at their own sites. Account directors who are responsible for a number of sites recognise achievement at that level.

The group health and safety officer champions Driver of the Year competitions which take into account safety, courtesy, economy, technical expertise and other factors. The response to our Driver of the Year competitions has been reflected in a reduced incidence of accidents and improved fuel consumption.

All divisions have awards for Depot and Contract Managers of the Year together with the Customer Care Awards. These competitions are highly publicised via posters, inhouse magazines and briefings. Awards are presented by divisional and group directors.

In administration we measure invoice queries, credit notes, debtor weeks outstanding and overdue debt. Local administration teams are always recognised for achieving targets by the director of credit and administration. The chief executive has always sent a handwritten note each month to each successful team and this practice continues.

For the various sales teams weekly newsletters are produced to update product awareness and sustain interest in our various incentive programmes. Above average results are publicised and successful individuals and teams are recognised and commended. The CEO sends numerous handwritten notes to high achieving and improved performance.

National sales conferences are held each year to introduce new products and incentive and review our achievements. Prizes are presented by the sales director and divisional managing director and individual and team achievements are celebrated with the conference in January being a particularly motivating experience.

Weekly customer feedback covering the eight elements of Expressing Excellence is circulated to all the depots. The sales director writes an accompanying letter highlighting the outstanding achievements and improvements. Each depot now logs its own progress against these and numerous other key indicators on the prominently displayed wallcharts. Locally produced newsletters are circulated with key performance indicators.

Each quarter the most successful team in each region is presented with a Customer Care plaque by the regional director. The top national team receives an annual award from the divisional managing director. Individual customer care performance is recognised with a certificate. Winners are selected by a panel of directors and employees and receive £250 each. An annual national winner receives a trophy and £1 000.

Individuals are nominated for our Hall of Fame in recognition of outstanding performance. Nominees are invited to lunch with the chief executive and have their portraits hung in TNT head office. The occasion is also celebrated in our inhouse magazines.

In 1995 our CEO served as juror for Coffee Limited's internal quality award. In 1996 we introduced our own TNT Excellence Award. This award is based on the three TQM principles of customer focus, involvement and continuous improvement. Three individuals and one team received the inaugural awards and cash sums from the chief executive in autumn 1996 to recognise exceptional endeavour and enterprise in achieving service excellence. Over 100 peer nominations were received. In 1997 over 120 nominations were received.

When reviewing our approach to recognition in 1997 we decided to make recognition even more timely and to reinforce the use of this tool as a way for management to demonstrate their commitment to company principles. In 1997 our 'I Made it Happen' awards were introduced. These awards are designed to help local managers encourage our 'must get through' attitude and are made immediately where outstanding individual instances of this are shown. We presented 57 regular 'I Made it Happen' awards to staff in 1997 and a further 146 special awards to each person at our Bradford depot for their fantastic effort in handling the Silver Ltd flotation in June.

Our purchasing director runs a supplier accreditation programme based on a scoring system of 40 per cent quality, 30 per cent cost and 30 per cent service. Each year he presents the TNT Supplier of the Year awards for the highest score.

TNT managers regularly recognise customers' success and celebrate joint achievements. Notable examples are the successes of our collaborations with Black Ltd and Sage Ltd. We regularly ask our customers to appear in TNT videos and feature in inhouse magazines. Each year we invite selected customers to join us at quality related events such as the UK Quality Award presentation, the EFQM Business Excellence Forum and conferences organised by Midland's Excellence.

Need for control

We dislike being in situations where we cannot exercise some control over our own destiny. When placed in these situations we feel fear, apprehension and concern. These are not conditions in which we are creative or highly productive. They are however the conditions found in most organisations. We have built rules and created hierarchies that place people in little boxes, and with no space to exert real influence over what they do, they are powerless.

This need for control underpins the syndrome found in most organisations – resistance to change. People resist change because they see change as a threat. Given the experience of the late twentieth century, that is not at all surprising. But people do not resist change, they resist being changed. Participation brings understanding which in turn minimises the sense of being out of control. Such control does not remove resistance to change which can be deeply embedded. It does however provide a strategy that reduces its effect.

Need for interaction

Homo sapiens is essentially a group animal. We hunted in groups, farmed in groups and we work in groups. We raise our children in groups and we teach them in groups. Many of our sports are team based. Whilst we can enjoy periods of solitude, we need interaction with others. Studies of health show that people who lack a social network, a community with which they can identify, are more likely to succumb to illness. Our desire to belong is strong; we have always been relationship orientated animals.

This need for interaction is because collaboration is the only way to achieve essential goals. Hunting for food was more successfully achieved in groups, even if this involved sharing the spoils. Through this interaction, we learn to trust others and identify those who cannot be trusted. Learning is also underpinned by interaction. We see how others do things and take those lessons on board. We express our opinions, take actions and then watch for the reactions of others. In this way, we enrich the picture we have of ourselves. We see our impact on the wider environment. These interactions help to shape our character. Indeed it can be argued that we are defined by our relationships. So important are relationships that we often define our sense of meaning in terms of our relationships with other people. Relationships – our interaction with others – are a fundamental part of our make up.

In many organisations, the focus has been exclusively on tasks with little thought to relationships. As a result, people have felt they have been pushed aside, and are of secondary importance. Relationships have been essentially ignored. It is therefore of little surprise that so many people complain that their work has no meaning when relationships, the foundations upon which meaning is built, are essentially ignored when we design and build organisations. Organisations provide a community for their people, but few make any real effort to foster a community spirit. Work is separated from socialising; personal relationships from professional relationships. This is not universal. Many eastern cultures place friendship above professional relationships, building networks of family related businesses. The need for relationships might be innate but how we implement it is learned.

Aversion to risk

Based on our basic instinct for survival, most people avoid placing themselves in risky situations. True, there are people that seek out danger but they are a small minority. People who are comfortable have more to lose and therefore are less likely to take risks. Paradoxically, when people are under great threat, they will take great risks, on the basis that there is probably little to lose.

Putting people in an environment where they are constantly personally threatened will cause the wrong behaviours. This environment will encourage win:lose behaviour and work against collaboration. People will play the political short game, keep information and ideas to themselves and look for other, safer opportunities. What is needed is an environment that heightens the threat but also depersonalises it. This will encourage collective risk-taking to beat the external threat.

Ability to learn

We have an in-built ability to learn throughout our lives. Whilst we may learn more in the first 12 months of our lives than the remainder, we never lose the ability to learn. An old dog *can* learn new tricks.

Learning at the physiological level is about setting down chemical pathways between neurones in the brain. These pathways are the response to stimulus from outside. The more stimuli the brain receives, the more pathways are created. If there is a physical limit, we certainly have not reached it. The real limit is created by restricting the stimuli we receive. We do the familiar things, particularly if our risk threshold is low. In many organisations the restriction is imposed. People are forced to do the same thing in the same way. The ability and desire to learn still exists, but it is not allowed to flourish. In time, the desire to learn becomes suppressed, the effort involved in gaining the stimulus is not rewarded.

This ability to learn has a negative side – a difficulty with un-learning. As the patterns within our brain become entrenched as a result of the very practice that is essential in establishing learning, the work required to break those patterns increases. It is perhaps wrong to think of un-learning, which often leads to punishment or negative strategies. Better to focus on consolidating the new learning through recognition and reinforcement.

Some of these characteristics of human nature are contradictory. We seek control, but shirk from bad news even when that will open up our possibilities and give us greater control over our destiny. We have an ability to learn but we shy away from situations that will provide learning opportunities if they involve personal risk. It is perhaps these contradictory traits, these in-built checks and balances, which have been part of our success as a species. It is the contradictory nature of these traits that makes managing people in organisations such a demanding task.

It would be wrong for people to assume that these traits exist in exactly the same way in everybody. Like many things in life people exhibit these traits to differing degrees. What we are is a complex melée of human nature, the cultural traits we absorb from our surroundings – our family and country – and our own personality. This richness of interacting factors makes us unique. It also makes us difficult to understand and our actions unpredictable.

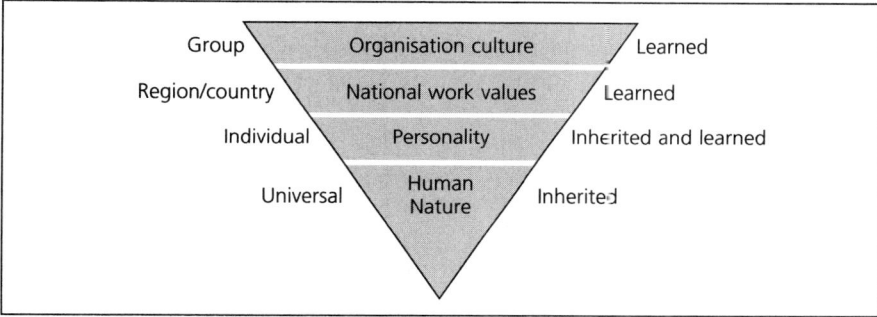

Fig. 4.3 Layers of cultural complexity

I have used these learnings in my work and in the development of the process for building dynamic organisations. You will see these underpinnings appearing throughout the rest of the book. They can be very powerful ways of getting people to think outside their normal frame of reference. I have found that people will more readily consider new ideas if they can relate it to things that they recognise, albeit in other walks of life. We have always used metaphors as a way of communicating. These are new metaphors for organisations and change that I commend to you. I also counsel you to look outside the everyday world of work and organisations and discover your own new metaphors.

Part II
Dynamic Change

Bounded vs Dynamic Change

*Things work out best for those who make
the best of the way things work out.*
ANONYMOUS

In organisations there are two distinct but closely interrelated cycles of change. Every organisation needs to continually examine its products and processes and find better ways of doing those activities that are necessary. New systems have to be introduced, new products brought to market and improvements to the way the organisation does business implemented. This type of change, I will call it bounded change, is bounded, with a clear end goal; the process delivers a change. The change may vary in scale or scope: a small team working on improving one of their processes, the introduction of a new organisation wide accounting system, or the delivery of a company-wide branding are all examples of bounded change. By bounded I do not mean that the change is necessarily easy to effect. Few changes are. I use the phrase because change of this nature involves bounded problems and end-points. There is a known goal to aim for, even if that goal is developed as part of the process of change.

Dynamic change on the other hand has no end point. It is about building an organisation's ability to change. It is a problem of an altogether different nature. Achieving dynamic change is about creating an environment within the organisation where people are encouraged to take on the responsibility for change. It is about creating an environment where bounded change happens continuously, much of it without any top down direction. Dynamic change means building an organisation that is closely in touch with the outside world, using the stream of information and insights to fuel improvements and changes.

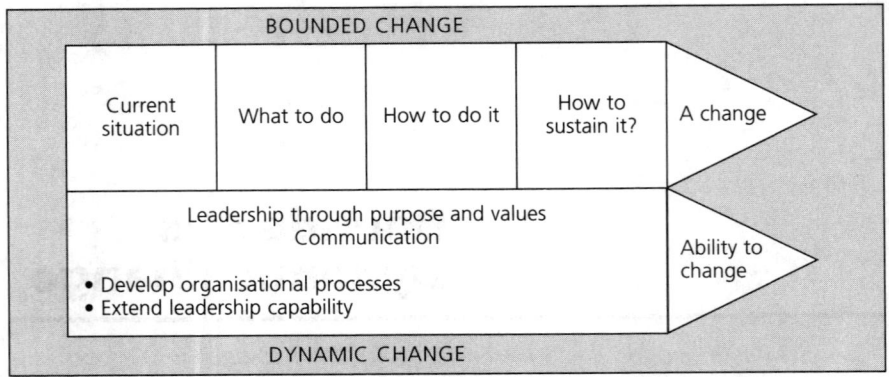

Fig. 5.1 Bounded vs dynamic change

Bounded change can be fostered and developed by teaching people an approach to change; providing them with the tools, capabilities and opportunities to develop and implement change projects. Dynamic change – building the capability to change – only happens when the organisation takes on an eternal sense of curiosity and desire for improvement coupled with an intention to be the best at its chosen business, traits that have to be deeply embedded in the culture.

The difference between bounded and dynamic change is more than academic. The process for introducing bounded change is totally different from that required to enact and sustain dynamic change. Bounded change can address a problem or issue within a part of an organisation but dynamic change is always an organisation wide and all embracing issue. It is impossible to build a dynamic organisation without addressing all the aspects of the organisation. It is a perfect example of holistic change. The other important difference between the two is the nature of the change process. Bounded change is essentially a linear process. Whilst the steps may overlap and merge, there are a series of steps to follow for a given end. In dynamic change, the steps overlap hugely and the goal continually changes. Many organisations have sought to achieve dynamic changes using a process that is ill-suited.

Navigating bounded change

The concept of dynamic change is about building an organisation's ability to change. The core of this is the organisation's ability to deliver change time and time again. Dynamic organisations ensure that a process of change is available to everyone and everyone has the ability and freedom to use it. This process of bounded change is about delivering a specified outcome. Providing people within the organisation with the tools often encourages application and development of the change skill. Each time the skill is practised there is an opportunity to reflect, learn and improve. In a dynamic organisation these learnings are shared, refined and embedded, further ratcheting up the change capability.

Some organisations have primed the building of their change capability by providing people with a framework for bounded change. GE developed its 'Workout' programme to provide people across the organisation with an approach to continuous improvement. The Unipart Group of Companies has a programme called Ten(d) to Zero which it uses across its organisation and encourages suppliers and partners to adopt. Other organisations have adopted proprietary change methods. Whatever the approach, the goal is the same: provide staff with the means to identify and deliver continuous improvement.

The power of continuous improvement is undervalued by many organisations. They seek the big breakthroughs that redefine their industry. They are not wrong to do this but they are wrong to rely on it to the exclusion of all else. The whole organisation should be looking for entirely new ways of doing things. But by definition, breakthroughs are not an everyday occurrence.

The second reason that continuous improvement is so important is the scale of improvement that can be achieved by cumulative action. Let me illustrate this with a simple example. Place one grain of rice on the first square of a chess board, two on the second, four on the third, eight on the fourth and so on. Now guess how many you would have on the 64th square. One million? 10 million? More? The answer is a staggering 2^{63} or 9 223 370 000 000 000 000 – over 9 million trillion. Assuming each grain of rice is 1 mm thick and was stacked one on top of each other, the pile would reach to the sun and back 30 827 times! This is the power of continuous improvement when each improvement adds to the value of the last. Programmes such as workout are not trivial attempts to get people feeling involved; they are significant contributors to improved performance. High involvement with continuous improvement is one reason for Avis' record of 16 years of year-on-year productivity improvements. GE is now building on the foundation provided by Workout to introduce its Six Sigma programme across all the company's activities. When many organisations are happy to accept 99.9 per cent quality or 6210 failures per million, Six Sigma is the quest for performance that accepts only three failures per million. It is this awesome level of performance that world class companies seek.

Six Sigma at GE[24]

In 1995, the General Electric Company adopted and launched what is perhaps the largest quality initiative in corporate history: a rigorous, data intensive approach to quality called Six Sigma.

During the programme's first two years, GE realised savings of 150 per cent of its initial investment. A total savings and increased revenue of 250 per cent of the annual investment is expected for 1999. As a result, they set an aggressive goal to become a Six Sigma company – to transform our products and processes to a near-flawless standard of quality – by the year 2000.

Six Sigma permeates the GE culture and has become a major part of the company's multi-million dollar annual training and education effort. To meet the year 2000 goal, GE trained nearly 4000 individuals, known as Black Belts and Master Black Belts, in Six Sigma techniques. In turn, these mentors have trained more than 30 000 other employees in how to integrate Six Sigma projects and techniques into their daily work. By the year 2000, all GE employees would be trained in Six Sigma methodologies.

GE businesses reap the rewards of Six Sigma

Here are some specific examples of how various GE businesses have benefited from the Six Sigma approach to quality:

GE Medical Systems: in 1997, Six Sigma projects contributed $42 million to GE Medical System's operating margin.

- GE Power Systems: completed more than 2500 Six Sigma projects in 1997, with a benefit to the business of $94 million.
- GE Supply: achieved more than 40 per cent sales growth with customers targeted by a Six Sigma project focus; in addition, a 50–75 per cent reduction in defects was achieved for each Six Sigma project closed.
- GE Electrical Distribution & Control: in 1997, the Six Sigma programme delivered almost double the originally committed financial benefits with payback of 2.6 to 1.
- GE Plastics: a Six Sigma project cut lead time for colour matching process by 85 per cent, resulting in a key competitive advantage

Bounded change process

In setting out a process for bounded change, it is important to state that I do not believe that this is the only way. I have seen many approaches to change used with success. The purpose in setting out the bounded change process is to share something that I know works. My advice is that you use this and other approaches to develop something that works for you, something that reflects the needs of your culture and industry.

Let's start with the overall framework. It is predicated on understanding the gap between the current level of performance and what is required to meet customers needs and achieve an edge over the competition. The framework recognises that the world changes from the outside and that is where the focus of change efforts must be. The first question should always be aimed at building an understanding of the world around us, notably the customer. The second important point is that it is important to understand the starting point. Many changes fail because they have an inaccurate or incomplete view of how the current process or organisation works. The result is a change that is badly designed and does not achieve the goals set within the time agreed.

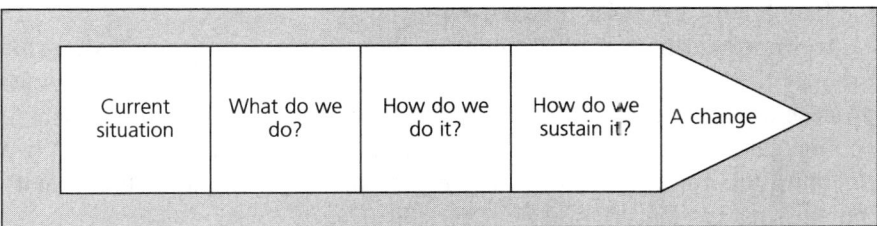

Fig. 5.2 Bounded change process

For each step of the process I have set out the key questions and identified a series of tools and techniques that can be used. This list is not exhaustive and you can doubtless think of tools and techniques that have worked for you.

In describing the steps of bounded change, I will us the word 'system' as the object of the change project. In this context system is used in its truest sense to decribe an organisational system and not just an IT system, although this might be one component.

Current situation

Understanding what is happening is the first step. This is all about collecting and understanding data and collecting information and insights about the world outside. Any organisation must establish a measurement process that informs people of performance trends. Internal measures are essential for tracking process efficiency but external customer based measures are needed to ensure that products and services deliver against customers' changing needs.

A vital first question 'Is this activity necessary?'. This question should encourage the search to minimise non-value added activities. There is no value in improving an activity that is unnecessary; indeed any effort here merely compounds the waste. Customer needs are a useful starting point. Data here will help to highlight activities that are not valued by customers and are therefore obvious candidates for elimination. Organisations that are curious also have an edge. They are constantly looking at how other organisations do things and therefore pick up ideas and tips that they use to improve their performance. When South West Airlines was looking at how it could improve flight turnround times, it studied motor racing pit stops where a car can be refuelled and have new wheels fitted in less than eight seconds. South West have not achieved that level, but have become the benchmark for aircraft turnaround.

An important part of understanding the current situation is to describe the way the current process operates. There is a variety of techniques for process mapping from the very simple (Post-It notes on brown paper) to sophisticated, computer based modelling and simulation tools. When mapping the current situation it is important to highlight problems with the existing system.

Key questions

- Is this activity essential?
- What customer data have we got?
- Who is the best in class performer and how do they achieve it?
- What additional data do we need?
- What opportunities can we exploit if we improve performance?
- Are there any threats from not improving?
- How is the current process/activity operated?

Useful tools

Voice of the Customer:	a matrix based on Quality Function Deployment used to identify the key requirements of customers
Relationship Scorecard:	a scorecard used to track the performance of key issues in a supplier/customer relationship
Dynamic Organisation Audit:	an organisational assessment to identify areas for improvement
Bechmarking:	a systematic comparison of performance of key processes
Statistical Process Control:	measurement of process performance using statistical techniques
Process Mapping:	depict and analyse the way the current system works

What do we do?

This is the stage where the solution is defined. Based on a thorough understanding of the strengths and weaknesses of the current situation and the possibilities gleaned from benchmarking and learning, the dreaming begins. At this stage it is important not to limit the possibilities. Many a crazy idea has turned into a great business proposition. The Japanese use a technique called contingent based thinking where they set an outrageous goal and then consider how it can be achieved. For example, the superb suspension on the Lexus was the result of asking how a car could operate with square wheels. The impossible question led to breakthroughs and a higher level of performance. Small improvements can be achieved by tinkering with the existing system. Outrageous goals shake people out of their frames of reference and help them consider the unthinkable.

Envisioning the new solution should lead to the creation of a number of options. Each of these can be compared to the existing way of working and the gap between old and new assessed. This gap can then be used to calculate the performance improvement gained. All too often people fail to do the sums. The gap between the old and the new is also the basis of the project plan.

Key questions

- How can this process/activity operate most effectively?
- What benefits does each option deliver?
- What is our chosen option?
- What are the priorities for change?

Useful tools

Process mapping:	depict the way the future process/activity works.
Scenario planning:	the development of scenarios of the future as the basis for learning and action.
Brainstorming:	development of ideas and options.
Trade-off analysis:	quantification and assessment of alternative options.

How do we do it?

This stage is about moving from thinking to doing. The gap between the current and future state is used as the basis of developing a project plan. The plan should cover the major milestones but should not be so detailed that it removes any opportunity for interpretation and adjustments. Detailed project plans fall foul of changing circumstances and the larger the scope of the project, the greater the chances it will be impacted by circumstances. Plans often invoke a strange behaviour. People blindly follow the plan, even when the circumstances make such acts folly. It is the behaviour that leads companies to continue to invest in projects even when the expected benefits are no longer achievable. Blind allegiance to a plan is a sign of an organisation where thinking is only done at the top and the rest of the organisation are expected to follow orders. Plans should be sufficient to identify the major activities, milestones and dependencies.

A key part of this phase of the change is the building of the appropriate skills, but flexible enough to accomodate changes.

Key questions

- How will the changes be effected?
- What skills are needed and do we have them all?
- Are changes needed in information systems?

- What is the timetable for change?
- When will benefits be reaped?
- What tools and techniques will we use to effect the change?
- How will we track and manage progress?

Useful tools

Project planning:	development of project plans.
Competency frameworks:	identify the skills needed.
Learning sets:	develop the skills and behaviours required.

How do we sustain it?

Many changes are successfully implemented but do not stick. There are three reasons for this. First, the people who have to do the work are inadequately involved. As a result they lack real commitment to the change and, in extreme cases, will work against it. Secondly, the change is ill thought out and does not deliver the expected benefits. Finally, the change is successfully implemented but the systems and processes it interfaces with are unchanged. The changes are squeezed out by the inertia of the greater system. Measurement systems in particular have the potential to derail change. New systems are designed to deliver a different mix of results that are not recognised by the measurement and incentive systems. The change team have to ensure, as far as is possible, that associated systems are also changed.

Like a plant, if any change is to succeed in the long term it has to be carefully nurtured in the early days. It needs the support of leaders to provide space and time to iron out teething problems that will inevitably arise.

Key questions

- What associated systems need to change?
- Do measures reflect the new system?
- Is performance in line with expectations?
- What feedback and reinforcing loops can we use/introduce?
- Do people have the right skills and the opportunity to practise them?

Useful tools

Scorecards: ensure measures reflect the new system.
Appraisal systems: embed the new skills and behaviours.

Towards dynamic change

The process of bounded change is of little value if it is not widely practised. Encouraging the spread of the bounded change practice is one of the key organisational processes found in dynamic organisations. Indeed the wide use of bounded change is an essential component of a dynamic organisation. The approach, tools and techniques contained in a bounded change process form part of the capabilities a dynamic organisation needs. The widespread application of bounded change constantly ratchets up performance of all elements of the organisation. Learning and development programmes provide the basic skills of change and on-the-job coaching provides continuous support, encouragement and further improvement. Leaders encourage teams and individuals to establish change projects. They practise the skills and deliver results. Their experience encourages others to set up change projects. A self-reinforcing cycle is established; success begets success and the seeds of dynamic change are sown.

As people across the organisation practise change, the bounded change process becomes second nature. Anyone can initiate a change: they have the skills, the tools and the confidence. They know that they will be heard and supported. Over time people across the organisation begin to make a real, visible contribution to improving performance. They are more involved in the organisation and develop their understanding of how the organisation works.

Providing a bounded change process and toolkit is not in itself a guarantee of success. People have to be encouraged to use it and take responsibility. Pizza Hut in the UK expresses this through their 'Accountability Triangle'.

Much of Pizza Hut's organisational and individual development is aimed at creating the skills and the conditions where everybody can operate in the top slice of the triangle. That requires not just talented individuals but an organisation that:

- Helps people understand the business environment in which the organisation operates.
- Ensures people are clear about the vision and goals of the organisation.
- Reinforces the values that the organisation holds dear.

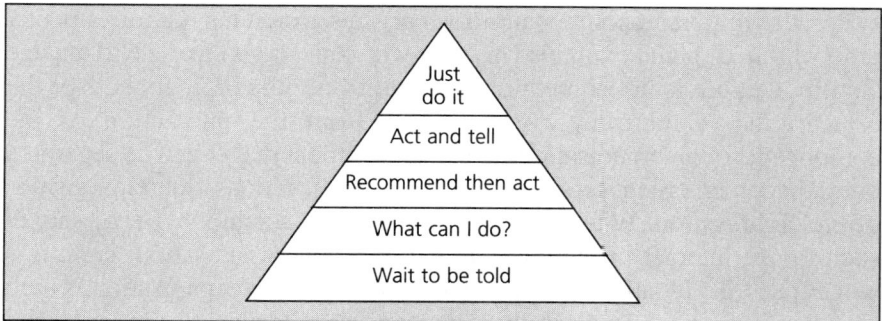

Figure 5.3 Pizza Hut (UK) accountability triangle

- Trains and develops people in the skills of change.
- Creates leadership that encourages and coaches people to move up the accountability triangle.

Only when people are clear about the issues facing the business and what is happening in the outside world, are they equipped to identify the necessary improvements. This is of limited value if they do not also know where the organisation is headed. Understanding the organisation's vision and goals is the second piece of the jigsaw. Unless people know this, equipping them with change skills will result in full speed ahead in every direction. It will encourage activity but not necessarily improvement. Non-value added can only be effectively defined if the organisation's staff knows its goals and therefore the actions needed to deliver value to the customer. Leaders need to encourage people as should rewards and recognition. We now begin to see the essential role of the other elements of dynamic change.

Dynamic Change

Dynamic change is about changing the culture of the organisation towards one which is much more in touch with external environment and where continuous performance improvement is a way of life. It is an organisation where the ability to change is an inherent part of the culture.

Understanding culture

People talk of culture as if it were a component of an organisation. They list culture along with strategy, structure, leadership style, processes and systems as important components of an organisation. This is a fundamental error of thinking and explains why many organisations struggle to change culture. Culture is not something separate from other components of the organisation. Culture is what emerges from the interaction of the components of an organisation. It is not a component that can be separated but rather an emergent property of the decisions, actions and relationships of the organisation. When strategy, structure, leadership, systems and all such things interact in the daily activities of the organisation, culture is what arises. To identify culture as a component of an organisation is a bit like saying that a cake is in the same category as flour, eggs, milk and sugar. You can see a cake when it is finished, but you cannot improve a cake by changing the cake; you have to change the ingredients and/or the method in which they are combined. You cannot change culture by changing culture, you have to change the ingredients and/or the method.

Let's look therefore at the ingredients, and in later chapters, a method of crafting the sort of culture that typifies dynamic organisations.

Extending leadership capability

Every great organisation has great leadership. I intentionally use the word leadership rather than leaders because I believe that leadership has little to do with position in the hierarchy and everything to do with what people do. Leadership is activity, not role. We expect people in senior positions to be leaders and many are; others however are merely senior managers. They do nothing to excite and energise the people working for them. They do not encourage and promote change. They do little to develop the talents of their people.

Perpetuating a role-based view of leadership makes it more difficult to develop the strategies needed to expand leadership capability because it focuses on developing a few individuals. Recognising leadership as activity makes it a capability that anyone in the organisation can practise. Indeed the very essence of leadership is that it steps forward when the need arises. This activity-based view of leadership is essential at times of rapid change. New ideas or threats don't conveniently present themselves to senior managers for action. They arise when and where they arise and that is precisely where leadership is needed.

The focus on activity is not to ignore the individual. It is people that deliver leadership. The mistake is to assume that all managers, even senior managers, have leadership talents. The mistake is to assume that people cannot work together to deliver leadership. The mistake is to assume that only one person can be a leader. It may take the spark of one leader to ignite and nurture the flame of leadership but dynamic organisations ensure those flames spread and grow to the point where they become self-sustaining.

What are the vital leadership activities? I believe there are five:

- Developing a shared vision
- Exemplifying the values
- Fostering involvement
- Nurturing innovation
- Balancing stakeholder interests

I will examine the whole subject of leadership in greater detail in Chapter 11.

Developing organisational processes

Talented people and a 'traditional' organisation are not a recipe for success. One of the founding fathers of the quality movement, Edward Deming, said that in most organisations poor performance is the result of the 'system' not the individuals. He believed that people wanted to give their best but the organisation's processes and systems often constrained them. Many training and development programmes fail to deliver the expected results not because people do not learn but because they return to an organisation that does not reflect and enable the learning they have acquired. People attend learning programmes with new skills, ideas and intentions but then return and run into the treacle of the organisation.

Consider what is a common scenario in many organisations. The organisation is underperforming, bogged down by bureaucracy and systems that were designed for a time when change was an occasional interruption to business as usual. One reason for this is that people lack the essential business and leadership skills to make the necessary organisational changes. The need to upgrade these skills is correctly identified as the key to success. Senior managers are sent on excellent leadership development programmes. They return fired up with enthusiasm and new ideas. They try to implement their new ideas but are constantly held back by the very processes they are supposed to change. The old culture, its processes and systems make change difficult. Sometimes even the most enthusiastic people are dragged down by organisational treacle that is so thick they give up. That is why it is vital that for dynamic change to succeed the old processes and systems must be obliterated.

There is however a real paradox here. Changing organisational processes demands the determination and perseverance of a cadre of leaders willing to tackle sacred cows and entrenched views. This is why dynamic change can only succeed if there is a group of people with the skills and the commitment to make change happen and tackle the reformation of organisational processes early on. By doing this, the way is cleared for people to tackle change across the organisation. But those same people work within the culture that is the anchor they are seeking to change. It is why culture change demands courage. This is not a new observation.

> One of the difficulties in bringing about change in organisations is that you must do so through the very persons who have been most successful in that organisation, no matter how faulty the system or organisation is.
>
> GEORGE WASHINGTON

Developing organisational processes involves removing the obstacles and building effective support for the new way of working. The key processes that need to be put in place are:

- Sensing – how the organisation gathers information about the world outside, notably customers, as a basis for action.
- The three Rs – how the organisation recruits, rewards and recognises the talent it needs to succeed.
- Change and improvement – how the organisation encourages and implements bounded change across the organisation to improve value to customers and minimise non-value added.
- Learning and development – how the organisation increases the skills, knowledge and behaviours it needs to succeed.
- Communication and involvement – the methods employed to keep people informed and engaged in the success of the organisation.
- Measurement – how the organisation measures performance.
- Strategic agenda – how the organisation establishes its goals and priorities.

I cannot stress enough how important it is that these processes must not be bureaucratic. Simplicity and speed are the watchwords. What is also vital is that they are practised across the organisation and become part of normal activity. Repetition is essential for learning. A new driver thinks about each individual action when they are learning to drive. An experienced teacher focusing on simple instructions such as 'mirror, signal, manouvre' help them to learn. In time, practice embeds those routines and what was once a significant thinking effort becomes second nature. The processes become implicit. The analogy holds true for developing organisational processes. Deep organisational learning involves the development of tacit learning from explicit actions.

Primacy of values

Organisations that develop leadership and their organisational processes require one final piece of the jigsaw of dynamic change – alignment with values. In times of rapid change values provide guidance without rules. Further, values encourage creativity. People with different backgrounds operating in different contexts will develop different solutions. A dynamic organisation encourages this diversity when it is coupled with mechanisms that enable these solutions to spread across the organisation. This approach to management is typified by successful organisations like Avis Europe and GE. Many organisations see organisational alignment and the freedom of action granted to diverse parts of the organisation as conflicting objectives. They misunderstand the power of values to provide clear guidance in totally different circumstances. People might do different things, but if they do them for the right reasons then the likelihood that their actions will destructively conflict are low.

Values are found at the heart of everything a dynamic organisation does. Leadership style and actions closely reflect and encourage the values. Organisational processes are designed to reinforce them and people are selected as much for their support of them as they are for their technical skills. Indeed when change is rapid, technical skills have a short life whereas support of the values is a necessary capability with a long shelf life. Picking people that reflect the values is vital. You can train skills and develop knowledge but it is extremely difficult, if not impossible, to change people's values. That is why great organisations place such a high regard on the values of the people they employ.

Building Dynamic Organisations

I am a firm believer that people have an innate need to understand the 'big picture'. I will therefore begin this section by providing an overview of what a dynamic organisation is and the process of driving fundamental culture change required in building one.

Dynamic organisations

Let me begin by describing the characteristics of a dynamic organisation.

Change everywhere

A dynamic organisation is one where the ability to change is deeply embedded in its culture. Change is a way of life, something that is, to a greater or lesser degree, practised by everybody across the organisation. These changes are not always large-scale organisational changes, though some may be. Many are the actions of people seeking to constantly improve their performance. This improvement is aimed at delivering the best possible product or service to the customer at a cost which competitors cannot match. To achieve this, there is a constant quest to reduce or eliminate those activities that do not add value to the way the customer experiences the organisation. This accumulation of improvements creates a position competitors find hard to match. It is sustainable because individuals in the organisation are constantly looking for improvements. They don't have to be told to improve something, they just do it.

Customer aware

Information about the needs of customers and how well the organisation is doing in meeting them permeates the whole organisation. No one is in any doubt about which customers the organisation serves and what their hot buttons are. People know they have the freedom to go outside the rules to satisfy customers. Senior managers pay close attention to the way the organisation is serving its customers. They monitor results for customer satisfaction and retention and spend time with customers – with the people who buy and use the company's products and services. They seek to experience their company as the customer does, to understand any weak links in the company.

Externally focused

In addition to close attention to customers, dynamic organisations pay close attention to changes happening in the world at large. They monitor the activities of their competitors to ensure they are not blind-sided by a new product development or the introduction of a new channel to market. They also spend time studying other organisations and how they work. They participate in benchmarking forums, spend time at conferences, and read widely. They study the changing socio-economic and political situation looking for new opportunities and threats. This constant vigil on the outside world, including customers, provides a stream of new information upon which the change machine can work.

People centred

Dynamic organisations know that it is people that make a difference. Therefore they pick the best, invest time and money in developing them and, most importantly, give them challenging work and opportunities to make a difference. They keep all their people informed about the progress of the company as a whole and give them opportunities to have their say on matters local and company-wide.

Leadership intensive

To build the sort of working environment described, dynamic organisations invest heavily in building and developing leadership capability. They understand that leadership is about what people do, not what title or position they hold. In a dynamic organisation leadership is a set of activities that can be practised by anyone in the organisation. Leaders therefore arise at any point of the organisation according to the need at the time. Leaders in one context are followers in other contexts.

Values driven

Dynamic organisations operate around a set of clear and well-understood values. They are not simply words on posters but real beliefs that guide the daily actions of the organisation. They are embedded in the way the organisation works. The organisation's leaders (and remember that is a very broad constituency) work to ensure that the values live each day. They are referenced, sometimes consciously other times sub-consciously, when making decisions. Starting with induction, development programmes include discussion and debate about the organisation's values and what they mean. Values become more important in a fast moving environment where rules have a short shelf life. In such circumstances, values help people by forcing them to think and interpret the values. They create a level of coherence of action without the need for cumbersome rules.

Dynamic mechanisms

Dynamic organisations are capable of changing constantly because they have embedded into their cultures a series of dynamic mechanisms. These mechanisms are reflected in the actions of leaders and the processes used to guide and develop the organisation. The mechanisms reflect the natural processes of evolution and learning found across the natural world. They are:

- External focus and curiosity: all successful living systems, of which organisations are one example, are aware of their environments. The five senses (sight, touch, hearing, smell and taste) are all designed to provide us with a continuous flow of information that guides our actions and reactions. Dynamic organisations also have a keen sense of what is happening in the world around them. They are constantly listening, in an active way, to their customers, suppliers, competitors and other organisations. They monitor and discuss changes in the society, economics and politics. This is not some centralised bureaucratic intelligence system but rather it is a way of life for all parts of the

organisation. This heightens the sensitivity to change, backed up by an ability to tackle change at all levels of the organisation.
- Restless pursuit of improvement: the Chinese can only express the concept of learning using ideographs representing study and practice. Only when both have been completed has real learning taken place. Dynamic organisations build into their companies systems that enable individuals and the organisation to learn and improve. This continuous learning is the vital force that drives performance ever upwards in the same way that evolution uses natural selection to continually develop species.
- Value diverse views: great organisations recognise that there is often more than one way to skin a cat. They encourage people to speak their minds. They encourage open and honest debate and are not afraid of giving and receiving feedback. This continuous dialogue and debate builds a deeper understanding and commitment. It is also essential to nurture the creativity that all organisations require.
- Encourage experiments: when the world is moving fast there is not time to plan in detail, to work out all the possibilities, and design the best solution. Learning by doing is essential. Who knows what the right answer is? Success demands that organisations try different things and back those solutions that work best.

These mechanisms will ensure that the organisation has a flow of information which it can then turn into ideas and improvements. They will take different forms in different organisations but it is important that they are present in some form. Creating these mechanisms is a central part of the process of building dynamic organisations

Building dynamic organisations – a roadmap

Building dynamic change into an organisation is a long term task. It is about fundamental culture change and that requires years rather than months. Some results can be seen within a short period of time but it takes time and perseverance to build the attitudes and mechanisms into the fabric of the organisation. But where to start? What can experience teach us about the path to building a dynamic organisation? Sufficient organisations have gone down this path to suggest some common steps that I will outline here and describe in more detail in the next few chapters. I do not suggest it is the only way that this type of fundamental change can be effected but it is an approach that I have used with some success in a number of organisations.

There are four main phases in the process of building a dynamic organisation.

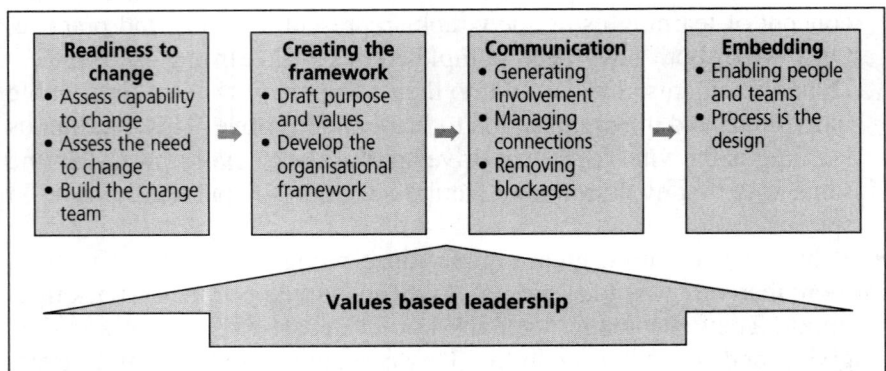

Fig. 6.1 The dynamic organisation roadmap

There is a flow to the process but each phase is not discrete, they overlap and blend into each other. They are presented discretely only for clarity. Other commentators believe there is a strict order to the steps required. I do not. The starting point and situation of each organisation is different. Some will have several of the pieces already in place; others will be starting with almost a blank sheet. There are however some dependencies in the process. It is unwise to begin the change process with no clear view of the organisation's ability to see it through. People across the organisation can only be effectively involved if they understand the big picture. This is not however a process where action is only taken when a detailed plan has been produced. It is values led change where the answers and next steps arise from the actions taken. It is essentially a learning process where actions create results that create learnings that lead to new actions. Such processes are rarely clear cut and linear. What is required is like the natural growth process that people experience. We are born essentially complete but over time different parts of the body grow and mature at different rates. The process of growth and renewal never stops; even up to death we are still replacing the cells in most parts of our body. And remember, no one grows up without experiencing some growing pains and setbacks. There will be broken bones and bruises along the way, but most people survive.

The change must reflect the future

One of the features of building a dynamic organisation is that the process of change required to deliver the desired results cannot be achieved using techniques and attitudes that reflect the old culture. It is not possible to dictate to people that they should be empowered or creative. Commitment and trust cannot be ordered; they have to be earned. The approaches that are part of a dynamic organisation are the same approaches used during the change process. It is an example of living the future today. The process of change is therefore a proving ground for the ideas, tools and techniques that will form the basis of the new organisation. Given that the basic philosophy of a dynamic organisation is the continuous search for improvement, the processes and techniques introduced to facilitate the change will themselves evolve and develop as the change itself progresses. In this way, the change is itself a model of the culture the organisation is seeking to develop.

The starting point for the change and the central thread of dynamic organisations are shared values. They act like a red thread through the organisation. They are reflected in the leadership of the organisation. They are reinforced through the organisation's processes and management mechanisms. They are fundamental in the selection, development and promotion of people. In dynamic organisations values are omnipresent; they must also be equally visible, if still developing during the change.

7 Preparing for Change

Preparing for Change
- Assess capability to change
- Assess the need to change
- Build the change team

KEY CONCEPTS

- Organisations have to build their capability to change. This requires attention to people, processes and values.
- There is a marked difference between simple and dynamic change.
- Capability to change is different from the recognition of a need to change, although as need grows, real capability becomes apparent. Dynamic organisations focus on strengthening capability. This includes heightening awarenesss of the need to change.
- The team may start small, but success lies in rapidly expaning it.
- Building the team is part of the process of change.
- Now is the time to be ruthless.

ACTIVITIES

- Assess the need to change using (for example):
    - Dynamic organisation benchmarks
    - Competitive benchmarks
    - Cultural profiling
    - Industry future scenarios
    - Process maps (current state)

- Assess organisational change capability:
    - Leadership capability audit
    - Change readiness audit

- Build initial change team:
    - Enabling change workshop
    - Change agent selection

> *Fortune favours the prepared mind.*
> LOUIS PASTEUR

Fundamental organisational change is a major undertaking, not to be taken lightly. The first questions should always be 'Do we need to change?' and 'Are we equipped to succeed?'. The purpose of asking the questions is not to make a go/no go decision, but to understand the organisation's strengths and weaknesses and thus be better prepared to take on the change. The most important issue is an organisation's ability to change. It is a paradox that the very capabilities that define a dynamic organisation are also the capabilities needed to drive the sort of change envisaged. Every organisation has some of these capabilities but to a greater or lesser degree. This first step therefore seeks to understand how well the organisation is currently operating. Jumping into fundamental change without this background information is to invite failure.

Assess the need to change

A dynamic organisation is always in a state of change in some way – large or small. The question therefore is not 'Do we need to change?' rather 'Where do we need to change?'. At the beginning of the process of building a dynamic organisation, these questions are particularly important. An organisation that lacks a real capacity to change is likely to be playing catch-up. It will have lost ground to the competition; be struggling to maintain its financial strength and may even be in danger of going out of business completely. These are never the best circumstances from which to begin a root and branch change of the organisation, but it is exactly the time when such change is needed.

Change has always been viewed as a necessary evil; something that has to be done occasionally if the status quo is no longer acceptable. Many organisations have fallen behind in the competitive battle because they have sought stability over constant appraisal and improvement. As we have seen in Chapter 1, the world around us is constantly changing. The failure to change at least the same rate as the outside world is the cause of failure of many organisations. They are typically blinded by past success and fall into the trap of believing their own propaganda.

The first stage of the process is therefore to assess the way the organisation is currently operating. There are many ways of doing this but they fall into three basic categories: benchmarking, envisioning the future, and intuition. Intuition has value but can be wrong and one person's intuition is another person's unsubstantiated guess. More robust and widely accessible methods of assessing the organisation are advisable.[25]

It is also important to get a real feel for the cultures operating in the organisation. Many senior managers believe they understand the culture of the organisation but their understanding is often inaccurate and incomplete. They experience the culture as senior managers and as it is presented to them by people in the organisation. It is essential that the cultures in operation are fully understood. Seek answers to questions like: 'How do front-line people experience the organisation?', 'What values does the organisation really promote through its actions?', 'What makes a winner in this organisation?', 'How effective is communication?'. These are questions that a dynamic organisation is asking all the time. Again there are more structured and effective ways of profiling organisation cultures of which my preferred choice is the profiling toolkit provided by DOCSA.[26]

The information provided by this internal and external assessment will suggest a focus for the change. People will more readily accept change if they understand the reason behind it. Being able to communicate a rationale behind the change is vital. Doing this with anecdotal evidence alone is insufficient. People will need to see hard information about the state of the organisation's competitiveness. Like doubting Thomas, they will need to see reality.

Capability to change[27]

Building the capability to change is a continuing focus of dynamic organisations. Understanding this capability is an essential part of the process. Paradoxically, to carry out dynamic change requires the very capabilities that are lacking. The only way forward is to learn by doing. It is important therefore to understand how well equipped the organisation is to begin the journey.

From my research, I have identified three areas which can be assessed to give an indication of the ability of an organisation to undertake change of this nature. They are:

- The existence and use of organisational processes. These are the processes that inform the organisation about the outside world and keep its internal activities synchronised with the changes it perceives.

- The existence and use of basic skills for managing projects and finances. These include negotiation, relationship building, project management and managing bounded change. These basic skills are required in a wide spectrum of managers in the organisation. They are the sort of skills that form part of the basic management development curriculum of most organisations. As the change process progresses these skills need to form part of the skill set of those individuals acting as change agents. The change process is itself an opportunity to upgrade and embed these skills. This focus on individual development is another characteristic of the type of organisation that needs to be developed.

- The management team's track record of managing change. Change is always a process that creates uncertainty. Confidence in the leadership team is essential. Over time, people judge their leaders by what they do, not what they say. Where they have seen leaders who have both integrity, which is nothing more than doing what they say they will do, and a track record of delivering change, the propensity to believe and follow is heightened.

I have developed a Change Capability Assessment – a tool developed specifically to help organisations assess their readiness to take on fundamental organisational change. The assessment is not a precise measure but an aid to thinking through the potential for change. Its purpose is to highlight areas where the organisation might need new blood, where individuals could benefit from development, and where outside help can be valuable. In particular, it is a mechanism for creating a dialogue in the organisation about its change capability. The full version of the assessment provides companies with the capability to benchmark different parts of the organisation and compare those results with a growing database of organisations.

Problem or opportunity

The desire to effect fundamental change and begin building a dynamic organisation is usually prompted by one of two things: crisis or vision.

Whilst the two threads follow a very similar process, the focus of the change is very different and this has real implications for the make up of the team (see below).

In my experience, most organisations consider the need for fundamental change because they are faced with a real problem. Often the business is

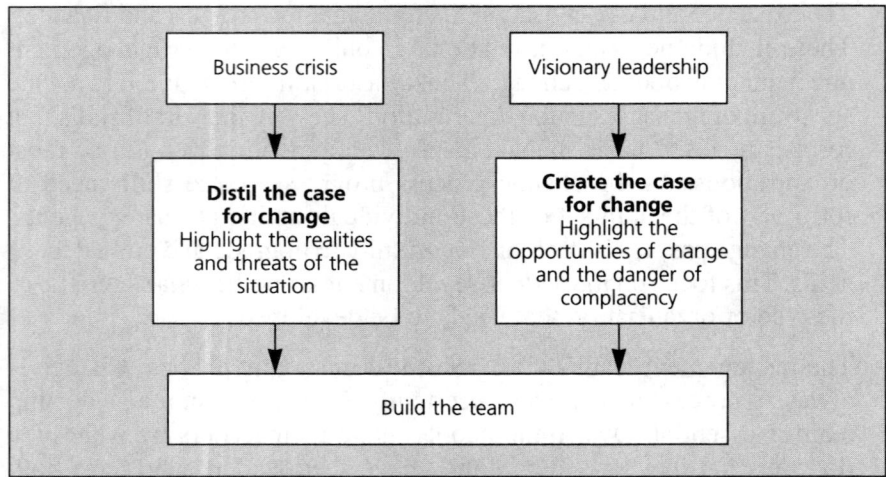

Fig. 7.1 The causes of change

under-performing in some significant way. It is a case of change or bust. This creates a sense of urgency and need that spurs people to review the way they work. They know that if they don't change the survival of the business and with it, their jobs, are under threat. The urgency focuses people's minds.

The really exciting development over the last few years has been the emergence of a number of organisations where change is not driven by the threat of losing the business, but by visionary leadership encouraging ever greater levels of performance. GE in the US and Avis and Oticon in Europe are organisations that have continually ratcheted up performance by building cultures where continuous improvement, customer focus and the development of people are deeply embedded; where change is not something that hits the organisation every few years but is a way of life. These organisations have achieved outstanding financial performance as a result and it is not through luck. They have intentionally built their organisations to succeed and change. No one can guarantee that they will be forever successful, but all the evidence to date suggests that they have the ability to succeed in the long term. They already have such a track record. More importantly, they have made the investments in leadership, learning and culture to continue that success. It takes a true visionary to take an already successful organisation and change it.

Leaders of organisations that are facing severe problems have a unique opportunity. They can work to change the business around and, at the same time, sow the seeds that will make the organisation dynamic. In some respects introducing the concepts of a dynamic organisation is easier in a crisis. The fact that there is a crisis makes it obvious that something has to be done. In organisations that are comfortable, there is no obvious need to change. 'Don't mess with something that works', people will argue. And there is always danger when introducing fundamental change. Indeed the whole goal behind building a dynamic organisation is to make change part of everyday life and therefore not something special that disturbs the organisation, its people and its customers. Managing the process of building a dynamic organisation so that the required change is made without damaging the business is a real challenge. That is why it is vital early in the process to take actions that reinforce customer focus and the investments needed to strengthen the relationship with them.

Building the change team

Dynamic change is never a one man show. To think of it as such is actually a contradiction. No organisation can survive if it relies on one person. There may be a great leader at the head of the organisation, but he or she is no more than first among equals. A dynamic organisation demands a large cadre of capable leaders. It may take a strong powerful figure to begin the process but success with such fundamental change can only be delivered by an ever growing team of people. In many cases, strong figures are pivotal in effecting the change. They often come from outside, but not always. Lou Gerstner was hired to turn IBM around as was Mike Jackson at Birmingham Midshires Building Society. Jack Welch, who has done more than most to build a dynamic organisation at GE, was an insider.

What these leaders do is build around them a team of capable determined people through whom the early stages of the change are driven. They handpick individuals who have demonstrated a willingness to go out on a limb to do the right things. These are not always colleagues on the board. Change requires a broader constituency drawing on the ideas, talents and networks of people across the organisation. They seek talent, not position. The team therefore is unrelated to hierarchy, although many will be drawn from the echelons of management.

Dynamic change cannot be undertaken without the support of the top management team; indeed they should be the people driving it. It is after all the top team's job to build an organisation that can thrive and grow. What else are they responsible for? Today's business is the result of yesterday's decisions. But not all top management teams have either the desire or the capability to effect fundamental culture change. Some are just too comfortable in their positions. They look at yesterday's success and can see no reason that it should not continue. They are sheltered from reality, choosing not to listen to bad news, dismissing it as a blip, or the fault of uncontrollable circumstances. They ignore the fact that competitors are seemingly able to grow market share profitably. It sounds strange to think that a group of highly paid, senior managers responsible for a large organisation can be so complacent. But it happens. The board of one major company did basically nothing as profits slumped and market share slipped away. This was despite the protestations of the majority of managers pleading for leadership and change. Some of the board refused to recognise the dire nature of the situation. Others saw the need but felt helpless to do anything. The result was stultifying confusion and inaction.

Can change be effected when the top management team is, at best, giving only passive support? I believe it is possible, but not easy. Even in the most complacent top management teams there will usually be at least one or two individuals who see the need for change. They can provide the opportunity for change and give tacit support to any initiatives. A group of managers who clearly see the need to change (and in any organisation there are always people who know what the problem is and how to solve it) can start the ball rolling. They can begin to create the framework for change (see Chapter 8) and take some of the actions needed. It must be said however that even a group of talented and determined people will have little success if they are working against a board who are actively against change.

At the very beginning of fundamental change I have found great value in getting the top 100 senior managers together in cross functional groups of 15–20 in workshops to discuss the issues. Over three to five days they are asked to consider what is wrong with the organisation and how it might be fixed. Challenge them to be brutally honest and realistic – no sugar coating to the facts. Use the data gathered in any assessments to bring some reality to the discussions. Challenge people to support their assumptions with real data and examples. It is also useful to provide examples of how other organisations have tackled fundamental change to provide role models and ideas. If possible, give them the opportunity to visit and talk to companies that have successfully changed their organisations and expose them to new ideas and tools for leading change. Finally, get the groups to develop action plans to begin to effect some of the changes that are needed in the business. The goal here is to generate some momentum and show that success is possible. Do not worry that at this stage there might not be a clear sense of direction. Many of the actions will address problems that need attention under any circumstances.

The workshops bring home to people the reality of the situation and builds and deepens the recognition of the need to change. The goal is to create a force for change. There is a second benefit of such an event; it helps to highlight those people who are both capable and willing to drive change. They stand out through their honesty, realism and passion.

Change agent

There is no perfect change agent, but a team can be (with apologies to John Adair). No one can possess all the qualities needed to drive fundamental change, nor should they. Dynamic organisations are not about heroes and egos, but team players. That is not to say that people should not be proud of their achievements and confident in their abilities. But that confidence should never reach the point where it prevents other people from meaningful involvement or blocks the ability to learn. Dynamic change needs a team of people who bring competence in several overlapping areas. These are:

- **Courage and perseverance.** Change involves taking risks and slaughtering sacred cows. People will fight back against the ideas. Setbacks are inevitable. Be prepared to take the knocks and come back fighting.
- **Goal-orientated.** People need to set themselves challenging goals and throw their energies wholeheartedly behind achieving them.
- **Open to learning.** Dynamic change is an emergent process and the only way to deal with the unknown is to be willing to recognise that you don't know everything and learn as you go along.
- **Business understanding.** The team needs people who know about business. That does not mean that everyone in the team has to know about this business, or even this industry. Indeed there is great merit in having people who have no preconceived ideas about how the industry should work. The team will however need some insiders and a very large dose of business acumen; people who have run successful businesses and know what it takes to win in the market.
- **Experience of change.** Firsthand experience of the process, tools and techniques of change are essential.
- **Leadership skills.** Leadership is one of the cornerstones of dynamic organisations. It is essential therefore that the team can demonstrate how leadership can make a difference during the process of change.
- **Management skills.** Planning, finance, project management, negotiation and other basic management skills will be needed throughout the change.

Creating the Framework for Change

> **Creating the Framework**
> - Clarify purpose and values
> - Develop the organisational framework

KEY CONCEPTS

- Purpose and values are the overarching design parameters.
- Recognise that purpose and values will take time to determine. Their ongoing development is part of the makeup of a dynamic organisation.
- Organisational framework is a starting point for further discussion and development, not a final design.
- The framework creates starting points for bringing others into the design and implementation process.
- The framework is holistic at the outset. Effort is needed to keep it holistic throughout implementation.
- The techniques and ideals used to develop the framework need to model the desired culture.

ACTIVITIES

- Clarify purpose and values
  - Desired cultural profiling
  - Purpose and values workshop

- Develop the organisational framework
  - Change mapping
    - Agree organisational principles
    - Define organisational processes
    - Identify values gaps

> *The only limit to our realisation of tomorrow will be our doubts about reality.*
> FRANKLIN D. ROCSEVELT

The understanding created by a thorough assessment of the state of the organisation is the foundation for change. It creates a picture of the compelling need to change and identifies the people who will form the core of the team to drive the change forward. Now it is time to think about what the future look likes for people in the organisation. The starting point for this is a framework that describes the organisation as it will be. That framework is holistic. It is a sketch that has all the elements but where most of the detail is missing. That will be filled in over time and by a wider constituency. This framework forms the vision that will drive the change.

What is vision?

Much is talked about the role of vision in change, particularly in the context of organisational change. It is not complex, though developing a good vision is not an easy task. For many, it is a statement that describes some future state of the organisation. Some say it should be no more than 20 words that describe the essence of the future of the company. This constraining view leads to endless sessions of wordsmithing where senior managers argue about the precise form of words. I believe this is to misunderstand vision. The word has it roots in the graphical and visual world, not the literal. Vision should inspire a picture of the future and whilst words can paint pictures, they are a poor substitute for the real thing. I am a great believer in the power of visual techniques and believe they are underused in business. One of the most powerful and best used visions I have seen was developed by Cendant Membership Services, the provider of credit card protection services in the UK. The company's vision is a picture (see Figure 8.1).

Later in this chapter I will describe how they use the vision as the centrepiece to their operational planning.

What makes a successful vision is not that everyone can recount the same phrase or draw the same picture but that everyone can describe the same intent. To get everyone to recount a phrase is not difficult. We gain this ability early in life when we learn nursery rhymes. Developing a common clarity of intent is much more difficult to achieve. This requires real, two way communication. It can only be achieved if people can really see themselves in the vision; if it becomes part of their own personal

Figure 8.1 Cendant Membership Services Vision

vision. This cannot be achieved 100 per cent. Some people will not buy into what is being proposed. They will see their own constituency threatened or be unable to see the benefits inherent in the vision. People are conservative creatures. Change has to be sold and sold hard.

The second mistake that many people make when talking about vision is that they restrict it to describing the business of the organisation and not the organisation itself. This results in phrases that lack the emotional energy that is an essential component of any change. Such visions are often an attempt by traditional strategic planners to usurp the process of change. They see vision as the top-level statement in a detailed strategic plan, rather than an aspirational statement against which people can plan their own activities. It is an attempt to maintain a level of central control that is not part of a dynamic organisation. Discipline is essential, but that does not imply centralisation. In a dynamic organisation, that discipline comes from knowing and understanding the big picture, the vision and values, and being clear about how you and your team play in that. The emphasis is on self-discipline.

Vision as strategy	Vision as aspiration
Emphasis on activities	Emphasis on outcomes
Actions centrally planned	Actions developed locally
Broken into substrategies	One vision to all
Establish what and how	Focus on what and why, leave how to others
Control through project management	Control through dialogue
Management of activities	Management of connections
Low ownership	Personal commitment

Figure 8.2 Two types of vision

As the world around us changes more rapidly, centrally planned and directed systems lack the flexibility to react quickly. There is not the time for information to feed up the system for a decision, which is then communicated back down. The larger the organisation, the more difficult this becomes.

> In a changing and uncontrollable world, any company with the desire to succeed over longish periods would be ill advised to rely on a management policy of high internal and external controls. The Shell study showed that successful survivors created internal space and freedom to cope with a world of changes which they had no hope to control. They had policies of high tolerance to people and ideas both from the inside and from the outside.[28]

As Arie de Geus states, long-term survival and central control do not go hand in hand. Vision as strategy constricts speed of movement. Vision as aspiration allows people to do what they think is necessary given the changing circumstances.

Even the US Army recognises the value of vision as aspiration. In a fast changing battlefield where every soldier can be given the big picture the US Army no longer wants soldiers to follow orders. What they are trying to develop is a system where soldiers 'understand and enact the commander's intent'. The argument for this is a simple one, and provides a real lesson to other organisations. Technology now allows each soldier to be continually updated with the major events of the battlefield as a whole. This and a clear understanding of the overall goal of the battle commander provide the backcloth onto which the local soldiers can paint their knowledge of the local situation. It is therefore the local soldier who is best equipped to decide what action to take. This represents a major shift for the US Army. It demands soldiers who are both competent and confident in their decisionmaking as well as having the skills of soldiering. It also requires a substantial shift in the skills of the army's senior managers. Ensuring that the troops understand the big picture both at the outset and as it changes requires much greater skills of communications. One of the keys to developing this culture and the ability to operate it is the open feedback they encourage at and across all levels of the organisation.

The organisational framework

The organisational framework is a powerful way of creating a vision that people can understand. It is a rich picture of the main components of the desired organisation. The emphasis is on breadth not depth. The initial framework is developed by a group of people drawn from the advocates of change identified earlier. In my experience, the framework can be developed quite rapidly, with one exception – the values, which are more likely to emerge and develop as the process unfolds.

There are three major components of the organisational framework.

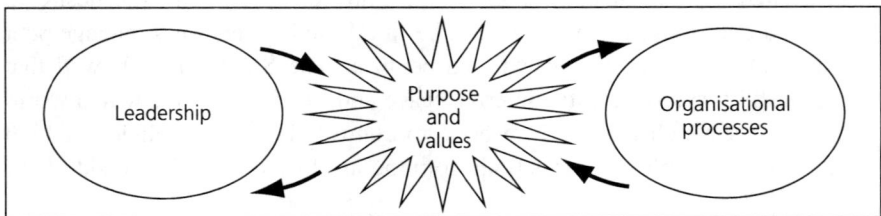

Figure 8.3 Organisational framework components

Purpose and Values

This is the heart of the framework. They are the design guides for the other components. They are the central component because they have to be designed into the organisation as a conscious act. It is essential, therefore, that purpose and values are understood by all involved in the process. Purpose answers the question 'Why do we exist?'. Values are the few guiding beliefs or inviolable principles that the organisation holds to be of great importance.

Organisational processes

Organisational processes are the systems that are used to guide and monitor the organisation. They are the vital mechanisms that keep the organisation in touch with the outside world, track performance and encourage learning, improvement and change. They are the way an organisation translates its values into the everyday activities of all its people.

Leadership

Dynamic organisations practise leadership that delivers results and work hard to bring the company's value to life. In dynamic organisations, the focus is on action not role. Leadership activities consciously reflect the value, building integrity into the organisation.

Developing shared purpose and values

Purpose

Purpose answers the question 'Why does this organisation exist?'. It is an easy question to ask, but a difficult one to answer. It is the organisation's raison d'être. It says something about the customers the organisation serves and what it does for them. It is not a statement of some desired state that can be achieved at some point in the future but a more timeless description of what the organisation is all about. Procter & Gamble states its purpose as; 'We will provide products of superior quality and value that improve the lives of the world's consumers'. It defines their customers – consumers around the world. It expresses the need to clearly understand what customers value. It positions the company as a supplier of quality products.

The timeless nature of a purpose that is well thought has more power than the traditional view of a vision statement as a 'desired future state'. I believe that visions are about more than where the business is in three or five years' time. Vision should encompass the whole gamut of what the organisation does and how it operates. It is a vision for the organisation and not just the business. It is the framework in its entirety, not just the business. Purpose has the ability to encompass both business and organisation. I must add that I am not interested in semantic arguments. I know of many organisations that use the words vision or mission instead of purpose. What counts is what it says. Xerox for example has a mission statement that says its strategic intent is 'to be the leader in the global document market, providing document solutions that enhance business productivity'. That does not state any end date or express any specific strategies for becoming leader in a market that itself is only broadly defined as 'document solutions'. But it does answer the question 'Why does Xerox exist?'.

The power of purpose is that it creates a common starting point and a focus for discussions. It is this desire and ability to create dialogue across the organisation that dynamic organisations seek. They do not look for prescribed answers but seek mechanisms to generate conversations and dialogue. They provide forums for people to meet and talk. Purpose provides a jumping off point for people to talk about what and how. So why not skip the 'why' question and get on with the tangible things that describe what the organisation is going to do and how it does them? There are three reasons.

First, explaining the company's raison d'être enables a broad constituency to be involved in discussions and decisions about what and how. Anyone can propose a 'document solution'. There is no fixed formula in Xerox for what is or is not a document solution. The suggestions arise from across the organisation. That discussion however is not overly constrained. Document solutions can cover anything from paper to complex computer based business processes. If Xerox's mission had stated what and how, then there would be limited opportunity for others to express their ideas about what and how. The company might have ended up with a similar product line and go to market strategy but the ownership of those strategies would have been diminished. Focus on purpose creates space in the organisation for the good ideas to come forward. Who knows where in the organisation sits the person with the next great idea.

Secondly, whilst purpose may remain relatively constant, the strategies used to deliver that purpose will change, and change with increasing regularity in a fast moving world. Purpose enables an organisation to provide a degree of continuity yet does not stifle the need for change that is so essential. Continuity of purpose provides an anchor, an essential element of people's emotional well-being.

Thirdly, purpose helps to provide meaning to work. The question 'why?' is the most frequently asked but least answered question in most organisations. Purpose goes some way to answering this question and enhances the sense of meaning associated with work. Work without meaning is drudge. People need to know that they are contributing to something they value. As work is increasingly related to people's ideas and brainpower, the future success of the organisation rests even more on the commitment of its people. People who lack meaning in their work, work less well. Nurturing meaning is therefore of real importance. It is why dynamic organisations place emphasis on it.

Values

Every organisation operates with a set of values, whether they are explicitly stated or not. Most have two sets: one is the values in operation, the other is the organisation's stated values. The gap between the two is one measure of success in introducing dynamic change. In a dynamic organisation, the gap is much narrower. The words and deeds have a high degree of coherence.

The preparation stage will have identified the culture currently operating and the values that underpin it. What is important as the organisation moves forward is that a shared understanding of what values it holds dear is developed. This is not a short exercise where a group of senior managers get together for a couple of days to come up with a set of words, although that is often a useful place to begin. Rather, it is a lengthy process of dialogue that must, over time, embrace the whole organisation.

The thinking has to start somewhere and that is the role of the initial change team. There is no magic formula for this; but whilst it involves some hard thinking, the process itself is not rocket science. The starting point is to consider the heritage of the organisation. Great organisations regularly reinvent themselves but they do not lose the values that made them great. This understanding is a useful foundation for thinking about the future. The key is to carry forward the best of the old and couple that with the values that the organisation needs to succeed and grow.

The values an organisation selects are of course unique. They are shaped by the heritage of the company, the values of the leaders of the organisation, and the demands of the environment. I have collected values statements from over 150 companies and am struck by the similarity of the values from companies in diverse industries and circumstances. Whilst they are all different, there are a number of common threads that each contain. These are:

- **People** are at the heart of the values of great companies. Hewlett Packard states its intentions:

    > We have trust and respect for individuals. We approach each situation with the belief that people want to do a good job and will do so given the proper tools and support. We attract highly capable, diverse, innovative people and recognise their efforts and contributions to the company. HP people contribute enthusiastically and share in the success that they make possible.

    Great companies recognise that their success is down to their people. They also have, and always will do their best to attract, develop and keep the best talent. As HP states in its values, a key part of this is giving people the opportunity to make a real contribution. Avis Europe stresses the need to develop people stating: 'To this end, we will provide the environment to help employees improve and develop themselves'. Avis Europe has one of the most sophisticated training and development programmes for frontline sales people found anywhere. Consequently, 85–90 per cent of senior managers are internally recruited, having started at a hire station around Europe.

- **Integrity and ethics** are widely cited as being at the core of the values of many great organisations. They behave in an ethical manner not just because it is the right thing to do, but because it is essential to sustainable success in business. Reputations are founded on ethics. To explain what I understand by integrity I can do little better than quote American philosopher Henry David Thoreau. In 1870 he said 'I cannot hear your words for the action that thunders above your head'. Integrity is about saying and doing in concert. One of HP's values is 'We conduct our business with uncompromising integrity'. They explain that:

    > As a practical matter, ethical conduct cannot be assured by written HP policies and codes; it must be an integral part of the organisation, a deeply ingrained tradition that is passed from one generation of employees to another.

- **Creativity and innovation.** 3M is innovative because it values innovation. In describing their innovative culture, 3M state 'Innovation is required at 3M. Thirty per cent of each year's sales must come from products less than four years old'. Avis Europe has evolved its 'We try harder' ethos to mean 'innovating ahead of the competition'. This value requires Avis Europe to continually look for new ideas and put them into practice. As their values statement notes, 'The only mistake is not to try something'. As a result of the actions taken to bring that part of the values to life, Avis Europe were the first car rental company to introduce a loyalty scheme, rapid return through remote check out, and first on the world wide web.

- **Excellence and improvement** are closely coupled with creativity and innovation, for without them, excellence and improvement cannot be sustainably delivered. GE simply states 'We have a passion for excellence and hate bureaucracy'. It is the driving force behind the introduction of Workout and Six Sigma, techniques for getting the whole organisation engaged in constantly ratcheting up the level of performance. "We try harder" is more than a badge worn by over 4700 Avis employees. It is a way of life expressed in their values:

'... we look for continuous improvement, no matter how small, in everything we do and at the same time quantum improvement in the way we do business. We will never hesitate to adapt to new and more profitable ways of working provided that the integrity and honesty we apply to our business is not compromised'.

These values lie behind an organisation that has delivered 18 continuous years of year-on-year productivity improvement. Procter & Gamble express one of their values as a 'Passion for Winning'. They go on to explain that

We are determined to be the best at doing what matters most. We have a healthy dissatisfaction with the status quo. We have a compelling desire to improve and win in the marketplace.

In the company's 1997 annual report to shareholders, Bill Nordstrom, head of one of the most profitable US retail chains said:

Our goals remain the same. We want to be the best. Our customers want to shop with the best. Our employees want to work for the best. Our communities need us to be at our best. And our shareowners want to be part of the best. Being the best at what we do has always been Nordstrom's goal and always will be. How we become the best is what we must all be willing to question, and moreover, be willing to change.

It is interesting to note that customers do not appear explicitly in the values statements of many great organisations, although some, like Avis Europe and Xerox do include reference to customers. I would argue that even when customers are not explicitly stated, they are implicitly present. Excellence in delivery, which is an almost universal value, is only possible if customers' needs are satisfied.

I have included in Appendix A examples of values statements from a number of leading organisations. As you study them, you are struck by their similarity. If they are so alike, why do they lead to such different outcomes? Surely this degree of consistency would lead to increasingly similar results.

The main reason is a significant difference in the quality of implementation. I know many organisations that have similar values to HP, GE and Avis, but are nowhere near as successful. For these organisations, values are another task completed in the tick in the box exercise of the management curriculum. The values are launched at a razzmatazz roadshow along with the posters, the mouse mats, and the little cards that everyone is expected to carry in wallets and Filofaxes. Once this is completed, senior managers can get back to the real work. I have no time for such charlatans. Real leadership has the posters and the mouse mats, but they are an insignificance compared with the effort invested in building values into systems for appraisal, measurement, reward and recognition, and learning and development. Little cards may well be printed but they are issued to people who spend time at development programmes, peer discussions, and company events generally discussing values and what they mean.

Quality of implementation is a conscious act of organisation design in its truest sense. Every organisation is perfectly designed to achieve the results it does. Some organisations succeed in the long term because they have built an organisation that thinks long term. Excellent organisations continually improve their performance because they have designed into their culture organisations systems that encourage continuous improvement. This is not some chance result but a conscious act of design. It sometimes begins with the ideals and values of the company's founders, as in the case with Bill Hewlett and Dave Packard. In other cases, a crisis calls for a different approach and up-steps some like one John Townsend at Avis. Sometimes a visionary individual like Jack Welch at GE steps into a position determined to make a difference. Whatever the cause, careful and considered thought lies behind the design of a dynamic organisation.

Programming not directing

The real power of values is that they are guiding, not directing mechanisms. They help people think through situations and in that way influence their actions. This brings a degree of coherence that actually encourages people to think deeply about what the value means in the context of a particular situation. People are all different, they think differently. Well-crafted values encourage creative thinking. Using values in this way means that leadership is not about directing the organisation, but about programming it to behave in a certain style. Values are to an organisation what fractal equations are to mathematics; simple rules that generate rich patterns of behaviour when they interact with their environments. Programming an organisation is very different from telling it what to do. It requires a different form of leadership – teaching rather than telling, providing opportunities for people to work things out for themselves.

Describing the changes at Ford, CEO Jacques Nasser said:[29]

> We realised that the change had to be understood on the individual level. Every manager, every designer, every engineer, every person in the plants had to change his or her way of thinking. And the only way to change at the individual level, I believe is through teaching. Teaching, we've found, is an amazingly effective way to change an organisation.

He adds that

> ... many executives intuitively lead by teaching. In both formal and informal settings, they share their perspectives on strategy and competition, for instance, or they coach individuals to build their skills.

This characteristic of a dynamic organisation has significant implications for the style of implementation that is used to effect the change. It requires people who can lead by teaching and by example. That requires a great deal of integrity in the people with the responsibility for change. Their actions, how they describe and implement the change, will be seen as the biggest indicator of the style the new organisation wants to encourage. That is why the identification of the advocates (see Chapter 7) is so vital. If they do not demonstrate the required culture, people will interpret the exercise as just the latest programme that will go away if they keep their heads down.

Whilst Nasser describes the process as teaching, I believe it is more useful to think of it as learning. Teaching is about giving people knowledge and skills. Learning is about study and practice, which is what much of Ford's programme is about. Providing people with the skills and knowledge and not the opportunity to practise them is futile. Also, much of the change is about changing how people do things, not just what they do. Behaviours cannot be taught. They can be modelled and coached and encouraged and thereby learned, but not taught.

To some, programming sounds like some Orwellian truth police driving out anything but the official version. Values don't programme the organisation in that way. They actually encourage debate and dialogue. Because they are high level statements of intention, people have to think about what they really mean. This leads to a rich diversity of views, something that is invaluable in a world that is changing so quickly. But values also encourage a lack of willingness to accept something or someone that acts against these basic tenets of the organisation. People who value involvement, empowerment, and the commitment they generate will quickly make an authoritarian manager uncomfortable. He or she will find pressure from all sides to change or go. It is not that they are bad people, or necessarily wrong, but they just don't fit. Values act like the T cells in the body's immune system. They identify and eject harmful substances. Dynamic organisations are hard nosed about the people they employ, particularly those who supervise or manage other people. The wrong people can quickly set the organisation back. They may get results in the short term, but they do so at the risk of the long term health of the organisation. This again reinforces the need to pick and develop the 'right' people to lead the change.

Organisational processes

Organisational processes are the mechanisms that translate purpose and values into the daily activities of the organisation. They provide the dynamic mechanisms described in Chapter 6. The aim at this stage of the exercise is not to define in detail the processes. That is a role that other people in the organisation are often better equipped to do. It is also a useful way of getting other people involved in the change process. I have split the processes into three domains: related to work, people and change. It is perhaps too grand to call some of them processes as many of them are simple methods. What matters is that they exist, are consistent with the organisation's values, and are coherent, that is, they work together.

Work Processes

These processes enable the organisation to translate its direction into the daily work of people across the organisation and monitor performance. In all the interest with change it is important to remember that any organisation has to deliver its products and services. Without effective methods of translating intention into action, change will never become embedded in the work of the organisation. One organisation I worked with had a very good strategy but no way of translating that into the operations of the business. Consequently, change plans remained as plans. Business unit heads continued to manage their businesses but struggled to integrate changes into the business. The organisation had two entirely separate systems, one for running the business and another for strategic planning and change. A multinational company operated two separate planning systems, one for financial budgeting and a second for strategic planning. The same group of senior managers got together twice, within a space of two months, to develop two sets of plans. For many years, the company struggled to bring its strategic plans into being. Budgets never reflected the strategic goals of the organisation.

Operational planning

Operational planning takes its lead from the strategic goals for the period. This is typically expressed in a business plan which contains the goals and the resources and investments required to achieve them. A number of well practised techniques for this exists, the best known of which is probably Policy Deployment or Hoshin Kanri. This uses a complex matrix to tie together the strategic goals for the period, specific targets, benefits and long term goals (see Figure 8.4)

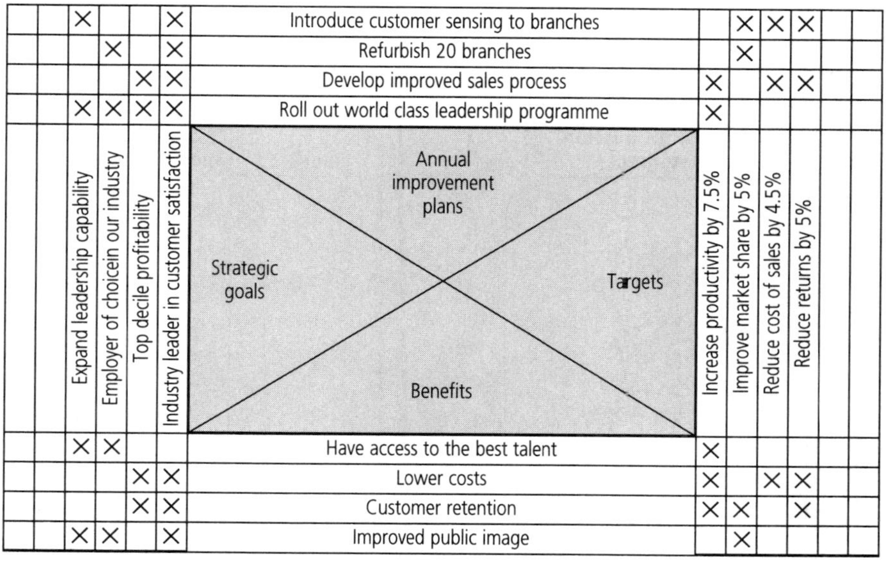

Figure 8.4 Hoshin Kanri Planning Matrix

Cendant Membership Services in the UK uses a much simpler, but equally effective approach. As part of their annual planning process, they develop and issue to every member of staff a booklet that contains details of the complete business plan. On the cover of the booklet is the vision picture (see Figure 8.1). Inside the booklet are:

- Introductory letter from the managing director;
- Purpose statement;
- Key business objectives and goals;
- Departmental objectives.

Each department lists its objectives and plans under the same headings as the company. In this way, the whole company is aligned to the same goals. Owners are identified for each of the actions and are responsible for putting together detailed action plans. The booklet is not simply handed out. All members of staff attend workshops where they discuss the company's plans and work on the development of detailed plans in their own areas. At these workshops, each member of staff is given a piece of paper with a copy of the vision picture on it. In the margin around the picture they are asked to identify where they contribute to the vision. This is a very simple but powerful way of helping everyone to see themselves in the overall scheme of things. In *Dynamic Organisations*, I described the Pentagon campaign operated by Mitsibushi Heavy Industries.[30] When visiting their plant at Sagamihara, Japan, several years ago, posters were visible all around the shopfloor.

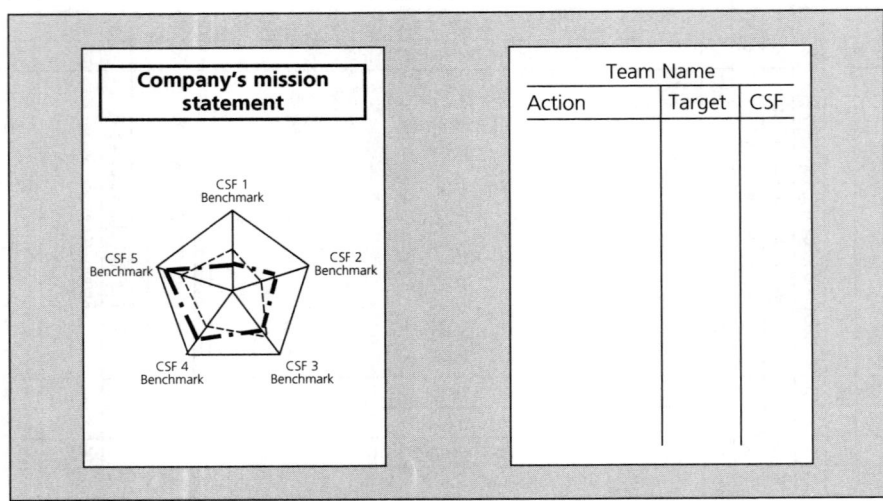

Fig. 8.5 Mitsubishi Heavy Industries – Pentagon campaign

The left-hand side of the poster was common, preprepared; the right-hand side handwritten. Managers explained that the posters were about the company's 'Pentagon Campaign'. The left-hand side described the company's mission and critical success factors (five). These CSFs were shown as a polar diagram, with the world leading benchmark at the end of each arm. Each arm then showed the company's target for the year, overall performance, and actual results for the section of the plant. The right-hand side described the improvement activities devised by work teams to improve performance. This simple mechanism combined direction, goal setting and performance mechanism in a simple chart. An excellent example of what the Japanese call visible management. It is also a simple way of aligning the organisation yet leaving significant freedom for people to identify and shape their response to the company's competitive challenges.

What is important in the operational planning process is that they leave room for people to shape and create their own plans. All too often operational plans are highly detailed. This not only leaves no room for people, it is often overly bureaucratic. All that is required are the goals, major milestones, and any key events or investments needed. The complete operational plan for Cendant Membership Services comprises the equivalent of 14 pages of A4 paper. It is also important that the plan is holistic, addressing all the major parts of the business.

Performance measurement and review

The operational plan determines the run rate of the business and the changes to be delivered. On the basis of what gets measured gets moved, the organisation needs a process for reviewing performance and amending the plans as appropriate. The understanding of business measurement has developed significantly in the past ten years. The work of Peter Drucker, Norton and Kaplan and Karl-Erik Svieby has brought new ideas for measuring performance in a knowledge business.

If an organisation's values are truly important then business measurement should be one more way that they are introduced and reinforced in the business. If customers and people form part of the values, then that should be reflected in part of the scorecard.

Working with a business unit within a major IT supplier, I helped to develop a scorecard as part of a holistic organisation design. The foundation of the design was a set of organisational principles that described how the organisation should work. To help bring these principles to life, we developed a scorecard that mapped onto the principles. It was not necessary to develop a one-to-one match, but the major headings were all addressed (see Figure 8.6).

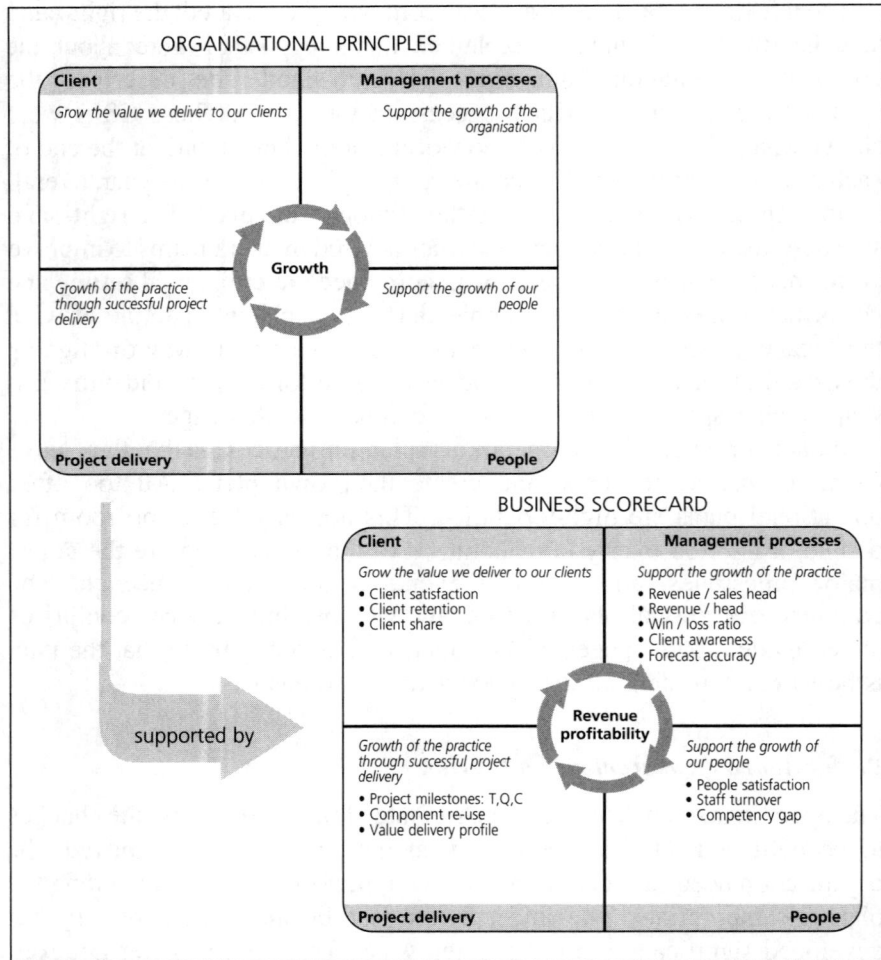

Figure 8.6 Linking values and measures

The linkage not only forces senior managers to think more deeply about the values they are proposing but also sends a clear message to the organisation that the values matter.

Measurement is of course done for a purpose and that is to inform people about performance so that they can take any corrective action, to recognise good performance, and to examine how the organisation can get even better. Measurement is one of the essential elements of a continuous performance culture. Records must be kept and accounts filed but these are but a small part of the reason behind performance measurement. The prime purpose of measuring performance in a dynamic organisation is to enable learning and improvement. I find that successful organisations measure more things more regularly than other organisations. Tom Bell, Managing Director of TNT Express Parcels, once told me that they have league tables for just about everything.

Measures are of little value unless they are reviewed and used as the basis for learning and improvement. There is, of course, a relationship between the frequency of the cycles of measurement, learning, and the opportunity for improvement available to an organisation. An organisation that measures customer satisfaction only once a year creates only one real opportunity to learn how it is performing and has only one real opportunity to generate improvements. Dynamic organisations know that the competitive environment is too aggressive for this complacency. They work on weekly and monthly measures and reviews with new ideas for improvements being generated by the continuous flow of information about performance. This approach can only work if the measurement systems are non-bureaucratic, the data is easy to access, and people have the skills, tools and motivation to do something with the resulting information. TNT Express Parcels, GE, Avis Europe, PHH and many others teach all their people basic problem solving skills (see Chapter 4 – Six Sigma at GE for one example).

Reviews are a real opportunity for different parts of the business to get together and share problems, issues and solutions. One organisation had a quarterly business review where business unit and country managers were required to spend a day each reviewing, in detail, the performance of their business. It was described by one senior manager as 'the pat on the head or the directory down your trousers session' depending on how well your business unit was doing. Man months of effort went into preparing figures for the review. It was the work of what was once described in GE before Jack Welch took over as the 'police:'

> The cadres of professional nit-pickers and second guessers on the strategic planning and finance staff, who reviewed every operating decision and supervised the allocation of capital'.[31]

Dynamic organisations seek to build measurement into everyday work and processes of the organisation, thereby minimising the effort and cost of collecting it. Teams are provided with the performance data they require. Data generated by systems is made easy to access and manipulate. Wherever possible the information is provided to the teams for them to analyse and act on. They do not have to wait for approval to act, they just do it; indeed they are expected to act.

One area often neglected in the field of measurement is change itself. Change has to be actively managed and should also be measured. In the same way that business performance is rightly reviewed to see how adjustments and improvements can be made, so too should change. Change plans are, quite rightly, often subject to review. But such reviews are often ineffective because they lack real data on the progress of change. Anecdotal evidence has its role, but can be misleading when people pick up one or two isolated examples and claim that to be a trend or an issue. And in an organisation where change is a continuing theme it is surely essential that the organisation develops measures for change. These might be people related, such as the number of people that have acquired change skills, or business related such as revenues and profits from new products or channels. Periodic reassessments using tools such as cultural profiling or organisational benchmarks such as the change capability assessment (both referenced in Chapter 7) can inform progress. The vision is the starting point. What should the organisation look like when the changes start to take effect? What will have changed and which of these can be measured to provide useful insights into the progress of change?

People processes

People processes are the vital processes that help to motivate and develop staff. They are particularly important in embedding values as they affect the issues that are of direct relevance to people. They are highly visible and therefore particularly influential in changing culture and creating the new organisation. If people do not experience the organisation's values in the mechanisms that play a significant role in how they are rewarded, recognised and developed by the organisation, then they will have little faith in those values. They will perceive the change as a meaningless management ploy. And they will be quite right to do so. As I have previously stated, values should only be adopted if people believe they are vital to running a successful business. If they are vital, they must be enacted.

All processes require the active support of the leadership of the organisation but none more so than people processes, which are central to the relationship between people and their managers. I will address the issue of values based leadership in Chapter 11.

Recruitment

Dynamic organisations begin their focus on people before they arrive. They take great care in the people they recruit. Values form a key part of the recruitment process. The people with whom the new recruit will work are often actively involved in the recruitment process. They know that fit within the team is as important as academic and vocational skills. They understand that whilst skills and knowledge can be taught, the same cannot be said of personality and values. In early discussions about the values at GE, a group of senior managers said

> We encourage the sharing of these values because we believe they are both fair and effective, but we realize they are not for everyone. Individuals whose values do not coincide with these expressed preferences will more likely flourish better outside GE.[32]

Dynamic organisations also recognise that they are increasingly in a fight for the best talent. They understand the best people have choices and will choose those organisations that can not only provide a good reward package, but also provide challenging and interesting work and the opportunity for continuous development. Bright people know the world is changing and understand the need for lifelong learning.

In the past, organisations have often undervalued the contribution their people make. GE's Six Sigma process has contributed in excess of $3 billion net of costs in the four years since its introduction in 1996. That is a contribution of approximately $10 900 per employee on top of the value of their 'normal work'. Picking people with the tenacity to drive change is not just nice to do, it is crucial if you want to build a world leading performance culture.

Performance management

Every organisation has access to the same talent as GE. What marks GE out is that they intentionally recruit and, more significantly, develop the right people. Few people doubt that change is part of the everyday cut and thrust of business today. Nor is their little disagreement that the ideas and contribution of people are increasingly the source of competitive advantage. Why is it then that so many organisations still fail to invest adequately in the development of their people? I recently worked with the top 100 managers of a multi-billion pound organisation. For most of the people on the programme, it was their first training and development activity for three years. No sports person would seek to compete at the highest level without an exhaustive and comprehensive training programme. We rightly would complain vehemently if we sent untrained soldiers into battle. Development is not an option; it is a competitive necessity. TNT spend almost five times more on training than their nearest competitor and 66 per cent more than the national average according to a survey by MCG.[33] In a study involving 540 US corporations, the American Society for Training and Development identified links between investment in training and learning and corporate financial performance.

The study, the first of its kind in the performance arena, compared companies' expenditure on workplace learning during 1996 with their performance during the first half of 1997. By creating two sub-samples in the study group – those that invested an average of $900 per employee on learning and those that invested an average of $275 per employee – researchers found that, among 40 publicly traded companies in the sample, the top group outpaced those in the bottom group by:

- 57 per cent higher net sales per employee ($385 000 vs $245 000);
- 37 per cent higher gross profits per employee ($165 000 vs $120 000);
- 20 per cent higher ratio in market-to-book values.[34]

As the old saying goes, if you think education is expensive, try ignorance.

Dynamic organisations place great emphasis on the monitoring of performance, giving constructive feedback and ongoing development using both on- and off-the-job of all their people. They have appraisal systems that are tightly linked to their values. People's performance in the areas of values are assessed alongside their performance in delivering business objectives and other areas of competence. The focus of the review is personal development. At Intel, each employee is told three things during their formal annual review:

(1) how they rate against expectations of the job – outstanding, successful, or improvement required;
(2) how they rank against others performing similar work – top, middle, or lower third;
(3) how they are trending – faster, equal to, or slower the others.

If there are sustained performance problems, a corrective action plan is developed with a three- to six-month timetable. 360 degree feedback is given to everyone, even the CEO. The employee then puts together and drives the process of preparing development plans.[35] Appraisal does not have to be formal or annual: Triple A Animal Hotel and Care Centre based near Newcastle in the North East of England have a one page weekly assessment. Once a month, each of the 25 employees writes a one-line assessment of each of their colleagues. Doing this in an organisation of 50 000 people is clearly impractical, but the idea could be of great value in teams within a large organisation.

The development of people is particularly crucial in the early stages of the change process. Development programmes will be needed that provide people with the opportunity to understand and challenge the values that are being proposed. It is through this dialogue (a process that never stops) that they are honed. More importantly, learning and challenge are effective ways of helping people to internalise the values – to help them understand what they really mean. Getting senior managers to openly debate the values, what they mean for the organisation, and how they are to be implemented, is part of the process of communicating the change.

Reward and recognition

Money matters. It is never the only the way to provide incentives to performance but it is always part of the toolkit. In dynamic organisations it is performance that matters, not position in the hierarchy. The grade systems that limit pay based on position have no part in the dynamic organisation. Dynamic organisations build cultures based on merit. Pay systems need to allow for customised packaging of salary, incentives, training, benefits and other perks that the very best talent demands. They know their value in the marketplace and are increasingly in a position to demand it, given the talent shortage. Inflexible, grade based pay systems are often the excuse for bad managers who are unwilling to address the issues of merit and performance believing they will cause disharmony amongst peers. But it is exactly this type of weak management that causes the problems. People know who amongst them is not pulling their weight and who is going the extra mile. They know who deserves the lion's share.

The change process has to introduce a pay system that rewards performance. This will typically involve a shift towards a greater element of performance based pay. That places a great responsibility on managers in the organisation to provide the environment in which people are clear about what performance means; objectives are crystal clear and managers deal with people supportively, equitably and push more decision making to the front line. Pay is no exception. In an organisation where collaboration is required to drive organisational performance, performance related pay will have to reward collaboration. That implies a shift to team-based performance pay. That does not mean that everyone in the team will get the same, but that will be a decision that the team makes.

Equality also means providing the same access to reward packages and that includes stock options. If the company is growing, all those who have contributed to it should have the opportunity to share in its growth. That does not mean equal rewards for all, but equal access. Why should only the executive suite have the opportunity to share in the capital growth that results from their combined efforts.

But remember money alone is not enough. Several hundred millionaires at companies like Microsoft and Cisco continue to work. They don't need the money but they relish the challenge those companies continue to provide for them.

One of the most underused motivational tools is recognition. From a 'Thank you' to a structured programme of 'Employee of the Month' recognition is simple but highly effective. Here are just a few examples:

- Birmingham Midshires operated a scheme where an employee each month won the use of a car of his/her choice for a week. I remember visiting one week when the award was being presented. The winner had picked a two-seater convertible and was taking a week off to drive around France. It was a week he would remember, along with the company that made it possible. The same company regularly springs surprise awards on people that have gone the extra mile and make a 'Magic Moment' award. Presented by a manager often in fancy dress, with balloons and party poppers, the whole team around them will celebrate the individual's success.
- Avis Europe have a company-wide scheme 'The Spirit of Avis'. Any member of staff or a customer can nominate someone to receive an award. Each nomination results in a certificate and an award. Nominations are accumulated up to a Gold award presented by the Chairman.
- At Pizza Hut UK, managers carry awards cheque books. At any time, they can give an employee a cheque for outstanding performance. The cheques accumulate and can be exchanged for prizes. A number of employees have gathered enough points to earn a holiday in the US in the 12 months since the programme began.
- The most telling story of the power of recognition comes from Chris Atkinson, Sales Director of TNT Express Parcels in the UK. Chris, himself a former driver, tells the story of a driver he met on one of his depot visits. The driver received a recognition award from Chris many years ago. During the visit Chris was introduced to the driver who said he had met him previously. When asked when, the driver pulled out of his top pocket a tattered piece of paper – the recognition letter Chris

had presented to him many years earlier. Pride had driven that man to keep a piece of paper. He was proud of his achievement and a simple thank you letter had maintained that pride for years.

The letter that driver received is not unique in TNT. Recognition is a part of the culture, as it in all great organisations. It is one of the things that makes them great. At TNT it is not just the winners who receive awards. Any individual, team or depot that achieves their best ever result is recognised. This plays directly to TNT's values which include: 'Leadership: Inspiring all members of the TNT Team to be outstanding achievers ...' and 'People: Recognising individual and team achievements ....'.

Whilst recognition schemes are of great value, the thank you note that is so commonplace in TNT cannot be systematised. It is an example of values-based-leadership in action.

It is also important to recognise that not everyone responds to formal recognition in the same way. People from different cultures value different things. Many Scandinavians think some formal schemes are crass and will prefer informal but sincere recognition. People know best what will encourage that extra effort; why not ask them? Many of the best schemes are designed and operated by the people themselves.

Issues management

In any organisation there are always going to be things that affect people. Whilst good leadership is always the first line of addressing issues people raise, dynamic organisations also provide other vehicles. It starts with simple but effective monitoring of people satisfaction. These are typically corporate wide programmes that monitor a percentage of people across the organisation on a rolling programme. In this way, the morale and issues of concern to people can be regularly monitored.

In dynamic organisations, local managers often supplement this corporate survey with assessments of the health of their teams on a more regular basis. One part of a US multinational uses a team assessment comprising just ten questions. Completed anonymously, the quarterly feedback lets the manager know how people are feeling on issues such as trust within the team, communication, job satisfaction, development, and clarity of objectives. Results are discussed at team meetings and actions taken where necessary. This requires a level of maturity in a team, but paradoxically it will not develop that maturity unless issues of how members of the team relate to each other are discussed.

Leadership of dynamic organisations place great store on staying in touch with the front line of the business. They are intensely interested in how that part of the organisation that faces the customer is performing. They therefore spend time talking to people at the front line to understand what life is like for them. A UK TV series followed a number of managing directors as they went 'Back to the Shop Floor' to work for a week at the heart of their own businesses. In the reviews with their fellow directors at the end of the week, they were all amazed at what they had learned about how the businesses they run really work. Directors and senior managers of dynamic organisations do this all the time, not just when the cameras turn up. The information they glean about how the business is working, what conditions people are working under, and quality of the customer experience is invaluable in guiding their investments and decisions. For the same reason, the CEO of AT&T Card Services lunches with a group of employees each month on a no-holds-barred agenda. Jack Welch and his fellow executives at GE attend a session at the management development programmes where they answer questions on any aspect of GE.

Mechanisms of this type are helpful and informative, but they can never be a substitute for good managers who have the time to listen to people, the desire to see them succeed, and the courage to confront issues of performance. Dynamic organisations invest time and money in training, and more importantly in coaching people to develop their skills of giving and receiving feedback. They learn how to deal with conflict in a constructive way to use it for the benefit of performance rather than sweep it under the carpet.

Change processes

Establishing an understanding of the outside world and using the information it and internal performance measures provide is the fuel for change. Few organisations have effective and coherent systems for identifying the need for and effecting change. When these are designed in, the organisation builds its ability to change considerably.

Understanding the outside world

The world outside the organisation is what really counts. That is where the customer lives. It is where competitors dream up new ideas. It is where politicians make decisions that affect the daily lives of people and where fashions are set. A dynamic organisation understands that an intimate knowledge of this world is an essential requirement for surviving in a changing world.

It begins with the basics – understanding the needs of the customer and how well the organisation is doing in meeting those needs. Dynamic organisations use both formal and informal ways of staying in touch with customers. Some business-to-business organisations use Customer Advisory Boards, a group of key customers who meet to discuss issues affecting them and how the organisation can help in solving them.

Dynamic organisations don't just monitor customers. They watch what competitors are doing to ensure they are not blindsided by a new development. They track technology to identify developments that can underpin new products and services. They network widely to help build a rich picture of the world around them. Building scenarios is an increasingly popular way of pulling together views of the way the world is changing. Scenario planning requires people to collect data and opinions about how the world is changing and use this to consider how the organisation might respond. Shell has used scenarios to guide their strategic planning for many years. It was one of the factors that helped the company survive the 1970s oil crisis better than their competitors. They had seen the future; executives were prepared for the actions that such an event would require.

Developing the strategic agenda

The world changes a bit at a time. It only occasionally lurches suddenly in one direction. Our approach to strategy however is predicated on a model that says the future can be predicted and planned for. What nonsense. Market opportunities and threats do not obligingly wait for the next strategic planning round; they just happen. The best organisations are creating strategy all the time.

Dynamic organisations need dynamic approaches to developing strategy – an ability to experiment with a number of actions and see which produces the best result. It is the approach to strategy that has served the natural world well for millions of years. The strategic agenda fulfils this role for organisations. A fluid list of priorities is amended as circumstances require. The strategic agenda arises from the situations facing the world in which they operate. Senior managers listen carefully to the changes in the outside world and the real issues of their organisation. Those that listen well and widely pick up changes ahead of the pack and build them into the organisations' plans and actions, often as experiments. The real exponents of this art push this capability down into the organisation, allowing a broader range of people to initiate new ideas and experiment with new products and services. The role of senior managers shifts from developing and owning strategy to coaching and sharing learning. They spend their time encouraging people to pursue new ideas and share the good ideas developed in one part of the organisation with others that can benefit. The goal is then to move this capability from the domain of a few individuals to an integral part of the organisation's culture.

But what of budgets and business plans in the world of the strategic agenda? Business plans are important, business building even more so. The ability to transform an idea into a business can no longer be the domain of a few executives. Dynamic organisations teach and coach people in the art of business building. Budgets are different. I suggest that they are an increasingly bureaucratic irrelevance. What purpose do budgets serve? They set out, in detail, what each part of the organisation should earn and spend. They are predicated on a master plan and seek to impose an order and structure when order and structure are the very things that so often hold people back. What would happen if budgets were scrapped? A good deal of non-value-added work would immediately disappear for one thing. If there were no budgets there would not be any need for budgetary systems and budget reviews. Estimate how much time is spent in your organisation preparing and revising budgets and the monthly and quarterly reviews associated with them? How many ideas, good ideas, are dismissed because 'they are not in the budget'?

Budgets have been described as 'structured distrust'. They are a way of maintaining control from the centre. Dynamic organisations need mechanisms that enable, not constrain people. Budgets can be replaced by three very simple, but effective mechanisms that give people much greater freedom but protect the organisation from the extremes. Those three are:

- Clear direction and objectives;
- Values that guide behaviour;
- A simple operating ratio such as profit margin or return on capital employed.

This is exactly how Svenska Handelsbank, a Swedish based banking group, have operated since 1970 when they scrapped all budgets. This bank without budgets finds and develops talented people, gives them clear goals and values, and then asks them to deliver a certain margin percentage. The level of revenues and costs are set by branch managers. They are free, within broad limits, to expand their cost base if they commit to delivering a level of revenue that meets or exceeds the ratio. Managers do not review budgets. They use their experience to coach people in how best to achieve their goals. The bank is both profitable and growing.

Organisational learning

The processes of organisational learning and development are vital for increasing the efficiency and effectiveness of the practice. The whole approach to strategy and change described here is predicated on learning. To avoid continually reinventing the wheel an organisation has to have mechanisms that enable individuals to share what they have learned. Whilst technology can play a helpful role, the real key to organisational learning is to connect people emotionally as well as rationally. Technology can provide methods of communication suitable for some circumstances and build repositories for valuable information. Technology however cannot encourage people to share their ideas or to value and adopt other people's ideas. Indeed any attempts to force people to adopt other people's ideas usually fail. That requires processes that connect people directly and recognises people's efforts to share ideas with other people.

Learning is not what happens in the classroom, that is a minor part of it. Real learning happens when knowledge and skills are put to use in the workplace. Organisational learning occurs when people across the organisation use what one person has learned. The key to organisational learning is organisation design. The barriers to organisational learning are rarely technological. They are cultural and interpersonal. Only by working on those levels can organisational learning be truly developed.

Values fit

Every organisation will have its own set of organisational processes. Like cultures, they are not right or wrong, or good or bad. What is important is that they are coherent with the values of the organisation. Only by

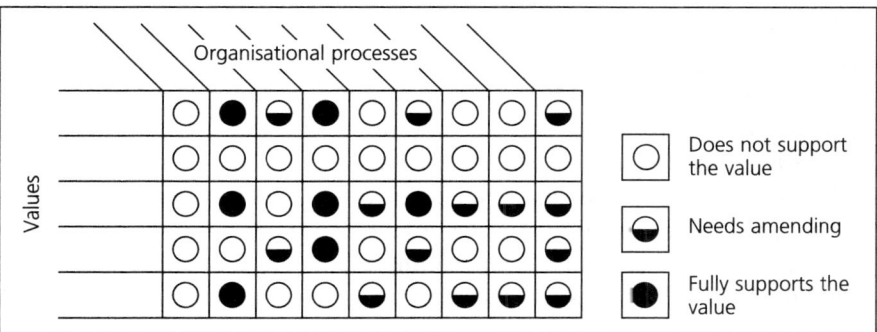

Figure 8.7 Values fit matrix

consciously designing processes that reflect and reinforce the values in the daily activities of the organisation will they come to life. One simple way of thinking through this fit is to draw up a matrix that compares values and processes identifying the nature of the relationship between the two.

The aim of the exercise is not to draw a matrix, but to challenge people to think through how the processes will actively support the implementation of the all-important values.

Communicating the vision

Whilst the thinking and doing might start at the top, they cannot stop at the top. People are most committed to things they truly believe in. They are more likely to believe in things they have thought through and had a hand in building. If you want people to share your vision, explain to them the thinking behind it and give them an opportunity to shape it. Be open to their ideas and use them to enrich your vision. It is through such dialogues and the actions they spur that shared visions are truly built. This is how the process of developing purpose and values progresses.

Real leadership goes beyond power drawn from position. Real leaders are able to perceive a different future and have the courage to act to make a difference. They have the ability to shape a view of the future and persuade people to do things differently. The vision thing counts; it is a cornerstone of leadership. But building a shared vision is a complex and often overly simplified process. It is complex because it is shaped by two paradoxes.

The first paradox is that you can only begin to build a shared vision when you are clear about what you value and what you want to achieve. It begins with an individual – you. Through careful thought, you have worked out what is important and what you want to achieve. It is your personal vision. But a vision that has clarity and robustness can only be achieved by being open; by being willing to having your vision challenged and tested; by being receptive to new ideas and perspectives. It is this process that helps builds the courage you need to match your convictions. The process of testing and refining is the source of the inner confidence that leaders have in their visions.

The second paradox is that real shared visions are not shared. They are a collection of individual visions each with a number of common threads, but each unique to an individual. Telling people your ideas, your vision, only lets them know what you want. This alone is no more than a vision shared. It does not generate the sense of commitment and passion that the vision inspires in you. And it is real commitment that makes the difference.

That will only come when people have the opportunity to go through a similar process of thinking and heart searching. In the words of the ancient Chinese warrior Sun Tzu, 'Of the really great leader the people say "We did it ourselves"'. The key is to both convince people of the value of your vision whilst at the same time helping them to realise their own vision by helping them paint themselves onto a common canvas. A leader's ability to persuade and cajole people to share their view of the future is what sets them apart. But they balance this with the knowledge that real commitment comes from doing something the individual values. Leaders engineer space for people to fulfil their own ambitions.

Shared vision is not some fine form of words that the executive team has wordsmithed for a couple of days. Nor is it some artificial point in the future. It is a continuing dialogue that allows each member of the team to see a way forward. It is a commitment to work together to make things better. Visions that are discussed live. I have yet to see anything that is nailed to a wall thrive and grow. Shared visions are about the thoughts and actions of people across the organisation. Building shared visions is a process of thinking, doing and rethinking. Thinking without doing is daydreaming. Doing without thinking is lunacy. Neither is advisable.

The key to solving both these paradoxes is conversation. Real leaders build shared vision by having the courage of their convictions and the courage to be persuaded – another paradox. They listen carefully and respectfully to the views and ideas of others whilst intelligently and passionately advocating their views. As they develop their own vision, they are also helping people develop theirs. The process of creating a shared vision is under way.

Many managers and their teams make the mistake of believing that you need an off-site, facilitated workshop to do the vision thing. At certain points in time, such an event can help. The truth however is that the creation of shared visions is most effective when it is a part of normal work. As situations arise, leaders prompt questions about what they mean for the future that they are seeking to build. They use everyday problems and opportunities to relate and develop their vision. In this way, visions are grounded in reality. This does not mean that they are about today. But visions that do not relate to the good and bad of today as well as paint a picture of the future are merely castles in the air. They may describe a future, but they provide no reference point from which the journey can begin. They do not inspire confidence in people. They are doomed to a life as posters hanging on walls.

People also fail to create shared visions because they lack the art of conversation. The following points will help.

Be receptive to others

Many people mistakenly believe a conversation is a one way street. Real leaders know the value of listening. They listen, observe, and watch as much as they talk. They are curious and question not just what people do but why they do it. They encourage people to express their opinions. They are interested in what people feel as well as in what they do and think.

Through their active listening, leaders seek to develop an understanding of the viewpoints and perspectives of the people they are dealing with. They try to put themselves in their shoes and understand their concerns and issues. They do not put down people with other ideas or opinions but seek to understand the reasons behind their views. They are also always looking for the ideas and perspectives that enrich their own vision. Skilful communicators look to gauge people's reactions. They watch their gestures and their body language for feedback. They assess whether people are confused, concerned, worried, interested, enthusiastic, sceptical, cynical or supportive. They test for understanding and seek feedback by asking questions such as, 'Is this of interest to you?' and 'Am I making any sense?'. They actively encourage feedback saying, 'What do you think?' and 'Do you see things differently?'. They use this awareness to reach out and involve people. Their own responses and body language are not defensive, further encouraging feedback. They avoid presenting black or white situations, recognising that the real answers often lie in the myriad shades of grey in between. Paradoxically, they do not fudge the essential issues. Their strong belief in their vision and values is reflected in the passion with which they argue their corner on the vital issues.

Good communicators encourage discussion. They seek the views of people. They encourage discussion rather than argument. They are diplomatic but never dishonest. They do not dismiss ideas and opinions out of hand but seek to understand the reasons or concerns behind those views. They use open ended questions to encourage people to express themselves. They know that God gave us two ears and one mouth as a model for communication. They recognise that discussion is a central part of the process of persuasion. It provides people with the opportunity to explore the thinking behind the basic ideas on view. One manager I worked for used to ask three questions of anyone presenting an idea. Why?, why? and why? His logic was that if someone had really thought through their idea, they could answer all three questions satisfactorily.

Express yourself

Leaders recognise that visions are personal and they invest some of themselves into the idea and its presentation. They do not just blandly present an idea. They begin by explaining the background, establishing the context. They use stories and analogies with a personal element to communicate their ideas. They powerfully express their own feelings and beliefs as well as the thought, engaging people's emotions as well as their intellect. Leaders recognise that people often buy the person as much as they buy the idea. They are not afraid of expressing their excitement, frustration, hope, worry or passion.

Share control

Having thought through their ideas, leaders are confident enough to talk about their vision without a script. Do not second guess how people will react; that leads one to prejudge people's reactions and act accordingly. Rather, be open and trusting. Skilful leaders express their ideas without telling people what they should do. They recognise the value of letting people develop their own path towards the vision. They provide advice and guidance rather than instruction. They respond to questions by saying 'What do you think we should do?'. They emphasise outcomes rather than method. The one thing they do not give up is their determination and perseverance to achieve their vision. They push through the difficult decisions always focusing on the necessary outcome.

Respect people

Leaders have a knack of treating people as peers. Their respect for people of all types comes through. Arrogance and superiority suppress people's creativity and commitment. When you try to help others, you put them in an inferior position and they feel less able to help themselves. Don't lecture or preach. Rather listen to people and encourage them to suggest their solutions. Talk to people honestly and frankly: it is how you want to be treated and they deserve no less. Respecting people does not mean that you treat everybody as equals. You will take cognisance of some people's views more than others. But you will be unwise to dismiss people out of hand, or be patronising or insulting. Some people are wary about giving bad news so they dress up the real message by sugar coating. Sugar coating bitter pills only makes them more bitter when their true nature is discovered. My experience is that people prefer the truth. They know where they stand. They can make decisions about their future. Respect is about enabling people to make up their own minds. Too many managers are scared of letting people know the real facts, fearing they will not come to the 'right' conclusions. Such managers don't respect their people; they probably don't respect themselves.

When criticism is in order, leaders begin by confirming a positive aspect first and then lead into the criticism. Criticise people for their performance, not their personality. Explain not just what went wrong, but the implications of their actions. Do not be curt or cutting with criticism. Remember that what you are seeking to do is to enlist the commitment of the individual. Helping them to improve, not put them down, best does this. People who are belittled will find it difficult to develop a positive vision of them within the canvas you are painting.

Have patience and perseverance

Building a shared vision takes time. It will not happen after one presentation or discussion. People need time to reflect and consider. They need to think through what it means to them. They need time to become comfortable with the new ideas. People rarely express their real concerns immediately but with time and opportunity the concerns will surface. The more conversations you have with people, the more opportunities there are for these concerns to be addressed. Work to frame your vision in their context. In this way, your vision will become richer and involve others. If your vision is right, persevere. Do not be deflected by rejection or apathy. If you have thought through your visions and truly believe in what you are saying, you will find the courage to persevere and the ways to get your message across. If you struggle with either it is probably because you do not really believe in what you are saying. If this is the case, get out of the way. The world already has enough pseudo leaders.

What of power? In any organisation, power exists. But in too many it is seen as a finite resource, which has to be retained at the top if the organisation is to be controlled. This misses the point. Creating shared visions is about sharing power in a way that enables it to grow. Compost will rot and stink if it is kept in a pile, but when spread around a garden, it creates wonderful results. Power works in the same way, but has one unique feature. When power is spread around, the power held at the centre does not diminish to the same degree. Leaders who share power find they receive the respect and trust of their staff, which gives them greater influence and power over the organisation. Dynamic organisations seek to maximise the power to make a difference to each individual.

Developing and communicating a vision is central to leadership. Conversations and the actions that arise from them are a simple but powerful mechanism to creating and communicating a shared vision. The process does not fit easily into a strategic planning process but from these conversations, strategies will arise. It is not a quick fix, but it does work. The power of a shared vision is immense. But it needs to be nurtured; it needs to evolve. Building a shared vision through conversation and action is not a process that takes place at the beginning of some change. In great organisations, it is a continuing process.

Taken together, purpose and values, organisational processes and thoughts about leadership style, make up the framework for change. They build together to form a vision of how the organisation should operate. They provide the foundation upon which people across the organisation can act and drive the change forward. It is important that the executive team express a shared view of this vision and the rationale behind it. If they are unable to agree, they will be unable to present a coherent, clear view of the future of the organisation. Any confusion will affect the ability to drive the change forward. Time that should be spent discussing and implementing the actions needed to move towards the vision will instead be spent trying to remove the confusion or argue for a different version.

The process of developing values and translating them into action is an iterative one. It is possible to quickly arrive at the values that underpin an organisation. As they are implemented, the organisation will learn more about what they mean, and will change their actions accordingly. Some situations will throw new light onto the values. The precise form of words is less important than the will to make them work. This comes from implementation and learning not from eternal philosophical discussion. Discussion is important in the first stage; thereafter, learning by doing is the best way to develop.

Now comes the most difficult phase – moving the vision into the greater organisation.

Communiaction

Communiaction
- Generating involvement
- Managing connections
- Removing blockages

KEY CONCEPTS

- Involvement serves five purposes:
  - Widens the intellect applied to
  - Models behaviour of the future
  - Communicates through action – communi-action
  - Helps identify leadership skills
  - Creates momentum for further change
- Exchange of ideas and experiences are essential to maintain connections.
- Coherence is sustained through the implementation of values.
- Establishing organisational processes early is essential to removing blockages.
- Some people won't want to make the switch.
- Top management must step back and provide the space for others to act.

ACTIVITIES

- Generating involvement
  - Change exhibition and communication
  - Establish and equip change teams
  - Create space and freedom

- Managing connections
  - Aligning outcomes and values
  - Establishing a change forum

- Removing blockages
  - Identifying advocates, abstainers and antis
  - Developing change skills
  - Revisit organisational processes

I cannot hear your words for the action that thunders above your head.
HENRY DAVID THOREAU

A vision that is not enacted is a dream. Building the framework for change starts the process of change but now it has to be acted upon. The first step is to communicate the vision to the whole organisation. This has to be done quickly but, more importantly, effectively. The people who have been involved in forming the vision understand it because they have worked through its development. They have considered the options and argued their views. They have invested emotional and intellectual energy in it. They have lived through the decisions and understand why they were taken. These are decisions that are going to effect everybody in the organisation.

So how do organisations communicate their vision? In many cases, badly. In one US organisation undergoing fundamental change only 0.58 per cent of all communication issued to staff related to the vision.[36] This critical information is typically lost in a morass of organisational data and trivia. And how is it typically presented? Most organisations turn to the tried and trusted methods of roadshows, presentations and company newsletters. These are all useful forms of communication but are bland and ineffective when it comes to generating the emotional and intellectual commitment to something as important as the future of the company. They are also only essentially one-way. There might be time for questions at the end, but never enough.

Constant communication is essential at any time. During a period of change, it is even more important. The success of any change is not visible until after the change has taken place. Psychologists can show that in networks of people, there is a time lag between a change taking place and the widespread perception of that change. An organisation is a complex system of people each operating with their own beliefs. This belief set causes people to be selective in the information they select and how they perceive it. If people are not convinced that change will take place, then almost any information will be interpreted as supporting that view.[37] Managers driving change have therefore to work very hard. Quantity, quality and consistency of communications are vital.

The only meaningful form of communication is *communi-action*, with the emphasis on *action*. People who are meaningfully involved in something take time to understand it. But there is a paradox in operation. They will only get involved in something if they both understand it and can play a meaningful role. Communication of vision therefore has to follow three main stages. In stage one, people have to become familiar with the framework for change – the vision that is guiding the moves towards becoming a dynamic organisation. This should include a call to arms by providing opportunities for people to get involved in driving the change forward. In stage two it is important to restate the vision and the progress being made towards it, with the emphasis on any success stories. Stage three is about embedding the change and therefore using the new mechanisms and leadership style to continually refresh the vision and values and keep them to the fore.

Communicating through action involves both the communicators and their audiences. The communicators, the team that have crafted the framework for change, have to be role models. Mahatma Gandhi said 'You must be the change you want to see'. People look to senior managers as role models. They have therefore to be seen to behave consistently with the values they are propounding. I will address this in detail in Chapter 11.

Communication through involvement is about getting people across the organisation to embrace the change in an active rather than a passive way. Something that they have a real hand in doing not something where they are passive recipients of the gospel from on high. Dynamic organisations are about meaningful involvement, and the change process has to reflect that. Involvement is important for five reasons:

- Bringing more people into the change expands the pool of ideas and experience that can be brought to bear. It is an attempt to tap into the collective creativity of the organisation. People from different backgrounds, countries and perspectives can bring new ideas to old problems. People think differently. It is important that the organisation recognises the value of these different perspectives and the roles they can play. Tools such as Myers Briggs Type Indicators, the Herrmann Brain Dominance Instrument and the Kolbe Index are all useful ways of helping people understand the value of different thinking and operating styles.

- Involvement in the change process models the behaviour required in dynamic organisations. If continuous improvement and creativity are going to be tapped, then people will have to be actively involved in a much more meaningful way. Why not start as you mean to go on?

- Experience is the chief architect of the brain. Doing is the best way of learning and communicating.

- Involvement provides more opportunities for more people to exercise their leadership skills. Dynamic organisations are continually developing their leadership skills and giving people the opportunity to put them to use. Getting people to exercise these skills at this early stage also allows talent to shine and then be given greater responsibilities.

- Every question answered raises a host of other questions. As change projects start to deliver results the effect on other parts of the organisation become clear. This spawns the need for further changes. Soon, change becomes self-initiating provided of course the right conditions, notably leadership, are in place.

Change exhibitions

The sooner the communication through change begins the better. I believe in starting right at the beginning. The team that develops the vision should already have drawn on people from beyond the board of directors.

The communication of this vision should do likewise. One very useful and effective technique is a change exhibition. A change exhibition is a way of presenting the change framework to the organisation in an active way. The exhibition sets out the case for change, describes the elements of the framework and how the organisation will look when the changes have been effected. It is not passive. The exhibition should be structured so that during it people have things to do. Here are a few ideas that I have found useful in such events:

- When describing the case for change, ask people to identify the things that most constrain their ability to perform and contribute.
- Ask people to give feedback on the framework. What do they think will work? What won't work? What don't they fully understand? What are their concerns?
- Give people dummy cheques and ask them 'If you were in charge of the change, where would you invest to make the values come to life?'.
- Give people a mocked up front page of a newspaper and ask them to describe what life would be like in the new organisation.
- Provide people with workmats that describe the need for change, and the new organisation through a series of exercises.
- Ask people to identify projects that would help bring the new organisation to life.
- Produce a mock up of a new style office or manufacturing cell and give people a chance to try it out.
- Produce a computer simulation of the new organisation that people can experiment with.
- Ask people to volunteer to help in some area of the change.

An exhibition is something that people attend at a time to suit them. The whole office or factory doesn't have to close down for the duration of a presentation, much of which goes unheard. People can take their time; focus on the areas that are of interest to them; revisit something that they are unsure about or want to think more about. They can visit a second time. They can go with colleagues. In most organisations, this style of communication is so novel and different from the boring old stuff they are used to, people will immediately begin to think that this change just might be different.

Four things are important in a change exhibition. It is important that a member of the team involved in developing the vision is on hand to answer any questions and receive feedback. The change must be described holistically and address the reasoning behind the decisions. I find the best way to do this is to storyboard the thinking process that the original team went through: what options were considered and why was this the chosen one? The exhibition has to get people active in the understanding process. They have to exercise their minds and not just their eyes and ears. Finally, the exhibition must provide a route to further involvement. That might be as simple as the opportunity to ask questions later, but I am a great believer in getting people to volunteer to help. If the organisation is suffering, many people will be keen to help in some way. At one exhibition, over half the 200 plus members of the business unit volunteered to help. Typically 20-30 per cent of the people that attend will want to get involved. It is not exceptional to have hundreds of ideas and suggestions. There are the occasional sceptical or odd comments. One person employed by a defence contractor when asked what his three wishes were to bring about growth to the business replied 'A return to the Cold War'. The vast majority of the inputs are practical, pertinent and sincere.

Following the exhibition it is vital that people's interest is followed up. Those that have volunteered should be contacted and given the opportunity to join one of the change projects (see below). The ideas and suggestions should be collated and circulated to the whole organisation together with the actions being taken because of them. The change team should spend time explaining to people what they have learned from the feedback and how that is influencing the change.

Education and learning

Communicating change is an education and learning process operating at different levels. At the simplest level people see changes to their work and the processes surrounding them. This often involves taking on new skills and knowledge. Fundamental change often requires people to change the mental models which shape how they see the world. All these changes require education. Best practice organisations aggressively use education and development to promote their values during organisational change. In a benchmark study, the American Productivity and Quality Center found that all the best practice organisations used education to promote organisational values compared to 50 per cent of the whole community. In dynamic organisations, education is not just about acquiring skills and knowledge. A great deal of time is dedicated to helping people understand the values of the organisation and how they are implemented in the organisation. A deep understanding of the organisation is important because it underpins performance. During the initial period of the change, this begins with the communication of the framework for change.

Training, both on and off the job are an essential part of the change process. Early in the change process it is important to build change skills across the organisation, not just for senior managers. In Chapter 7, I described the role of a change workshop in preparing the change team. This education needs to continue and reach right across the organisation. Here is an example of a curriculum used by one organisation.

SENIOR MANAGERS *Purpose:* build capability to lead large scale organisational change

Topics
- The characteristics of successful organisations
- The role of vision and values in change
- Understanding organisational culture
- Developing a framework for change
- Managing transformations
- Generating involvement
- Communicating change
- Dealing with resistance for change
- Sustaining momentum
- Coaching skills

MID-LEVEL *Purpose:* create a cadre of change coaches

Topics
- Understanding the big picture
- Successful change
- Making change personal
- Managing and coordinating projects
- Identifying and dealing with blockers
- Helping people let go
- Coaching skills

▶

> **FIRST LINE** *Purpose:* embed change into the organisation
>
> *Topics*
> Understanding the big picture
> How people react to change
> Driving continuous improvement
> Learning and change
> Communicating change
> Coaching skills

Each of these programmes should combine educational input with the opportunity to learn more about the organisation's change and develop actions that contribute to the change. Such events are also a great opportunity for the organisation's senior managers to explain their vision and listen to people's ideas and concerns. One of the threads running through the curriculum is coaching skills. In dynamic organisations, the drive for continuous improvement is dependant on people continually raising their own performance standards. That requires managers, supervisors and team colleagues that can coach people. Coaches focus on process and behaviours – how people do things. Classroom based activities can only scratch the surface. Coaching helps people take what they have learned in the classroom and apply it in the workplace. Good coaches use their experience to guide rather than instruct. The right question rather than an answer can be far more effective in helping people to learn.

The forums that these events provide are a valuable opportunity for people to participate in the dialogue about change. Senior GE executives continue to attend programmes at the management development centre with an open agenda session. This dialogue shaped the values over the years. Welch insisted that drafts of the values be exposed to debate at Crotonville (GE's management development centre) until thousands of managers had considered them and given their response.[37] This dialogue continues to this day with managers questioning the values, and more significantly, the actions of managers to live up to them.

It is again important to realise that the use of education does not stop. Dynamic change is a process that never stops. Values are continually being tested and the understanding of them developed. Change is always being practised. Education and development are therefore continuous acts. The types of programmes used to raise change awareness and capability early in the process will continue ad infinitum. People can always learn more and a dynamic organisation facilitates and encourages that learning. This is not an investment just to support a change programme. It is an investment in a new and different way of running an organisation.

Access to business information

People need to know how the business is doing. It is, after all, their future that is at stake. Dynamic organisations operate with an open flow of information and opinion. In the early stage of the change, it is important to keep the pressure up. If the change was initiated by a crisis then information about business performance is needed to reinforce the need for change. People should be provided with regular information about how the business as a whole is performing with the opportunity to ask managers what this means and how it affects the plans for the business.

But there is a much more fundamental reason behind providing people with meaningful information about business performance. Dynamic organisations generate significant increases in performance through the daily acts of all their people. Continuous improvement is a way of life. Information is the lifeblood of this process. Without real data, people cannot effectively plan improvements. For this, they will need detailed operating information about the activities of their teams. The team members themselves determine what information they need to manage their performance. Much of the information that is collected in organisations is for upward reporting. Senior managers receive detailed operating information when they are often in no position to understand the implications of the data. This detailed upwards reporting is characteristic of a controlling management system. It introduces unnecessary bureaucracy and interference. If organisations are to move quickly, they have to push decision making to the point where the work is done. If they are to generate the degree of improvement that GE generated from Work Out and Six Sigma then it is the teams that decide how work is done. Increasingly, the teams set their own targets and the measures. I will return to this point when I discuss teams in Chapter 10.

Changes will be needed to information systems to enable teams to capture and manipulate data for their own purposes. People will need the skills to analyse the data. Basic statistics is on the curriculum of all dynamic organisations.

Access to information is also a useful way of stimulating organisational learning. Information systems provide benchmarks. TNT Express Parcels operate league tables for everything. Everyone can see which team or depot is performing best in certain areas of performance. Teams in dynamic organisations ask why and how. Why is one depot consistently more productive? How do they achieve those levels? The teams then decide which improvement projects they want to initiate and will often talk to their colleagues in the best performing team to learn how they do it. Information therefore stimulates internal competition, enhancing the desire to do better. This is to be encouraged provided it is operated in an environment where sharing of ideas is the norm. In dynamic organisations, leaders spend considerable time and effort in identifying best practices and encouraging other parts of the organisation to learn from them. This is not restricted to ideas from within. The best organisations know that they can always learn and constantly seeking ideas from any organisation. They use schemes like the Management Today/Unisys Service Excellence awards, the European Quality Award and Baldrige to compare themselves with the best anywhere. Winning is always great, but dynamic organisations use these events because it gives them information about who might be doing something better. They check them out and learn. The performance ratchet is cranked up again.

Change projects

Communication is about getting people to understand the change by getting them involved. People can be involved in two ways: through the changes in their normal work and through involvement in specific change projects. I want to address the latter. The framework provides an initial focus for action. When this is communicated the opportunity arises to get people from across the business to participate in the projects that arise from it. The most important qualification here is willingness. The organisation needs people who want to make a difference.

The first step is to provide people with the basic skills of process improvement. One IT organisation took the people who had volunteered to help drive the change forward and gave them one day training in problem solving and process improvement together with a short introduction to team dynamics. They were also provided with a very simple but effective template for change projects. The bounded change process described in Chapter 6 is an example.

The team should comprise a small group of volunteers, some of whom have some knowledge of the area being addressed. Avoid teams that are made up exclusively of people from the area being addressed. They will typically be more protective of the old practices and may even be unable to think of radically new and different solutions. Timescales should be intentionally short. Challenge the teams to come up with solutions in 30 days with a target to implement them within another 60 days. Not all changes can be effected in such timescales, but setting tight deadlines adds to the sense of urgency. Each team should be given a clear objective and in addition be required to design and implement a process that is seen to actively support the values. In addition to the training in basic problem solving, it is helpful to expose the team to leading edge thinking in that area. Consultants can be helpful to provide short, quick updates on the latest methods and ideas. A recommended reading list can also serve to stretch people's thinking, as can visits to companies recognised for excellence in that field. Schemes like the UK Department of Trade and Industry's 'Inside Industry' are valuable and inexpensive ways of picking up the best ideas around.

Each project should be allocated a sponsor from the senior management team. The sponsor's role is to smooth the path for the team and review their plans. It should not be an approval role. The teams should understand that their recommendations will be implemented provided they have consulted those directly involved. They should therefore be clear about their responsibility to the rest of the organisation. Teams will need two types of support. First, they will need the time to carry out their work. They will need to be freed from their existing work. This is always problematic, as often the best people to work on the change teams are the best people at their normal jobs. Secondly, they will need time and support to both remove the blockages that will inevitably arise and to discuss the real meaning of the values as they apply in this context. Leadership needs to show its mettle by sweeping aside petty objections.

If the work of the project teams are to take hold, organisational processes have to be changed as quickly as possible. If the organisational processes do not reinforce the desired culture then change will progress slowly and might even be constrained completely as people try to wade through the treacle of the old bureaucracy.

Managing connections

Throughout the change, there will be much activity. The danger is always that the activities of different groups will overlap or duplicate each other. People will argue therefore that the organisation needs control systems that monitor the changes and resolve disputes about who does what. What is needed is a master project plan and a project manager. This is another attempt to impose control from above. It is a perfectly logical argument but is fundamentally flawed. For one thing, this is not a project but a shift to a new way of working. The initial projects are needed to kick-start the shift by removing the blockages and changing the way the organisation works. Those individual activities are just an example of the type of projects that a dynamic organisation has on the go all the time.

Attempts to impose control in this way will add bureaucracy to the change, which will stifle creativity and slow the whole process down. Planners will begin to determine who does what when and before you know it you have reintroduced a centralised control function to drive a change that has concepts such as empowerment and speed at its heart. The organisation will begin to whisper 'We told you so' and the end of the change is already in sight. Bounded changes, the individual projects, need to be managed as projects. Dynamic change needs leadership and conversations.

The desire for coordination of activities is not wrong. It is the method that is wholly inappropriate. Think back to the termite mounds and shoals of fish I described in Chapter 4. They do not have a central planning department yet they work with a degree of coordination far beyond any organisation I have seen. They do it through conversation. Central planning is replaced by communication. Organisations can work the same way. In dynamic organisations, people talk to each other. When tackling a project, the first question is 'What else is happening in this arena?'. People willingly share information about what they are doing. Leadership takes time to keep people in touch with the big picture. These very simple mechanisms will never flourish if the organisation continues to rely on central control methods. What are needed are the right leadership and the processes for sharing knowledge and information. Leaders need to constantly restate the vision and values and challenge people to ensure they are working to fulfil them. They need to be out on the road talking to people. Helping them solve their problems. The more this is done, the greater the possibility for people making connections between seemingly disparate activities and events.

People who want to control from the centre do so out of fear. A few control freaks seek control and power for their own sake but most have the best interests of the organisation at heart. They have been taught that control is the only way to achieve coordination. They overlook the fact that nature has developed highly interdependant communities, whose actions are coordinated to a degree most organisations could never imagine. The only form of control there is the invisible hand of Mother Nature. Dialogue based on shared vision and values are organisations' way of emulating nature. They work if they are given the chance.

Removing barriers

Change always generates resistance. The two go hand in hand. Resistance is most people's natural reaction to change. When faced with any change, the first question is always 'What does this mean for me?.' Until that anxiety is addressed, resistance in some degree is inevitable. There is one notable exception to this and that is when people themselves initiate the change. Then the commitment is much greater and resistance is never a problem. This is why involvement is so important to successful change.

Resistance to change comes in many different forms but there are only two real sources: processes and people.

I have talked at length about the need to have organisational processes that work to support and reinforce the values the organisation is seeking to embed. Because they exert a strong influence on the behaviours of people it is important that people see changes in them quickly. Change will struggle if reward and recognition systems fail to reinforce the behaviours expected. If customer and employee satisfaction are not measured, they will never attract the same attention, time and resources as market share or profitability. Removing any obstacles embedded in the processes is essential.

Taking the brakes off is an essential first step but minimising structural resistance can also be positively promoted. Organisations are systems and as such can be mapped. An organisational system map can help demonstrate how the different processes interact and combine to fulfil the organisation's processes. The map can also be of great value in helping people understand how the different systems need to work together. Increasingly, such tools are finding a role in not only planning change, but in helping people understand how the organisation works at the macro level.

The more challenging form of resistance to address is resistance from people. Logic has little part to play in this process which is about getting people to change the way they see the world and their role in it. Not all resistance is conscious. Much of what people do to block change is subconscious and not premeditated acts of defiance. Nor is resistance related to position in the hierarchy. The degree of resistance is about perceived threat, not position. The more someone has to lose the greater the likelihood that they will resist. This is why senior managers can often be the biggest obstacles to building dynamic organisations. They perceive that their power and influence will be threatened. For people who perceive power and influence as the ability to control and direct then there will be a loss of power. Dynamic organisations have power by the bucketload but it is not restricted to one group of people who happen to be at the top. In dynamic organisations the people who exert the power are those who can coach and enable people to overachieve. Their power is drawn from their ability to develop their people and thereby develop the business. They are not goody goodies, but leaders who know that success comes from improving the way people perform. They are rewarded with outstanding business results and even greater influence. Jack Welch would not have become the most respected business leader of the late twentieth century had he not delivered growth and prosperity to GE. He would not have delivered that growth and prosperity had he not built an organisation where every GE'er comes to work with continuous improvement in mind.

Blocking behaviour expresses itself in many ways. Here are just a few. Perhaps you can recognise some of them in your colleagues, or even yourself.

Talk an idea to death	Fail to seek/listen to feedback
'We've tried that before and it didn't work'	Group think
Failure to speak up	False enthusiasm
Ignore/fail to seek data	Close down discussions
Just do nothing	Ignore people and their ideas/views
Continuous sarcasm	Conform for a quiet life
'That's not the way we do things around here'	Divide and conquer
Rumour mongering	Follow your habits
Withhold support	Withhold access
Avoid confrontation	Fail to recognise effort and achievement
Don't trust people	Don't listen to people
Fail to stay up-to-date	Prejudice – unfounded beliefs about someone
Undervalue people	Keep useful information to yourself
Work in cliques	Selfishness
The eternal sceptic	Form a committee
I'm the expert	Lack of willingness to delegate
Analysis paralysis	Argument by position – 'I'm the boss'

Figure 9.1 Behaviours that block change

Dealing with resistance to change

The first step to dealing with resistance to change is to learn to spot it then develop strategies for highlighting it.

There are three strategies for dealing with personal resistance.

Vision and values

Because resistance to change stems from fear and anxiety, a major cause of resistance is that people are unable to see themselves in the brave new world. Sometimes people don't understand the change and struggle to understand how their role will change. Anything that delays the day when they have to face up to the future is to be welcomed. Why worry about the future if you can maintain the clarity and certainty of the present? In dynamic organisations, vision and values are continually debated because changing circumstances affect how people see the future. The aim is not to tell everyone that they will always have a job but to help them see the commitment to creating a future and helping them see their place in it.

Development and coaching

Some people resist change because they do not how to deal with issues. For example, many managers do not give good feedback because they are scared of causing conflict. Teaching them how to give feedback and use conflict as a constructive tool will help to address this issue. Coaching is a very effective strategy for dealing with people who subconsciously block change. Managers in particular often block change without realising they are doing it. A respected colleague can point out the behaviour and its implications and encourage the individual to consider how they might have dealt differently with the situation. Upward and 360 degree appraisals can also be tweaked to address blocking behaviour.

Execute the few

In any change there will be people who resist because they do not want to participate. These people are often amongst the more senior ranks. They are comfortable in their jobs and have often been involved in developing the culture as it now exists. The change is threatening the achievements on which their reputations were built. Whilst dynamic organisations respect their heritage, they have no place for people who live in the past. These people must go. Having listened to countless discussions about mistakes made in organisational change, one message consistently comes across. A failure to rid the organisation of senior people early in the change process who would not or could not make the shift. These are difficult decisions because it often means shipping out old colleagues. But keeping them in the organisation only leads to more tears. Change is tough. It involves making tough decisions.

10 Embedding Change

> **Embedding**
> - Enabling people and teams
> - The process is the design

KEY CONCEPTS

- Dynamic organisations are teams of teams.
- It is not just about enlarging the number of people involved. Expanding the team also involves growing the competence of each team member and the team itself.
- The process of forming teams is an important organisational capability – the emphsis is on teaming.
- Letting go is an essential part of empowerment.
- Continuous reinforcement is essential. Without constant pressure the organisation will revert to type.
- People need both skills and behavioural support.
- The process by which a dynamic organisation is built becomes the organisation design. Recognise that a dynamic organisation prefers verbs to nouns: for example, leadership vs leaders, planning vs planners, sensing vs surveys.

ACTIVITIES

- Enabling people and teams
  - Supporting individual learning
  - Establishing a teaming process
  - Establishing team support
  - Helping people to let go
- Process is the design
  - Redefining organisation design
  - Embedding purpose and values
  - Strengthening leadership capability
  - Strengthening organisational processes
  - Reflecting and learning

Embedding Change

Success is the sytematic destruction of failure
DUNCAN GOODHEW

Continuous improvement of the ability to profitably satisfy customers is the work of dynamic organisations. Values based leadership and organisational processes are not an end in themselves, they are an essential way of creating an organisation that competes and wins in a changing market. That requires a constant restlessness and dissatisfaction with the status quo. Perfection may not be possible but the constant search to find it leads to awesome levels of performance. This applies not only to the processes that deliver products and services to customers, but also to all the necessary processes of the organisation. The simple operating rule is to scrap everything that is not necessary and ensure that everything else operates at the highest possible levels of performance.

The change process in the early years is like a growing child: temperamental and full of unexpected surprises. American doctor Brian Epstein described the conditions for the successful development of the brain in a child's early ears. There are parallels for developing dynamic organisations.

Child development	**Organisational development**
A child needs:	*An organisation needs:*
to feel safe	to develop employable people
to know they are special	to recognise individual and team achievements
to feel confident about what to expect from their environment	equality and equity in its dealings with people
discipline	to encourage self-discipline in its people
a balanced experience of freedom and limits	to help people understand empowerment and the responsibilities it carries
to be exposed to a diverse environment filled with books, music and appropriate toys	to closely monitor and share information about its operating environment

Figure 10.1 Development parallels

There is another parallel between parenting and the creation of dynamic organisation. The result in both cases is something that takes on a life of its own. Children look to their parents for guidance and protection. As they grow up, they develop a life of their own. Dependence gives way to independence; the relationship changes. Dynamic organisations have grown up. So much of what their people do is self-generated and directed. Dynamic organisations have senior managers, but they do not tell the organisation what to do. The relationship is one of adult to adult, not parent/child. They use their experience and wisdom to guide and coach. Wisdom and experience are not strictly a function of age. Many senior mangers may have 30 years of experience, but that is just two years' experience repeated 15 times. In a fast changing world, wisdom and experience relate to ability to learn, not length of service.

The early stages of the change present their own difficulties. The task seems mammoth and there is no obvious starting point. Pulling a team together takes time. Difficulties seem to outweigh any possibilities and the world is full of sceptics. Progress is slow. For every two steps forwards, there is one step back, and the knocks always feel harder than the few successes. This is because organisations are collections of highly complex, inter-related components. Change one part and it has implications and effects dozens of other things. This is why organisations have to be changed as a whole. It is why the change framework has to be as holistic as possible. The whole situation is further complicated because the most crucial elements of an organisation are people. People don't behave rationally or logically, as I explained in Part I. They are conservative, emotional and irrational.

This is where leadership is called for in spades. The members of the change team have to support each other. As the change progresses, the organisation builds more and more of the features of a dynamic organisation, notably the organisational processes. Slowly, things start to happen. More and more people begin to understand and propound the vision. The project teams begin to implement the new processes. Abstainers come off the fence and begin to get behind the change. The momentum seems to be growing and success is assured. Wrong.

This point in the change is dangerous. People believe that victory is in sight and take their foot off the gas. This is the point when renewed effort is required. It is a shift from change as a programme to change as a way of life. If this shift is not made, all the efforts thus far will have missed their mark.

There are a number of things that can be done to reinforce the change and avoid slipping back to the old ways.

Business first

The most important thing to remember is that changes must be seen to make an impact on the business and not just in the way the organisation works. Leadership must continue to relate the changes to the way it delivers value. It is easy to get caught up in the process of change and forget that there is no point in changing an organisation if it does not make a difference to performance. Every opportunity has to be made to strengthen the change's impact on the company's purpose and strategic goals. Customer data has to be regularly reviewed and questions asked about how life for the customer can be improved. New people and teams have to be coached to identify projects that improve business performance. Measures that give a clear picture of the company's performance must be widely circulated and assistance given to help people understand them and their implications.

Any successes should be used to reinforce the value of the change. Success becomes a rallying cry for driving the change further. Indeed successes should be planned for. Setting short-term objectives are a useful way of creating success along the path. I am a great believer in getting people to think about what they can achieve in 90 days. This time limit forces people into action rather than interminable planning. Good thinking and some planning are important but it is very easy for people to slip into planning mode and never emerge. It is better to get something 90 per cent right, then work to improve it. Dynamic organisations are all about doing, learning and improving.

It is important that people are clear about the goals of the organisation. People cannot hit targets if they do not know what they are aiming for. Many organisations set their strategic goals at the beginning of the year and place great importance on communicating them across the organisation. Then follows a stunning silence. People are not told of progress towards the goals, or whether the goals have changed. Dynamic organisations however provide regular updates for all their staff and spend time explaining performance of the key issues on the strategic agenda and what it means for the organisation.

Enhance feedback mechanisms

A constant stream of information about performance of both individuals and the organisation is the lifeblood of a dynamic organisation. To embed the process of change it is essential that these mechanisms are broadened and improved. There are five areas of particular importance:

- Team Performance: each team should be encouraged to improve both what they deliver and how they work together. I will address the issue of teams later in this chapter.

- Individual Performance: learning is a cycle of taking in information, reflecting and, if appropriate, doing something different. This same cycle applies to the acquisition of skills and knowledge and to changes in behaviour. I have previously talked about the importance of coaching in providing feedback and improving performance. Equally important is how well the individual understands him/herself. I have found that I have improved how I work by better understanding how I think and relate to other people. A number of techniques give valuable insights into the relationship between how people think and the way they operate. At this stage of the change, the processes, and more importantly the intent, of performance management have to be operating across the organisation. A good system of performance management will mix informal coaching with formal feedback. A popular approach is a monthly one-to-one meeting between a member of staff and their manager to discuss any issues. The agenda should include work issues, personal development and other personal issues.

- Leadership: one area of personal performance that is particularly important for dynamic organisations is the activity of leadership. Leadership drives change. It is important therefore that this particular capability is carefully monitored. Leadership and its development are covered in detail in Chapter 11.

- Customer feedback: satisfying customers is central to the purpose of dynamic organisations. Improving the quality of the feedback gathered from customers builds the organisation's understanding of how this key constituency perceives the organisation. This of course has a direct effect on buying intentions and therefore revenue and profitability. (See below: 'Persuading customers – the need for patience'.) Leadership has to ensure that customer data is regularly collected and acted on. They must take a visible stand as customer champions. It is important that impact on the customer is considered as part of all decisions. I recall discussions about necessary redundancies in the sales and service force of one UK business equipment supplier. When discussing how the news should be communicated to customers, one director said that what they thought was unimportant; this was an internal matter and nothing to do with customers. The fact that most of the customers would notice a change of the person dealing with their business seemed to escape him.

His view was that customers were privileged to buy from the company and use their excellent products. The company ceased to exist shortly afterwards.

> **Persuading customers – the need for patience** [39]
>
> Like so much in life, networks of customers do not behave logically. Customers who have previously bought from a supplier often build an affinity with that supplier. Loyalty is not just based on excellent performance of the supplier. Customers have invested their support in that supplier and will therefore seek to justify their decision. If the quality of the experience changes, there is a feeling of frustration and annoyance in the customer. Nowhere is this better illustrated than by the public reaction of a large number of customers to the deterioration of Marks and Spencer Many customers talked about how they felt let down by Marks and Spencer. A reputation so badly damaged takes time to repair. The performance needed to recover that position has to be visible and sustained.
>
> Customers might be unconnected individuals but they do talk to each other. It is well known that a satisfied customer tells, on average, five other people, whereas a dissatisfied customer tells ten. Customers are another example of a complex system. There is a pattern to their behaviour. One of the ways this manifests itself is in their reaction to changes in the quality of the experience with a supplier. The experiences and activities of an individual customer may have little impact on a business. But as more customers have a bad experience, word spreads. The network of people who perceive the supplier as failing grows to a point when all of a sudden the whole network seems to act in concert.
>
>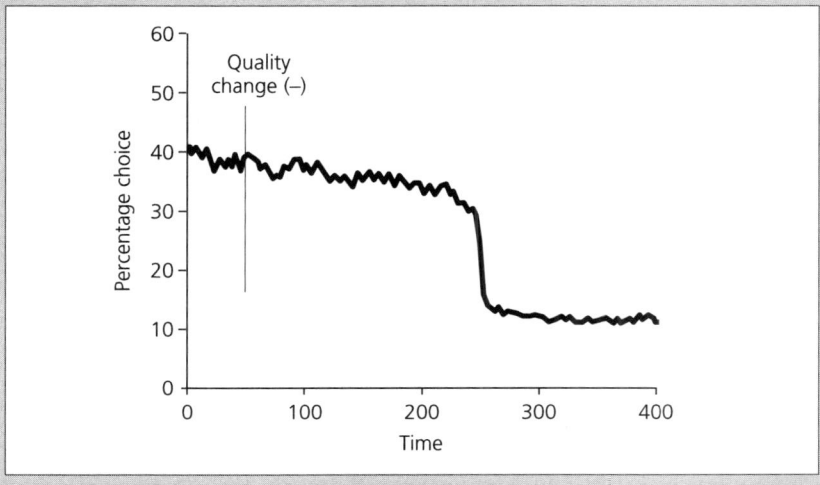
>
> *Figure 10.2* The impact of perceived fall in quality[40]

> This time lag between a change in quality and the impact on the business often causes businesses to misinterpret the reasons for the sudden failure and, consequently, take the wrong action. This is typical of businesses that do not regularly and actively monitor the actions and perceptions of their customers. Another sort of organisation does monitor customers, but management ignores or dismisses the data. Both are examples of the complacency, ignorance and arrogance that still afflict too many organisations.
>
> Turning a situation of this type around takes time for exactly the same reason that there is a delay in the reaction in the first place. The actions of individual customers take time to reach a critical mass and generate the necessary momentum for significant change.
>
> This time lag is why many organisations fail to make change stick. They have correctly diagnosed the problem and put in place solutions that will correct the poor performance. But because results are not instant, they lose their nerve. They change the solution, looking for another strategy that is more effective. They throw out the right solution just at the point where it may be about to produce the desired results. The approach is written off as another failed 'Quick Fix'. Some so-called quick fixes fail because they are just wrong; a knee-jerk reaction that results from a shallow understanding of the organisation and its problems. Other so called 'Quick Fixes' fail not because they are wrong, but because they are not quick. They need time to work; time that is often denied to them.
>
> At times like this, leadership has to be patient and help people to understand the nature of the system they are dealing with. In the longer term, helping people understand the systemic nature of the organisation helps to build an organisation where real understanding drives performance improvement. Once again we are back to helping people understand 'the big picture'. (See also Business Modelling below.)

- Business Performance: Amalgamated Banks of South Africa use encrypted broadcast TV to communicate with their people across South Africa. Every week one member of the Executive Board talks to the whole workforce to tell them what is happening and how the business is performing. Directors will talk about their own area of responsibilities but will always answer questions (phoned in) on any other issue. They have sought and been granted disposition to tell their people the financial results before they are released to the press. Compare that with banks in the West that have detailed schedules of interviews with the financial and general press on the day the results are announced. Staff learns of the results through the press, along with every other member of Jo Public. What does that say to staff about how they are valued? Dynamic organisations share information about business performance frequently and openly. The people are part of the team; they are trusted.

Embedding Change 167

And because they are also trained in business dynamics and basic finance, they can make sense of the figures and what they mean. This policy of openness does not apply just when periodic financial statements are issued. Company performance data is shared as part of the ongoing dialogue about how the business is doing and what can be done to improve performance. It is an essential component of the big picture that people need to understand. And it is a dialogue, not a monologue. Informed people can ask meaningful questions and that requires a management that is confident of its abilities and open to new ideas.

Whilst systems for performance management and team development are necessary, the heart of feedback is simple. At all levels, it is about answering three questions:

- What did we do right/well?
- What de we wrong/badly?
- How can we do better next time?

Central to strengthening the value of feedback is improving the quality of data. Data drives out assumption and doubt. So many decisions are made without reference to data, even when it is available. People prefer their own anecdotal evidence, mistakenly assuming that their experiences are of better quality and validity than other people's. They fail to acknowledge the filtering that is going on in their own minds (see Chapter 4). Dynamic organisations widely share available information to minimise data poor decisions. They measure more, listen more and study more. Above all, they share more. Because they share more, less effort is spent on collecting data that already exists. This also minimises the number of arguments between people about whose version of the truth is the right one.

At the US Army's National Training Centre in the Mojavia Desert, California whole battalions fight mock battles on an enormous scale. Video cameras, satellite tracking and laser weapons guidance systems track every detail of the battle as it unfolds. On completion of the exercise 600 observer/consultants – specially trained soldiers – conduct an 'After Action Review' (AAR) with each team involved in the exercise. At their disposal, the observer/consultants have a detailed picture of the orders and actions of every part and phase of the battle collected by the mass of technology. This makes up ' Ground Truth' – an accurate picture of what really happened. Ground Truth provides the backdrop of the AAR and stops people arguing about what really happened. There is only one version of events – that captured by Ground Truth. As a result, the AAR discussion about performance focuses on how the organisation performed, not about what happened. What orders were given? How well were they carried out? Did people fully understand the objectives? How well did the organisation function? The learning, and the concomitant improvement focuses on organisational performance. The battle experience and the After Action Review are mechanisms at the heart of massive culture change in the US Army.

Not every organisation can find the one billion dollars needed to build a one million-acre training centre. But every organisation can develop something with the same intent. Armies need mock wars to practise. Other organisations have the opportunity to learn from their everyday activities and the data they generate from the marketplace.

I believe data rich organisations are also more intuitive. Intuition is about spotting patterns and inferring something from incomplete patterns. Organisations that have more data can spot patterns earlier. Just look at the two pictures below. Both are extracts of the same pattern but it is much easier to guess what the second one is.

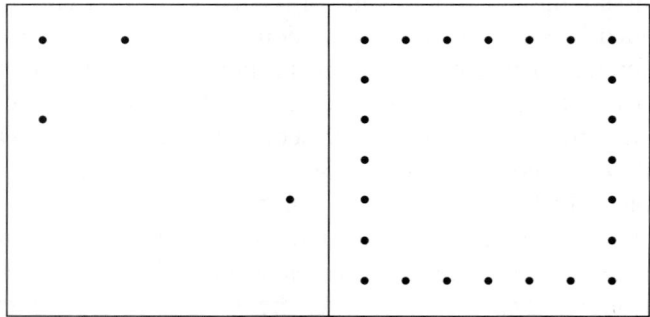

Figure 10.4 Data and intuition

Dynamic organisations spend time sharing information because they know no one person can gather the dots of information that help build up the rich understanding of their operating environment that underpins their ability to act ahead of the competition.

Business modelling

Organisations are complex things, full of interconnections. In dynamic organisations, people understand these interconnections. The diagram below is a simplified version[40] of a generic organisational model that I have used to help people understand how their organisations work. As people begin to understand the relationships between the so-called soft aspects of an organisation and financial results, they are more inclined to put time and money into building organisational capability.

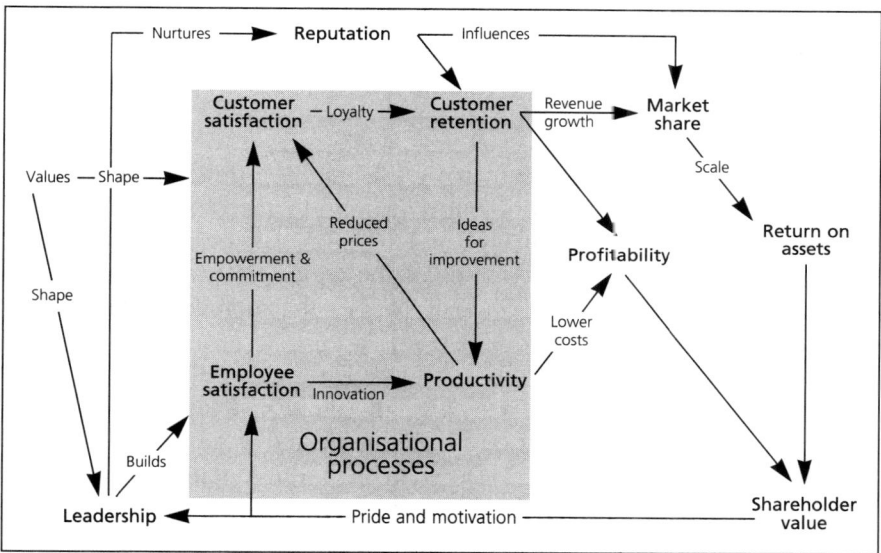

Figure 10.5 The interconnected organisation

There is great value in building a systems model of an organisation and using it to help people understand where they can make a difference. Dynamic organisations build the effectiveness of leadership and organisational processes not because it is worthwhile, but because it is profitable. By building these mechanisms, they know that they are creating the conditions in which a greater number of people can contribute ideas and effort to improve business performance.

As more people begin to initiate improvements, previously the realm of the few, a wider understanding of how the business works is essential. Teaching people the dynamics of the business is a way of getting them to understand how they can most effectively contribute. Formula One racing car drivers know how their cars work. This understanding is essential for them to advise on how to set the car up for each race circuit and conditions. Once people know how the company makes money and the levers through which that can be managed, they are better able to take decisions about changes. In many organisations, few people really understand how their organisations actually function. In dynamic organisations, more people have deeper understanding of organisational and business dynamics. Because they know how the organisation works, they are better equipped to change it. This understanding begins with the big picture – how the organisation as a whole functions. This is centred around purpose, values and the organisation's current strategic priorities.

Developing teams

Dynamic organisations are teams of teams and the development of the processes and capabilities to support teams are therefore crucial. The majority of teams are self-managed and therefore rely on processes rather than people to manage the activities of the team. There are two closely interrelated aspects of development to be considered by all teams: delivering results and working as a team.

Excellent teams have a strong performance focus. All that they do is about performance and improving it. This includes their development. Great teams do not view team development and performance as two separate things. Performance is the vehicle that identifies areas for improvement. It is also the vehicle used to improve the way the team works. Development activities are built around performance issues.

Excellent teams achieve excellence by design. Thought and effort is put into how the team should work, what skills it requires and how success should be measured. Dynamic organisations learn from this process and embed a teaming process across the organisation. Figure 10.6 is one example; a composite version developed from the experiences of a number of organisations.

The process aligns the actions and measurement with the purpose of the team. In dynamic organisations, teams review their performance regularly. How often depends on the tempo of the business. Additionally, teams should be trained to periodically examine how they work as a team and what this means for their performance. The goal is to improve the way the team works together, thus freeing up energy for the real work of the team. As teams mature, the issues tend to shift from weakness in team processes towards issues of personal relationships. All this is carried out with a clear focus on delivering the key results expected of the team.

Some of the issues of team performance arise not because of the effectiveness of the team, but because of the way different teams interact. Alignment of the activities of different teams comes from conversations

Embedding Change

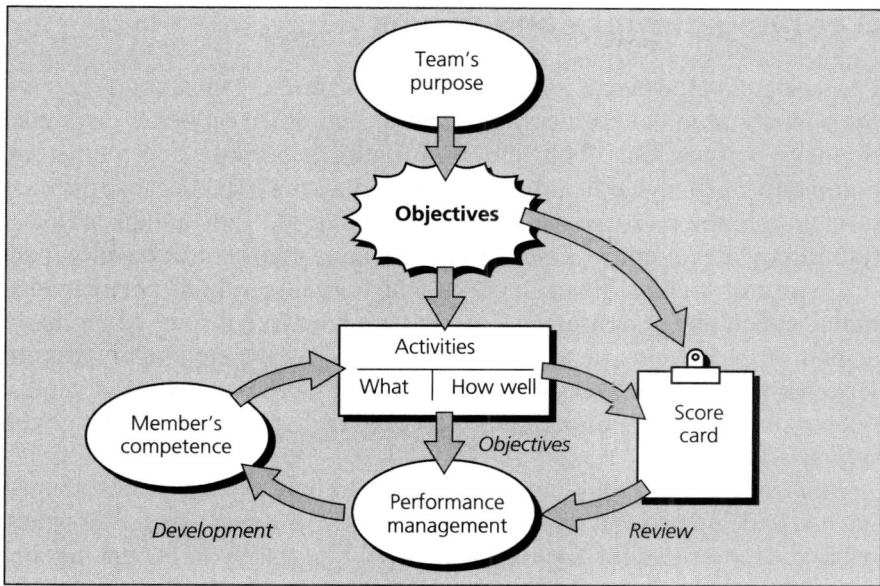

Figure 10.6 Team alignment process

between the different teams, not centrally directed from a politburo. One simple technique is to get the teams together for a day. Each team works together to identify the problems caused by each of the other teams. The 'offending' team is given a brief description of the problem and how it impinges performance. Teams are then asked to work out solutions to the problem and get approval for them from the team that raised the issue initially. It is surprising how many performance issues can be addressed in one day.[41] Dynamic organisations use techniques such as this to ratchet up performance.

Team performance rises as issues are addressed. The initial issues of performance will relate to the processes of work. As the team matures and these issues are addressed, driving performance up will require teams to address issues arising out of relationships between team members. Addressing these requires greater maturity of the individuals. This does not happen by accident. People are trained and coached in how to manage conflict and relationships with colleagues. Central to this is to get people to begin to value the contribution of their colleagues. For so often, organisations have been homes of structured distrust. In the words of one colleague,[41] we need to develop cultures of valuing the contribution of other people; focusing on how people can contribute, not on their shortcomings.

Clarifying purpose and values

Purpose and values are a living part of a dynamic organisation. They are not something that are brought out and dusted down on better days than Sundays. Discussions about the organisation's purpose and values are commonplace in dynamic organisations. Values are lived because they are brought into the discussions of everyday activities. They are discussed at training and development events from induction to executive development programmes. They form part of the organisation's performance management and appraisal systems and are therefore discussed regularly as part of the development of each individual. As the change progresses, leadership must take every opportunity to talk about purpose and values, notably the latter. It is important to talk about what the values mean to the organisation.

You cannot, and should not, train people to hold certain values. People have to understand what those values are and what they mean for how they behave. Understanding comes not by teaching, but by experiencing and discussing the values. Not everyone will agree with the values the company has chosen. Some will choose to leave.

This discussion of the values is all preparation for the time when they will be called upon to guide decisions. Values are not used to make routine decisions: those are guided by policies and operating procedures. Values are called upon when there is no procedure; when the situation is new, not previously encountered. That is why values are increasingly important. Organisations are more and more facing new and unique situations. They need well understood values to guide people.

Of course, none of this is possible unless leadership acts in concert with the values.

11
Values Based Leadership

Values Based Leadership

KEY CONCEPTS

- Leadership is about building an organisation around purpose and values.
- Leadership is a set of activities that help develop a sense of being.
- Leadership can be practised by anyone and is needed across the organisation.
- An understanding of human nature is the foundation stone of leadership.
- Leadership generates followership through conversations and dialogue from which action arises.
- Management, different from leadership, is an essential skill, but is not a substitute for leadership.
- Leadership at different levels of a hierarchy differs only in scope.
- Leadership is a team activity

ACTIVITIES

- Leadership development
  - Leadership through human nature
  - Leadership coaching and mentoring
  - Leadership assessment

A good leader inspires others with confidence in him.
A great leader inspires them with confidence in themselves.
ANON

Great organisations without great leadership are an oxymoron. An organisation can have great values that are clearly visible in the processes that guide the organisation. It can have a superb strategy that is clear and incisive; a sure thing to win huge advantage. But without great leadership, it will have nothing. Values and strategy will remain as ideas and intentions. Of the many companies I have visited and studied, I have never found a great company that does not have great leadership.

Activity not role

Throughout the book, I have used the word leadership rather than leader. This is intentional. Leaders are leaders because of what they do, not who they are or what position they hold. Much has been written about leaders and the world takes notice of a great leader in any field. In the search for greater understanding of leadership, many have gone down the path of identifying great leaders and then looking at their characteristics. People talk about leaders having courage, perseverance and integrity. Debates arise about whether leaders are born or made, how early life shapes their determination and will to succeed. These are often accurate characteristics of some leaders, but they do not explain how people who do not have these characteristics can also succeed as leaders. In my experience there is no one type of person that makes a good leader. Many are charismatic and forceful but others are quiet and considered. Some have presence, others have gravitas. There is no recipe for what makes a good leader because it is not who they are that counts. Whilst great leaders are remembered for who they are, they became recognised for what they did.

This focus on the individual limits the development of leadership capability in several ways. The focus on who, not what, makes it more difficult to train the skills that organisations need more of. Someone cannot be trained to be like someone else. It is difficult to train people to have different characteristics or behaviours. Activities however can be developed. Role centred leadership also reinforces the relationship between position and leadership. We make a big mistake by confusing leadership and senior managers in an organisation. It is true that we expect our senior managers to be leaders, but not all are. Some are just very good managers. Unfortunately, some are not even that. They were lucky (or devious) enough to be in the right place at the right time. Position is a very imperfect guide to leadership ability. People in an organisation want their senior managers to lead them, but they don't always get what they want.

Another problem with confusing role as leadership is that it acts as an invisible barrier to people. Great organisations see leadership as a capability that is needed across the organisation, at all levels. Situational leadership teaches us that different skills are needed to address different situations. Relating leadership to the role someone has in the organisation limits the best application of situational leadership. Role, not suitability is continually reinforced. Breaking the link between leadership as a set of activities that someone performs and the position they hold makes it easier for situational leadership to be developed and applied.

Finally, the focus on the individual rather than the activity precludes us from thinking about leadership as a team activity. Experience with self-managed teams shows that something that was once the domain of an individual role – the manager or supervisor – can become a team based activity. Why not apply the same thinking to leadership. If leadership is a set of activities, a team can carry them out just as well. This does not mean that leadership disappears, rather it becomes a shared activity. Leadership no longer relies on individuals. John Adair said 'No one's perfect but a team can be'. The same is true of leadership. Great leaders do not do everything themselves. Indeed to think that they can, or should, is to fundamentally misunderstand leadership.

Factor	Leadership as role	Leadership as activity
Focus	Who people are	What people do
Locus	Management	Everyone
Selection	Behavioural competence	Results
Involvement	Exclusive	Inclusive
Development	Personal characteristics	Results focused activities

Figure 11.1 Leadership as role and activity

Leadership activities

I have identified five areas of leadership activity that can be practised by anyone in the organisation.

Shaping the future

This is all about helping people identify and build the future.

The core of a dynamic organisation is the vision that describes purpose, values and the way the organisation works. The first job of leadership therefore is the process of synthesising and promoting the organisation's vision to build a deeper understanding of how the organisation will function in the future. I use the word synthesising because leadership in a dynamic organisation involves other people in the formation of the vision. Whilst it may begin with one person, vision is rarely a single person's idea of how the organisation will work in the future but a coherent collection of the ideas of lots of people. Synthesis recognises that visions are distillations of a host of ideas. That is why leaders spend time with a broad constituency of people. Without this network of contacts, access to information and ideas becomes limited and this impairs the ability to synthesise a vision. There is a particular responsibility of senior management to synthesise and promote a vision for the company, which I will address later in this chapter.

Developing vision is one thing but the real work of leadership is promoting a deep understanding of it. There is no point in having a vision that is not understood and therefore cannot be acted on. This has to be done in a way that helps people see themselves as part of that vision. In Chapter 8, I described the vision picture of Cendant Membership Services. They help people to understand their role in the vision by giving them a piece of paper with the vision picture in the centre and then asking them to identify the areas where they directly and indirectly contribute to the vision. I have used this same idea with a couple of developments. I ask people not only to identify where they play into the vision, but also where they see their future and therefore the development they need (see Figure 11.2). With a vision that describes the organisation, it easy for people to see how they can contribute and grow.

People can only effectively participate in this type of exercise if they understand what the vision really means. You cannot tell people what it means for them, they have to work it out for themselves. It is a process of dialogue that generates this understanding and, in turn, that understanding points to actions. This may seem like an overly-subtle and uncertain way of gaining alignment, but it has real power.

Even when the need to give people the opportunity to shape their own ideas is recognised this does not preclude leadership from giving guidance and suggestions. This is most effectively done by asking people questions that force them to think of new options, or providing examples of how

Values Based Leadership 177

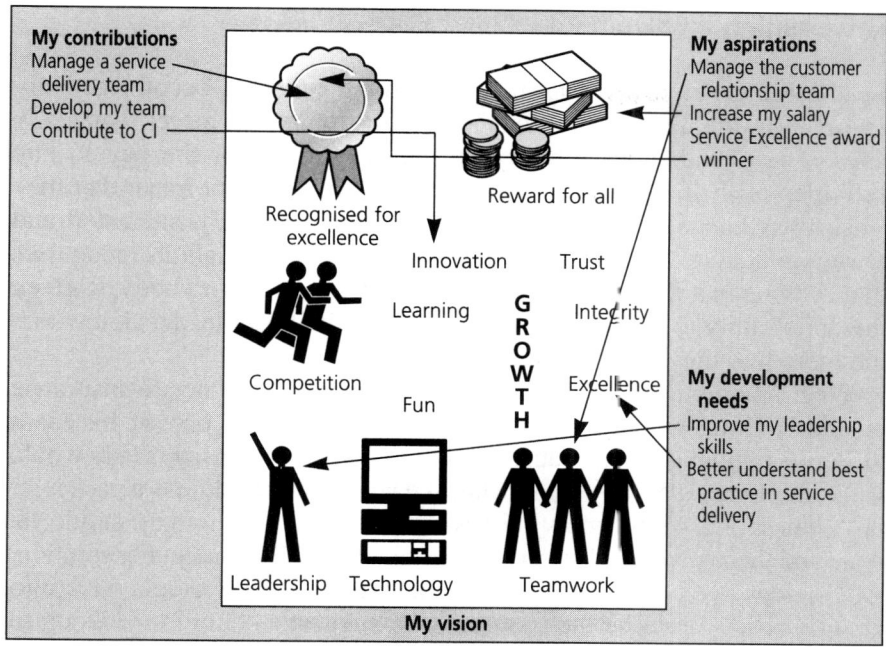

Figure 11.2 Enrolling people into a vision

other people or organisations have tackled similar situations. The art is to get people to stimulate people to generate their own ideas.

Leadership plays an active role in translating the vision into action. Change is not about what people do tomorrow, but what they do differently today. Leadership ensures that people focus on the actions that are needed to bring the vision to life by providing space and encouragement for people to act. To help bring the vision into being, leadership ensures that the resources needed to carry through the changes are available. This may involve some creative accounting and bending of the rules, but if that is what it takes, so be it. Leadership always involves risk.

Visions are not static pictures of the future. They cannot be as the future is always emerging from the actions different people take today. This is why the process of visioning is more important than a vision. To help people address this, leadership keeps people up-to-date with the changing environment; they spend time explaining why the organisation is following a particular path; why certain actions are necessary; what competitors are doing and how they might react to changes. By helping people understand the context, leadership helps to answer the question 'why?'.

Encouraging involvement

Leadership generates commitment by helping people to become actively involved in the design and management of things that affect their daily lives. They hand over authority and responsibility for the day to day activities of their part of the organisation. That does not mean that they wash their hands of the operation. They remain deeply interested and always available to help. Leadership in dynamic organisations recognises that thriving in a changing environment demands that everybody be given the opportunity to contribute to their full potential. But leaders know that the more that they do, the less scope there is for others.

When changing the culture of an underperforming health insurance business, Doug Cowieson once told me the story of one of his team leaders. Following the introduction of self-managed teams, this lady would walk into Doug's office asking what she should do to address a particular problem. Doug would reply by asking her what she thought should be done and then agreed and suggested she go off and implement her solution. After a few weeks of events of this type, the young lady would walk into Doug's office, describe the problem, and suggest a solution for Doug to approve. Doug would talk over the solution and then suggest she go back and implement her solution. After a few weeks of this, the lady stopped coming to see Doug. He saw her in a corridor one day and asked why she had not been to see him lately. She replied that on a few occasions she had set off for his office and half way there realised that he would only tell her to do what she was going to suggest anyway, so why bother asking. In this simple, but supportive way, she had learned what empowerment meant.

The biggest obstacle to involvement is lack of trust. Having spent their working lives in control based organisations that perpetuated the myth that 'management knows best' many managers are uncomfortable in giving up any control. They fear getting the blame if things go wrong. They believe that they are managers because they really do know best. They claim they do not have the time to let people work things out for themselves. These are all classic ways that managers block change. Leadership training is needed to help people work out how to let go. This is essentially about helping people understand the different roles of directing and coaching and providing them with the skills to do more of the latter. Much of this is simply about using questions rather than answers. Questions force people to think for themselves which in turn requires them to better understand their work and how to change it. When John Townsend took over as CEO of a troubled Avis Inc., he called in each of his direct reports and asked them how they could improve their operation and what they needed from him to do it. He then gave them 24 hours to come back with a plan for implementing those improvements. The vast majority were approved immediately. Townsend (the author of *Up the Organisation*) gave people the opportunity to take greater control of their own destiny.

In my experience, people do not want to be involved in every aspect and decision of the organisation. They accept that overall strategy is the domain of the senior managers. They do however believe they can and should be allowed to make a valuable contribution to tactical aspects such as procedures and work methods. People also respond well to being involved in planning on a greater scale. Reflecting the actions of John Townsend, Avis Europe still encourages people to develop and implement their ideas. Much of what the senior leadership team do is about providing the mechanisms and rewards for people to get involved in the planning, management and improvement of their business.

Promoting values

Dynamic organisations have values because they have real meaning for how the business should be run. They have real meaning because they provide guidance and continuity in a world where much is changing. It is vital therefore that leadership reflects those values in the things that they do. Describing the change at IBM, Gerstner recognises the need for personal leadership, 'If the CEO isn't living and preaching the culture and isn't doing it consistently, then it just doesn't happen. This is a sine qua non – this is not a sufficient condition, but a necessary one'. Promoting values is an area where leadership action is very visible.

Values can only be promoted by people who understand what they mean. This requires leaders to spend time thinking about them. One company tried to shortcut this process when it launched its corporate values by issuing a 30 page booklet that described the necessary behaviours required to comply with the values. No one internalised those values because you cannot tell people what they mean. You can help people understand them and reinforce their efforts to implement them by recognition and coaching.

Leadership implements values by using them to shape the organisational processes described in Chapter 8. They continually re-inforce them through their personal actions. Here are a number examples of how leaders have done this:

- At Avis Europe each of their senior managers spends three days each year doing a frontline job in order to better understand how their people and customers experience the organisation. They use this experience to guide their decisions and demonstrate the importance of people and customers.

- To focus employees on the importance of customer service, the chairman of one airline would arrive at terminals at 4:00 in the morning to talk with the check-in personnel, or check the cleanliness under the airline seats. Now middle-level managers do the same thing. Years later the chairman still stops by the terminals at 4:00 in the morning to check on things.

- Approximately every two years a large chemical company holds a Values Conference. The conference involves 150 to 200 leaders spending two and a half days on a variety of issues covering culture, environmental/community concerns, and learning about new segments. They constantly go back and realign the organisation around these values and the results they are looking for.

- Anyone can call TNT Express Parcels (UK) and ask to speak to any member of the management team. The personal assistant will not ask you the purpose of your call. This reinforces the spirit of openness that TNT is trying to encourage.

- A member of the senior leadership of GE attends an open session at every management development programme. They spend time relating GE's values to the issues and objectives of the organisation.

- Mike Jackson, formerly CEO of Birmingham Midshires Building Society, put his home telephone number on every customer satisfaction survey so that customers could contact him if they had a problem.

- Lou Gerstener, a great believer in performance and equitable treatment sacked his brother because he did not fit in with his plans for changing IBM.

- This company's CEO and his staff conduct employee training on customer service. This way the employees recognize that the company is serious about the training. It showed that there is real commitment – that the company means what it says.

The ability to promote values requires a deep understanding of the self. Each person has their own set of values which they bring to work each day. These values guide the behaviour of the individual in the same way that dynamic organisations use values to guide the behaviour of the organisation. Individuals that operate with values that are odds with those promoted by the organisation will struggle to work naturally and consequently will never be truly effective for the organisation. This is why Welch insists that leaders at GE are those that deliver performance and live the organisation's values. The values are important to GE and therefore have to be reflected in the actions of leaders. Equally, people operating against their values find themselves under stress. They are constantly playing a game; keeping up a façade. This consumes energy, which cannot then be put into the real work of the organisation. People have to work at being something they are not.

Getting people to live the organisation's values is a process about helping them internalise values. This is not achieved by some deep psychological process but by focusing on what they do – their activities. What people are – their being – and what they do are two sides of the same coin. The focus on doing is essential. It is possible to teach people how to do something they cannot do, but not how to be something they are not. This focuses on performance and has an impact both on the individual and on the organisation. This focus on what people do also provides new experiences for the individual and will therefore force them to consider the implications. Doing things differently opens up the possibility of the individual thinking of themselves differently. Changing what people do may lead to a change in their being. This is true learning.

Consequently, two essential traits of leadership are openness to feedback and a commitment to their personal development. Leaders will take on challenging assignments because they provide them with new opportunities to learn. They are as interested in their own development as they are of other people's.

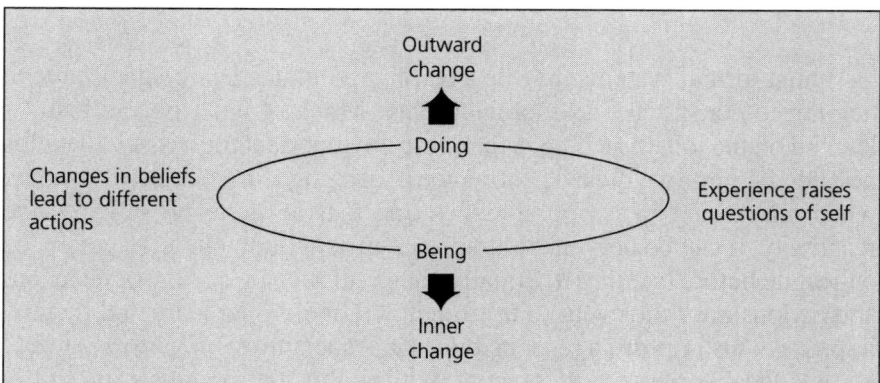

Figure 11.3 The Doing – Being link

Developing people

Getting people to fulfil their potential is central to leadership. It contributes to both the individual and the organisation. The individual grows in confidence and ability, able to take on added responsibilities and develop their career. Instead of staying in some job they know inside out, they are given the opportunity to take on new challenges. Few people perform well when they are bored. Like the brain, people without a challenge vegetate. That is when they become 'human resources'.

The starting point for development is to take an active interest in people and get to know their aspirations. What do they want out of life and work? Formal performance management systems can introduce this into development conversations.

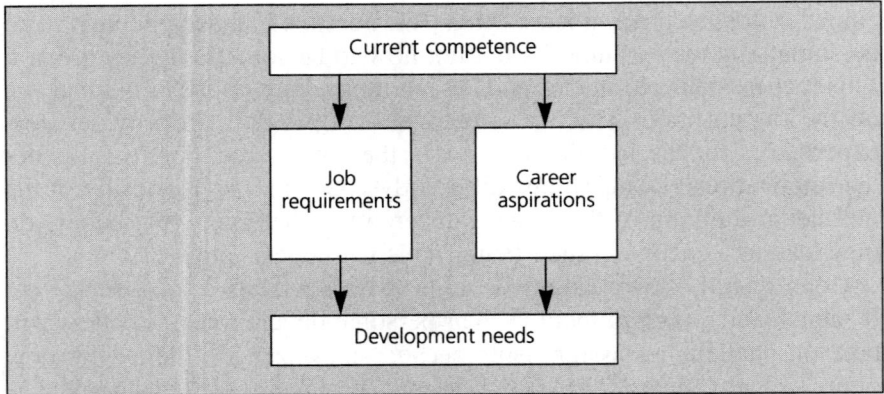

Figure 11.4 Development needs

Whilst formal systems may be a starting point, leadership goes beyond helping to construct a development plan. Much of what people learn is learned on the job. Coaching is therefore an important tool used to develop people and improve their performance. Coaching is particularly powerful when addressing behavioural issues and can be done proactively and reactively. It can be very useful to discuss a situation with an experienced colleague before tackling it. Equally, they will find the review of decisions and actions after the event to try to help the individual learn and thereby improve. This imposes a responsibility on leadership to stay up to date and knowledgeable about best practice both within the organisation and in business and commerce generally.

Central to leadership's coaching role is providing regular feedback to people. They publicly praise their successes and quietly discuss mistakes and failures. The public recognition also serves to illustrate and reinforce the role of values in the organisation. The Spirit of Avis recognition scheme is so named because the awards are given when people have acted in the spirit of Avis' values.

At the heart of leadership's focus on people development is a sincere interest in the development of people. The recognition of the emerging talent war described in Chapter 1 simply bolsters the recognition of the motivational value of development. Dynamic organisations worry less about losing good people. They know that the overall package of salary, challenging work and corporate culture positions them well to attract and retain good people. The fact that continuous development makes their people more employable is seen as an advantage. They recognise that as the world continues to change, people will place greater importance on joining and staying with an organisation that invests in their development. Increasing someone's capability and thus making them more attractive to other organisations may paradoxically be the best strategy for retaining people.

Focusing on performance

The work of leadership is about building a successful organisation. That means an organisation that delivers what is expected of it by customers and thus generates benefits for other stakeholders. My original definition of a dynamic organisation was one that 'profitably wins, satisfies and retains customers better than the competition'. That requires an intense focus on performance. It is why continuous improvement and customer focus are essential capabilities. It is why engaging the creativity and commitment of everyone in the organisation is needed. Jack Welch says that GE leaders are those people who live the values and deliver the results expected. Leadership is about both, not one or the other. Focus on performance is therefore central to the work of leadership. So many discussions about leadership leave out this vital element.

Focus on performance begins with setting clear and challenging objectives. People need to know what is expected of them if they are to perform. Achieving objectives should only be possible if people stretch themselves. Dynamic organisations know that well trained people relish a challenge. The supportive environment provided by leadership makes risk of failure less of an issue. As the Avis values state, the only mistake is not to try something. In dynamic organisations, objectives are not handed down. They are developed by the individuals, or more typically the teams responsible for delivery in discussion with their manager. The individual proposes the target. In my experience, this usually leads to more challenging objectives than when the manager alone sets them. One of the keys to success of dynamic organisations is their ability to identify objectives that avoid tradeoffs. Leadership focuses on the smart objectives that drive up performance in more than area: for example, improve quality and reduce cost, increase productivity and improve employee satisfaction.

Objective setting and the whole performance focus are only possible in an environment where accurate performance is readily available. Data is the foundation of improvement. Leadership ensures that people have access to the information and the opinions they need to carry out their jobs. To this end, leadership ensures that the organisation measures the right things. Scorecards are designed with a focus on the activities and processes that drive performance. These are typically the processes that most impact customer satisfaction and productivity.

An essential part of performance focus and the information rich environment it requires is a strong external perspective. Leadership encourages people to understand the world beyond the boundaries of the organisation, notably the world of customers. Leadership champions the voice of the customer and demonstrates the importance of contact with and understanding of this key constituency. Again, it is leadership by action and not just words.

This performance focus whilst important at all times has special significance early in the change process. It not only provides role models but also is instrumental in generating small successes. Reaching the level of change capability will not be achieved quickly. Early successes build morale and provide opportunities for recognition and reinforcement of the values.

Leadership and the boss

Whenever I talk about leadership as activity I am always asked the same question: 'Does this mean that no one is the boss?'. The answer is definitely no. There will always be a boss. Organisations need hierarchies with people in charge. Alun Cathcart, the Chairman of Avis is no less a boss although Avis has leaders operating at all levels. He has final responsibility for the organisation and its results. If things go wrong, the buck stops at Alun's desk. No CEO has invested more in building organisation wide leadership capability than Jack Welch at GE. That does not make him any less a boss.

Dynamic organisations have bosses. There are fewer of them (more self-managed teams) and they do different things Many people confuse consensus and consultative decision making. Consensus decision making is about seeking a solution to which everyone agrees. It is a weak form of decision making because it often ends up that the solution is the lowest common denominator. Consultative decision making involves people in the decision making process. It is about suggesting a solution, discussing it and other options and then making a decision. One person, perhaps the boss, may make the final decision. But other constituencies have been involved in that decision. Their ideas and concerns have been heard. The idea may have been refined and improved as the dialogue progresses. The people who contribute to that idea are those best equipped to make a useful contribution, and that has often got nothing to do with hierarchy.

Consider the following comments from Lou Gerstner, the man credited with bringing IBM back from the brink of disaster. Talking about calling a meeting to bounce around new ideas he said;

> I know the people I want at that meeting. There will be a dozen or more people who will be upset that they are left out of this meeting. The more vocal will come to my office and say 'My career is over. Why have you done this to me?' That is a problem. I will say to them 'Look I want to have a small meeting. I think that you can make contributions in other areas. I do not think it is critical for you to be at this meeting. You are part of the senior management team, so as the results evolve from this process, you of course will participate in reviewing them to the extent that they impact on your area of business. You will have a say in them. But this is an important brain-storming session and these are the people I want to have at this meeting.'

He went on to say 'We need to have more trust in one another – confidence that our colleagues can lead and do the right thing, so we don't have to attend every meeting and check every detail.'[43] Gerstner insists on having the right people at meetings because he recognises the need to bring the right brains to each situation IBM faces.

Perhaps the most significant difference between leadership at the top of the organisation and elsewhere is the scope of the challenge. The chief executive has responsibility for the performance of the whole organisation. In many organisations, this leads people to excessively reserve powers and decisions to themselves. Senior managers in dynamic organisations also have responsibility across the business but they recognise that responsibility can only be effectively managed by dispersing power and decisions. Bill O'Brien, former President of Hannover Insurance in the US once told me that his job was about 'the orderly dispersal of power'.

Dynamic organisations push more responsibility down the organisation's hierarchy, leaving senior leaders more time to consider issues of a truly strategic nature, including the development of the organisation. In fact in dynamic organisations senior managers spend more time on organisational issues than on issues of business strategy. They work hard at maintaining and developing the key organisational processes and fostering leadership capability. They remain the final arbiters of major decisions but because of the effort they put into organisational design and development, they are faced with fewer decisions that others in the organisation cannot resolve. Above all, chief executives are the chief architects of the culture of their organisations.

12 Case Study

This case study describes a successful approach to change in a business unit operating within a large multi-national information technology and services supplier. It explains how the change was planned and implemented. The issues of changing a business unit within the context of a larger corporation also undergoing change are also addressed.

Whilst the process of change is detailed as accurately as possible, some aspects have been changed to protect commercially sensitive information.

Background

The company is a large, global supplier of IT and related services. The work relates to a business unit serving the UK financial services market. At the time of the work, the company was recovering from large losses. There had been several changes to structure and profitability had been restored.

Relationships with major customers (which included many of the larger financial service providers in the UK) were handled through global account managers. The business unit provided complete IT solutions to these large customers and to a number of smaller companies. The work was undertaken in the late 1990s when the industry was facing two major IT related issues: the advent of the Year 2000 and the rapid growth of the Internet.

The business unit was amongst the most successful in the company and was set on a path of rapid growth. The director set a challenging goal of increasing revenue and profit 10 fold in five years. This stretch goal could only be achieved with substantial change. Incremental thinking would only achieve marginal improvements.

The business unit was very successful, ahead of both its planned revenues and profit. Revenue for the six months ending June 1997 was

64 per cent ahead of budget and profit was 300 per cent of the budget. This was a major achievement and a great tribute to the efforts of the people working in the organisation. There were however signs that this growth was putting strain on the organisation. Decisions were being made in isolation from the impact on the whole of the business. Systems were unable to provide the type of management information needed to run a multi-million pound business effectively. People were often unclear about what was happening in the business unit as a whole. The management team was spending a considerable amount of time and effort on fire-fighting activities and insufficient attention was being paid to the long-term development of the business – a critical activity where technology is a significant driver of change.

Customer satisfaction

The corporate customer satisfaction survey (conducted annually) rated the business unit 3.6 out of 5 overall. A significant proportion of customers were effectively indifferent to the business and its offerings. There was no indication from the figures to indicate why the score was so low. The UK survey covered broad relationship issues and provided little meaningful data at the level of the business unit. There was however some feedback that some customers did not like the fragmented business model established globally. They felt it left them dealing with different parts of the company. A reduction in the number of customers operating with dedicated account managers meant that many customers were not effectively managed.

Staff satisfaction

The latest corporate staff satisfaction survey also highlighted a number of issues. Staff working in the business unit returned the following results

- 44 per cent of staff understand the company's direction
- 59 per cent of staff are satisfied with management
- 40 per cent of staff are satisfied with their personal development within the company
- 35 per cent are actively dissatisfied with their personal development
- 22 per cent are satisfied with the reward and recognition they receive
- 44 per cent are satisfied overall

These figures did not paint a highly positive picture of the management team, particularly the figures for personal development and satisfaction with management. Although staff attrition rate within the business unit was 8 per cent (substantially lower than the industry average of 14 per cent), the survey figures showed a significant level of staff disaffection. One opinion was that high salaries were responsible for keeping staff within the company.

Year 200/EMU

Whilst revenues from the Year 2000 issue would remain strong up to the deadline, they would cease totally very shortly after the New Year 2000, although a peak could be anticipated early in the year 2000. The run up to the millennium would also see a growth in the work of creating systems that are Euro compliant. This too will dry up at a defined time. Recruiting to satisfy this demand was a real challenge. A greater challenge was to secure revenues that will ensure continuing work for staff. This special cause created significant problems for business planners.

Industry restructuring

The financial services industry is changing rapidly. Technology is changing the shape of the industry bringing in new forms of service and significant opportunities to offer new products and services. This is also bringing new players into the market. At the same time, the industry is undergoing significant consolidation. Demutualisation coupled with mergers and acquisitions is reducing the number of players in the building society and insurance markets. Globalisation is also increasing the likelihood of consolidation in both the retail and corporate banking markets. Each of these changes represents both a threat and an opportunity. The business unit needed to build a more deterministic future based on better market research and closer ties with key customers and partners.

Technology change

Whilst new technology creates new opportunities to generate income from customers, it also creates significant problems. The business unit's skills and knowledge have to be continually updated as new ideas and approaches to building solutions are developed. Given the staff's dissatisfaction with personal development expressed in the latest survey, this was a significant challenge for the management team. Evidence was growing in the industry that personal development was a significant factor in choosing an employer. The business unit would also need to be smarter at communicating to customers about the impact new technologies have on the industry and position the company as a leading player in the new technologies. The rapid change in technologies meant that the speed with which new technologies could be assimilated and built into customer solutions was vitally important.

Debt ratio and shareholder value

The company had substantial borrowings – running into billions of dollars and a weak credit rating, making borrowing expensive. On average, the debt attracted interest of about 12 per cent per annum. The corporation's P/E premium is between 10–15 compared to an expected loading of 25–40 for a services company. This disparity had depressed share values and affected its credit rating making the cost of servicing the debt higher than necessary. It was therefore very important to the company to raise profitability and improve the P/E ratio. An important factor is that all the business streams were bearing heavy interest charges caused by WIP. In the UK, this was predicted to grow by $10m in one year alone.

Whilst not responsible for the company's debt, there were actions that could be taken at the business unit level to help the situation. The staff reward system was linked to sales revenues not cash receipts or profit. This meant contract deposits were used to fund early project work rather than billing early in the project. This increased the requirements for working capital and thereby exacerbated the debt situation. It was important that the business unit built projects that delivered benefits across the life of the project and bill accordingly. They had to become as interested in income as they were in sales revenue.

A new structure?

The problems facing the business unit were essentially problems of success not of failure. The organisation was growing and was profitable. The feeling was that the business had outgrown the effectiveness of the organisation. The initial response was to look at changing the organisation structure. The director called for suggestions from the management team.

Case Study 191

The structure operating at the time was essentially a traditional functional organisation with separation of development, delivery and sales responsibilities. Sales directors had no responsibility for delivery of the projects they sold. Nor was there any clear responsibility for customer satisfaction and the absence of effective customer satisfaction data exacerbated the management of customer relationships. Profit responsibility existed only at the level of the business unit.

The directors each submitted their ideas on changing the organisation structure. Some of the suggestions sought to bring profit responsibility closer to the customer, others combined sales and delivery whilst some suggested retaining a functional organisation.

At this time the author was retained to advise on developing the business unit's organisation.

To better understand the issues facing the organisation a benchmark study was carried out using the Novius dynamic organisation model. The overall result for the business unit is shown in Figure 12.1 below.

Further analysis of the detailed findings showed that the issues facing the business unit were more than an inadequate structure. In common with many companies, the organisation had not been developed in pace with the growth of the business. This is a common failing. Growth in revenues and profitability is seen as evidence of a healthy company. Often however that growth outstrips an organisation's ability to manage. As an

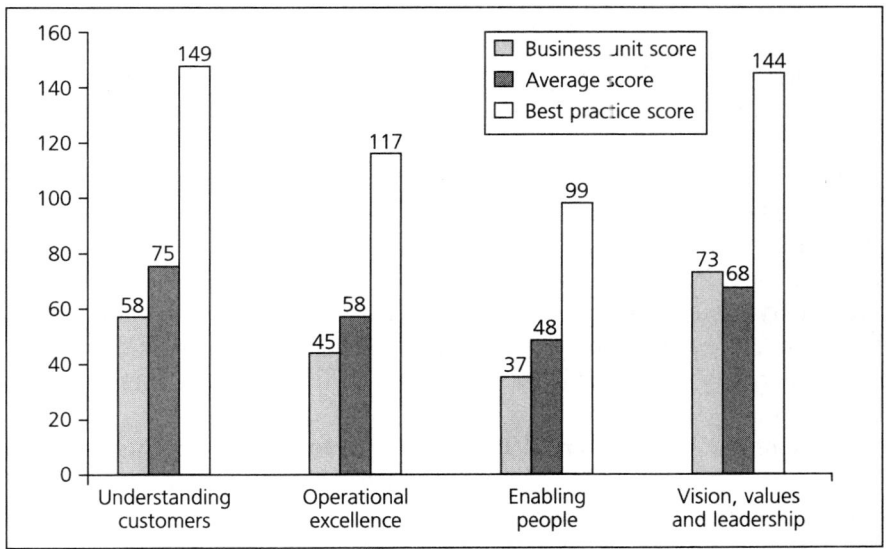

Figure 12.1 Dynamic organisation assessment

organisation grows, it has to develop organisational processes that match the shape and size of the business.

It is against this backdrop that change was initiated.

The change process

There were two linked objectives of the change. The first was to establish a new organisation designed to support the extensive growth being planned. The second, more fundamental objective was to develop the organisation's ability to manage change by embedding the necessary processes and values in the organisation.

The change process followed four broad phases:

- Creating the framework for change, establishing a broad design centred around the organisations values and principles
- Communication through involvement, bringing the whole organisation into the change process
- Implementation through many change projects
- Developing organisational processes to embed change and improvement processes

Change Mapping

To begin the dialogue of change, the management team attended a two-day workshop. The workshop used Change Mapping[44] a visual consulting technique. Change Mapping involves teams of managers developing map style pictures of their organisation. The mapping process is a very effective way of getting management teams to identify the real issues. The pictures allow people to get behind the issue. The act of building a map, considering who the players are, discussing the relationship between them and assessing the strengths and weaknesses of the organisation is a rich exchange of views that management teams seldom have. As a senior manager who had previously used this technique said, 'It sounds childlike, it is childlike but the effect of building those maps catalyses discussion amongst groups'.

The two-day workshop is an intense and highly creative experience that has two main outputs.

The tangible output is a rich set of ideas and design elements that provide the basis for the framework of the organisation. The maps, the discussions and the outputs of the various exercises contain rough drafts of: the principles, the organisation structure, the roles and responsibilities of the elements within the structure, the raw material for constructing a

Case Study

performance scorecard and a description of the organisational processes needed to make the whole thing work together. It is amazing what can be achieved in two days when intelligent people share their ideas and think together about change.

The second output, equally as important, is the shared vision that the workshop begins to build. In many cases, an event of this type is the first time a management team has collectively addressed the issue of how to make their organisation work better. They have had the opportunity to share their concerns, put forward their ideas and be part of the solution. The visual technique forces people to explain their views through a non-threatening, almost play-like vehicle. The pictures and the dialogue spark ideas. The gentle competition and banter between the groups encourages creativity and builds commitment. This result may not be captured in the work but is very real and very powerful.

The workshop began with groups building maps depicting how their existing organisation worked. An example of a change map is shown in Figure 12.2 below.

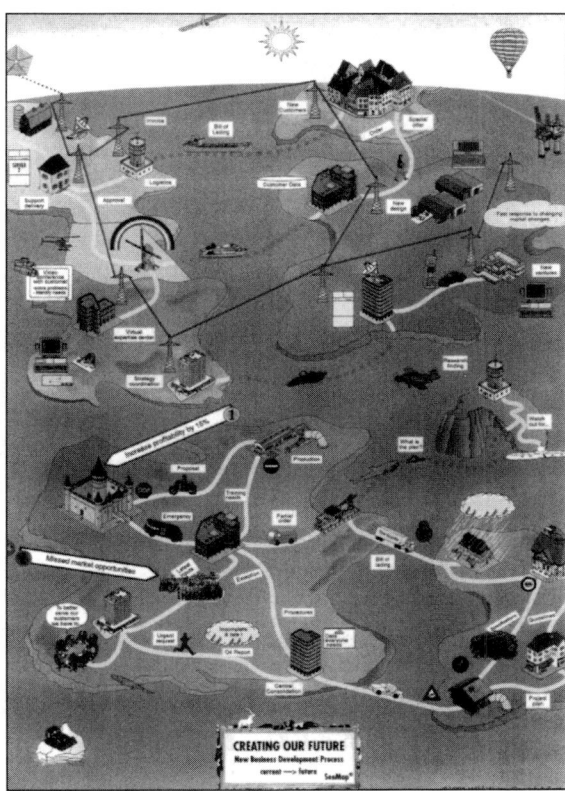

Figure 12.2 Change map[44]

Note: This map is a generic example. The real map cannot be shown for commercial reasons.

The maps of the current organisation highlighted a number of issues.

- The business was fragmented and disconnected. Project teams shared little information or common systems with each other leading to the constant reinvention of the same solution. Sales, marketing and the delivery arms were disconnected. There was no overall view of what was happening with each customer resulting in duplicated and isolated activities.
- Communication, or the lack of it, was also identified as a failing. Managers and their people felt they received too little information about the activities of the business unit and their colleagues.
- Fire fighting was the norm. There was little pre-emptive management of resources and the business. This was exacerbated by a shortage of resources, which meant that managers were usually embroiled in the daily work rather than managing the business.
- The business unit lacked any coherent strategy other than 'grow revenue'. Unfortunately, the sheer abundance of opportunity was leading to an undisciplined search for business. Many real opportunities were not properly pursued leading to the loss of significant business and further confusing the customer.
- Management lacked the information it needed to make effective decisions about the business. Key activities were not being measured. This contributed to the limited sharing of good practice.

These issues were discussed at length. The overwhelming feeling amongst the management team was that whilst the business was growing it was not achieving its real potential. Changing the structure was not enough; something more fundamental was needed.

The workshop went on to explore the way the organisation should operate in the future. As part of this exercise, they considered the principles that the management team wanted to operate throughout the organisation. They were guided to consider principles that were practical and relevant to the business of providing IT solutions. The mapping process lends itself to consider the processes that connect different parts of the structure. The groups were asked to identify and define these processes. Each group therefore produced all the elements of an organisation design – principles, processes and structure.

The four future maps were all different.

One group envisaged the establishment of a few Business Units, each having overall P/L responsibility for a line of business. The units were to have their own delivery and tactical sales and marketing. Some research and development activity was also to be directly managed by the business units. A team of business unit and functional heads would manage the business. This group would agree what business foci to adopt, how research and development funds would be assigned between the business units and what budgets each should achieve. A small central team would support the business units with specialist skills in strategic marketing, HR and finance. Their model called for virtual sales and marketing teams to be set up to deal with individual opportunities. A more effective resource management process would be required. The map also identified the major processes needed to manage the organisation. A central theme of this map was the importance of people and the management effort needed to support them. The group identified the important role of a 'Manager of Record' who is responsible for the development of staff.

A second group based their organisation around the project team – the key unit of delivery. Delivery people would sit in a resource pool from which projects draw the requisite skills. This approach would have great flexibility, but lacked the profit focus of the business unit model. The group also developed a clear differentiation between the role of sales and marketing; the latter responsible for generating leads and the former for closing them. Other key processes identified were technology management, resource management and performance management. To address the problems of sharing best practices, pooling knowledge and communication, the group identified a number of 'knowledge bases' designed to facilitate organisational learning.

The third group focused on an organisation designed to improve customer focus and establish closer links between sales/marketing and delivery. Their model called for virtual sales and marketing teams to be set up to deal with individual opportunities. In their view, the essential requirement was to improve delivery efficiency and capture knowledge for reuse within the organisation. Delivery and development resources would be based in product based business units. Central skills for resource management, technical directorate, finance management and marketing provide support for the business units under the leadership of a business management team.

Participants spent a long time debating the proposed organisation designs identifying the elements from each group that were worth taking forward.

Completing the Framework

The next stage of Change Mapping is to complete the framework. The workshop established the elements of the framework but they needed further development and, importantly, cross-checked to ensure they are compatible. This was done by defining a series of components of the organisation together with a matrix to identify any inter-relationships. This matrix is a useful way of defining the interface requirements of each component and of highlighting any conflicts in the roles and responsibilities of the components.

There were three types of components of this organisation:

Principle: statements of how the organisation will operate.
Structure component: a piece of the organisation structure such as a business unit or a role.
Organisational process: an organisation wide process that integrates the organisation.

Many people confuse structure and process. A training department is structure but learning and development is a process. That process may be under the guardianship of HR but is used by the whole organisation. Because organisational change has been dominated by structure, process is often ignored, or tagged on later. It is more appropriate to identify the organisational processes first and then consider how, if at all, they need to be structured. Structure has been used to conveniently underplay the need for process. By placing more emphasis on organisational processes, structure can be minimised. The organisational process approach recognises the necessity of complexity but uses process, not structure, to address it. Well-designed processes are better able to handle this continuous change than structure.

Principles

The framework that was agreed was built around a set of organisational principles focusing on growth. Whilst financial growth was at the core of the business' intentions it was recognised that it could only be achieved through growth in the capability of key activities. The four areas of the principles reflect the capabilities that the management team believed were vital for the successful growth of the business.

- Client – Improving the understanding of and relationships with the customers the business chooses to serve.
- Project Delivery – Improving the quality and productivity of delivering projects – the organisation's core service to customers.
- People – Improving the skills and motivation of staff within the organisation.

- Management Processes – Improving the effective management of the organisation.

Added to the top-level statements of the principles were short descriptions of the practices indicative of each area. This level of detail was to prove a very effective way of communicating to staff the meaning behind the words. They provide a very clear bridge between intent and action but do not impose detailed operating methods on the organisation. Leaving the space for people to interpret how the principles should be implemented was a key design criteria. Separating responsibility for what and how is essential if the change is to encourage greater involvement. The principles adopted are set out below.

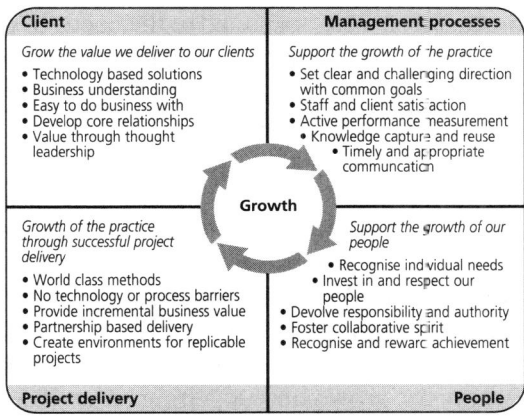

Figure 12.3 Organisational principles

In addition to communicating the intent and style of the planned organisation, the principles form the cornerstone of the design of the framework. Other elements are checked against them to ensure that the actions that will follow are consistent with the principles. One effect of this is to create a dialogue about the relevance of the principles, which is essential if they are to be effective in guiding the design and to remain relevant. Untested values and principles have little real worth.

Organisational Processes

Organisational processes are the glue that binds an organisation together. They are the key component of an organisation design. For each organisational process a purpose, an involvement matrix and measures of success were defined. The management team identified seven organisational processes.

- Manager of Record
- Customer sensing
- Staff recognition
- Understanding people issues
- Managing resources
- Organisational learning
- Internal trading

Some of the processes already existed in some form. Most however were either not practised or were not suited to the needs of the organisation as it was due to operate. For example the annual corporate employee satisfaction survey provided inadequate information about the needs and concerns of the people in the business.

Structure

A structure had to be devised such that it could accommodate a rapidly growing and changing business and support the principle of devolved profit and loss responsibility. The latter was essential if the business was to stay close to customers, grow without getting bureaucratic, and develop the next generation of leaders. There was much discussion about responsibility for P&L during the development of the principles. Devolved profit and loss responsibility was adopted because it removed the bottleneck of decision making from the centre. This had two major effects on the decision about organisation structure:

- A business unit approach was needed. Functionally based organisations do not lend themselves to the devolution of profit as its creation is split across the organisation.

- If business units were to have profit responsibility, they had to have control over the majority of the resources. This meant that any central functions had to be small and focused on supporting the delivery of profit in the business units.

Once the decision to adopt a profit based business unit structure had been made two issues had to be decided:

- What are the initial business units?
- What functions, if any should remain at the centre?

It was decided to adopt a mixed approach of service line and customer business units. Where relationships with major customers existed and involved multiple projects (and were likely to continue) a customer based business unit would be created. The remaining business units would be service line based. A process of customer relationship management was created to deal with customers of importance but not large enough to warrant a corporate account manager. This would co-ordinate the relationship between the practice and the customer, acting as the voice of the customer within the organisation.

In line with the principle of devolved profit responsibility, the centre was kept small. Only three strategic support teams were created:

- Marketing management
- Sales management
- Practice operations

These strategic support teams were charged with supporting the business units – their internal customers. To reinforce the internal customer principle, the business units would measure the performance of the support teams.

One important aspect of the structure was the rules established governing the life of business units. In a fast changing environment, reconfiguring the organisation to reflect the market needs is essential. Establishing rules for the birth, growth and closure of business units would enable the organisation to flex without having to continually change the entire structure.

The rules created were:

- A BU is created at a turnover of £4m with 40 staff
- The optimum size is £10m with 100 staff
- A business unit is a candidate for splitting when it reaches £15m with 150 staff
- Splits will provide for staff incentives and career growth

In addition to providing the ability to expand the organisation as revenues grow and the mix changes, this approach encourages entrepreneurial behaviour. It provides those responsible for delivering the growth a greater management challenge with associated rewards. Small, focused units also have a track record of performing better. This structure and approach brought to life the desire to get closer to customers and provide a challenging environment for staff where success would be rewarded. The structure and its growth rules also place greater emphasis on the organisational processes to integrate the whole practice.

The change team

As the change programme moved off the drawing board, it was important to establish clear roles and responsibilities.

Sponsorship of the project remained with the Director. He was responsible for delivering the change, providing the resources and most importantly, providing leadership. Major decisions were discussed with the Business Management Team and efforts were made to keep them actively involved in the change project.

Beyond this, many people from the business were involved in different aspects of the change programme.

Communicating change through involvement

In large organisations, change and communication have a bad name. Both are seen as something that is handed down from high. One of the concepts underpinning the change programme was that people do not resist change, they resist being changed. People are more sceptical of change when they do not understand and recognise the need for change and have no opportunity to shape the events that will affect their daily working lives. To overcome this scepticism and attempt to build wide-spread commitment to the change, the change was communicated in a way that gave everyone a real opportunity to have a say in both the change itself and to participate in making it happen. This not only removed some of the resistance normally experienced by change leaders but also brought new ideas, resources and energy to make the change happen.

A key part of the change programme was communication. This began immediately after the workshop with a letter to all staff informing them of what had happened and giving them a copy of the draft principles. The letter included a commitment to keep them informed at regular stages of the change. In addition to regular management feedback, a programme of change bulletins was used to keep people informed. However, the main vehicle for change was to be involvement. This was essential to generate the commitment any change needs and recognised the valuable contribution people and their ideas could play in improving the business. More importantly, it also modelled the culture the management team wanted to engender.

The vehicle for communicating the intent and framework of the change was a change exhibition. The exhibition was selected because it provided the opportunity for people to get involved and provide feedback, again reflecting the desired culture. It was also something new and different – important when dealing with staff who have become used to, indeed cynical of, corporate change programmes.

The exhibition comprised a series of large posters, which together built a storyboard of the change programme. In addition, staff attending the exhibition were provided with the opportunity to give feedback at every stage. People were invited to the exhibition through a personalised letter from the Project Sponsor. A brand was developed for the change programme that matched the brand that had been developed for the business. This brand and professional presentation of all materials helped project the intent that this change was an important and mainstream part of the business.

The central, unifying theme throughout the exhibition, and indeed throughout the whole change process, was the organisational principles. Everything was related to them. This showed staff that the principles were not a collection of nice words but a real framework for change that the business was going to live up to. Suggestions for change, the scorecard, working groups and investments were all aligned to and presented in the context of the framework of the four principles. Any successful change has a simple and clear message that is holistic in its scope and consistent in its presentation. The principles also formed a useful framework for staff in the business to question the actions of management and drive their own local improvements. If the actions taken were consistent with these principles then the organisation would achieve a degree of alignment that had previously been difficult to achieve. Alignment around principles or values also provides a degree of flexibility that cannot be achieved through other forms of alignment.

The exhibition was designed to inform and involve. A series of activities facilitated the generation of feedback, ideas and involvement. This began with the invitation letter that included two dummy cheques for £500 each which could be used at the exhibition to spend on the areas they thought change was most needed. This novel idea helped to spark interest in the exhibition and demonstrate to people that they had an opportunity to participate and influence.

An outline of the exhibition is set out on the following page (Figure 12.4).

People who attended the change exhibition provided feedback on the value of the exhibition and their thoughts on the proposed changes. The results (scored out of 5) follow Figure 12.4.

Stage	Key messages	Participant activity
Need for change	• Success to date • The expected growth • Customer and staff satisfaction • Need to build for the future	• Feedback form – what issues do you perceive?
Objectives	• The objectives of the changes • Design approach • Fit with corporate programmes and objectives • The organisational principles	• Ideas Bank – Under the headings of the principles feedback some of the changes you think are needed.
Structure and processes	• The new organisational processes • Proposed structure • Key roles and responsibilities • Measures of success	• Ideas Bank – Under the headings of the principles feedback some of the changes you think are needed.
The change areas	• Changes required listed by organisational principles	• Cheques – Where would you spend money on making changes.
The benefits	• What's in it for you • How the practice benefits	
We need your help	• Change involves everyone • Volunteer to join the project teams	• Volunteering Form – volunteer to join a group working in one of the areas of the principles. • Feedback form – provide feedback on the exhibition.

Figure 12.4 Change exhibition storyboard

Through the exhibition I gained a clear understanding
of the changes proposed   3.9

Following the exhibition I now understand:

    The reasons for the need to change   4.2
    The proposed organisational structure   3.8
    The proposed organisational processes   3.6
    The areas for change   3.9
    The way the changes will be introduced   3.4

Case Study

Over 85 per cent of people in the business attended an exhibition. Of those, 95 per cent thought the changes would improve the business, an overwhelming vote of support for the proposals.

The results of the exhibition in terms of communicating change were very pleasing. More important was the involvement that it generated. One third joined at least one of the working groups set up to design and implement changes within the framework described.

Encouraging Involvement

The areas identified for change addressed all four areas covered by the principles. The precise breakdown of where people wanted to see investment is shown in the chart below.

Volunteers had indicated which of the four areas of principles they wished to work on. The next step was to ensure these people fully understood the overall change programme and had the necessary skills and tools to carry out the work.

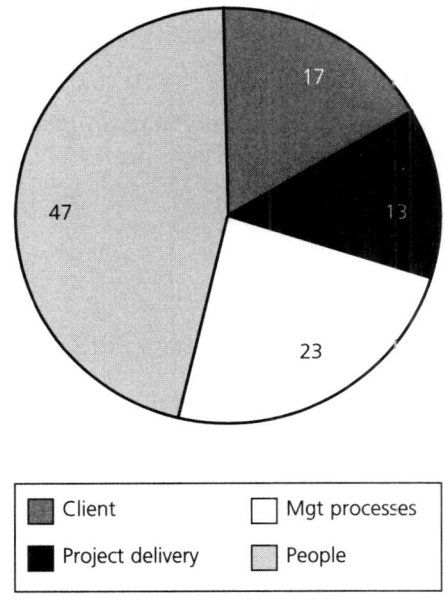

Figure 12.5 Change investments

The Change Workshop

All volunteers attended a one-day change workshop. At the workshop, specific teams were formed and a simple change process introduced. This step itself supported the principle of management processes by introducing a common change process for use across the organisation.

Each change group was given time to develop an outline of the change they wanted to initiate. A template prompted them through the following questions:

- What is the outcome the change will deliver?
- What benefits will accrue?
- What are the major stages of the project?
- Who needs to be involved/consulted?
- What resources are needed?

Within the template, a simple cost benefit model was proposed. (This considered intangible as well as tangible benefits, again related to the principles.)

Each change team had a sponsor drawn from the senior management team. The role of the sponsor, effectively the project team's customer, was:

- Open doors, provide contacts
- Provide an overview of/access to relevant company processes
- Supportive and constructively critical
- Open to new ideas
- Handles first level issue escalation
- Ensure progress
- Ensure relevance to business need

Sponsors were also coached to help them fulfil their duties effectively.

The issues addressed by working groups included:

Client

Financial services internet site
Customer contact database
Reorganisation of the marketing database
Targeted marketing plans on a page
Image awareness/PR campaign
Product portfolio and positioning
Customer satisfaction sensing

Project Delivery

Introduce a technology forum
Develop a common project estimating process
Standard project financial control methodology
Improve equipment and systems access
Develop and implement a best practice software testing method
Build a component repository
Develop a project information base

Management Processes

Executive coaching programme
Standardised management reporting
Monthly business team operational reviews
Who's who contact register for all staff

People

Forward resource planning process
Staff suggestion scheme
'Champions' recognition scheme
Practice recognition awards
Personal Financial Services training course
Improve staff re-assignment process
Microsoft certification training
Technical training review
Career development process
Project HR clinics
Investors in People accreditation

To show staff that their views really counted, the first Change Update included graphs showing the relationship between the priorities that staff had identified at the exhibition and the initiatives launched (Figure 12.6). This close correlation emphasised the value and notice that management placed on the views of staff.

This visible commitment to backing the views of the staff was a very powerful way of gaining further commitment to change and improvement. It showed people that their views counted and were acted on and encouraged them to participate and to initiate other ideas. At the time of the first Change Update there were 36 different initiatives generated from the change programme.

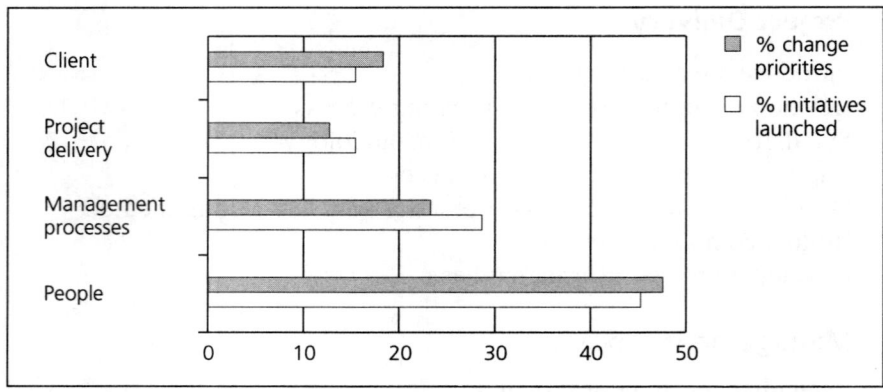

Figure 12.6 Alignment of initiatives and staff priorities

Implementing the new organisation

The new organisation was implemented through a series of projects, some led by the management team, others the result of the working group's activity.

Performance Scorecard

One of the key activities to emphasise the focus of, and embed the changes was the introduction of a new performance management regime. This was also aligned to the principles. The first draft of the scorecard is shown below:

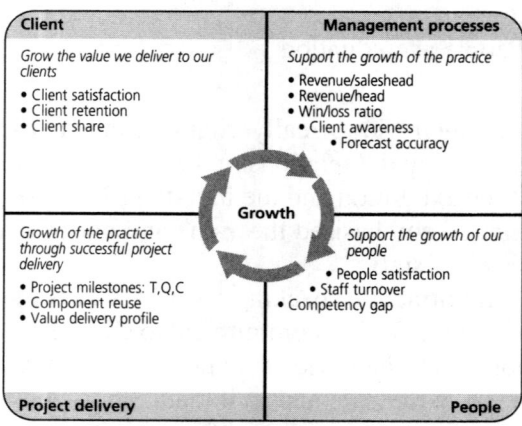

Figure 12.7 Balanced scorecard

New Structure

The new structure was one of the first things to be implemented. Heads of the various business units and support teams were appointed with the majority being drawn from the existing management team. Two appointments were external candidates. The business unit appointments emphasised commercial rather than technical skills. The role was described as that of a general manager with profit and loss responsibility. A number of changes were made to the management team to reflect this. It was however clear that several of the business unit managers needed development to sharpen their business management skills (see below).

Each business unit and support team head had to draw up a business plan. As the change was being implemented mid-year, the financial targets were re-cut to match the new structure. The management team committed to its bosses that the changes would not result in any reduction of the existing revenue and profit targets.

Organisational Learning

The organisational learning process was important if the business was to take better advantage of software previously developed. The return from investment made in developing software could be significantly improved if it could be repeatedly used across numerous projects. Such re-use would also encourage sharing of best practices and thereby improve the productivity of the software development process. Developing and implementing common methods and tools would also enhance organisational learning.

The initial thrust of the organisational learning process was to establish forums where people could share their ideas and developments. A series of Lotus Notes based knowledge bases were established to facilitate this.

People Development

A key part of the whole change programme was to upgrade the skills of the people. This was essential for three reasons:

- People development had been identified as an issue at the beginning of the project a view reinforced by the findings from the corporate employee survey.

- The new business leaders needed to improve their general management and leadership skills
- The constantly changing technology requires new skills to be constantly acquired

Induction

The company had operated an induction programme for several years but it did not explain the purpose and work of this business unit. Given that the plans called for a massive increase in staff it was decided that the business would have its own induction programme. The programme explained the work of the business unit and how it fitted with the rest of company. Based on feedback from staff much more time was spent addressing the factors that make life easier: where to find information and how things like expenses and time recording work. Presentations from the Management Team reinforce the fact that people and induction are important. The new programme has been extremely well received. Several new starters said they had never previously received an induction of this quality.

Manager of Record

A key component of the organisation design was the role of manager of record. This was not a full-time position but a vital role in the management and development of people in a project-based organisation where tasks change regularly. The manager of record, by being divorced from managing the daily tasks of the individual, would provide continuity of support and be better able to focus on the needs of the individual. Managers of record were drawn from the management cadre of the business but there was no assumption that he/she was from the same business unit.

The purpose of the manager of record was simply to develop people. They were to be the primary source of advice and guidance to staff. They would carry out formal and informal appraisals and coach staff to help them achieve their potential and develop their careers. Success was measured by the growth and satisfaction of the individual.

Introducing the Manager of Record role was more than just housekeeping. When carried out correctly it introduced a mechanism into the organisation that focused on people development. By emphasising the importance of this role, development was seeded into the culture. Once established it would be difficult to dislodge it.

Leadership Development

It was clear that the some managers lacked the necessary leadership and business skills. Many were new to profit and loss management and most were unfamiliar with the role of leadership in a modern business. A programme of management development was put in place which included attendance at programmes at Insead and Harvard business schools. The development was focused on the role of a general manager and the work of a leader.

Corporate changes

Shortly after the change programme was started the company appointed a new CEO. The CEO began his own change programme. Whilst there was nothing in the change programme that contradicted the corporate actions, there was concern that staff would be confused by mixed messages. To address this, great efforts were made to position the two changes as complementary. The fit between the corporate and business unit changes were explained and corporate initiatives were included in the business unit's change programme.

The organisation continues to operate with this principles led approach. Whilst they have evolved since their inception, the organisational processes continue. The business continues to grow although it suffered from not adequately investing in a core product.

In a fast changing industry like information technology, the need to build change into the organisation is clear. This case study shows how that change can be kicked off and how real involvement can be generated to drive the change forward. The basic approach set out in this case study has been used successfully with other organisations.

13 Dynamic Organisations

Considering the directions things have been going it is impossible to predict in which direction they'll go next.
ASHLEIGH BRILLIANT

There is a new breed of organisations that are changing the rules. They are building organisations that are far better equipped to cope with the rigours of a continuously changing world. They are better equipped because they are designed to better respond to change. They are not perfect, no organisation is, but they pursue perfection relentlessly. These organisations know there is no one future. Rather than follow specific visions, they build powerful organisations that constantly improve performance in every way. Their vision is to be the best at everything they do.

This pursuit of perfection is achieved by adapting a totally different approach to change. An approach that mirrors how the brain works in its constant search to grow and develop. The whole approach is one of continuous experiments from which learning and results flow. Chris Turner of Xerox Business Systems said: 'I think of our organisation as a dynamic living system, like an environment. You can't treat a natural system like a machine. All you can do is create experiences that disturb a natural system and then it decides how it responds'. This view of organisations as natural, social communities opens up new possibilities for management. A community operates with a set of shared values. They characterise who fits and who doesn't. They define who 'we' are. In a dynamic organisation, values take centre stage. They are the touchstones that guide everything the organisation does. Through leadership and organisational processes they are translated into powerful corporate cultures. Cultures where the organisations and the people in them cycle between assessment and development in an effort to improve both business performance and change capability.

The Primacy of Values

Values are the central driving force at the heart of dynamic organisations. They are the reason these organisations are quick to change and are immensely effective. More than any other mechanisms, values provide the means to solve the paradoxes that organisations struggle with.

Continuity and change

Organisations have to change much more readily if they are to cope with a world that throws new challenges at us all with increasing rapidity. In such an environment, rules are of limited value. In many industries, success is going to those organisations that rewrite the rulebooks. Yet despite the changing world, people want stability and continuity. Change breeds anxiety, as people are unsure of how to act when the rules change. Values solve this paradox. They provide touchstones or beacons that, if not timeless, have an enduring quality. They act as a reference for decisions and actions when rules no longer hold true. They provide a mechanism whereby people can generate new solutions to new problems yet still act in accordance with the best traditions of the organisation. This ability of values to bring together the past and the future provides the continuity that people seek without imposing restrictions on what they can do. The discussion in dynamic organisations is not 'Are we acting in accordance with policies and rules?' but 'Are we acting in accordance with values?'. Rules can only cope with a limited number of situations and in a world that is changing, many of the situations just haven't been imagined, no matter how clever the planners are. Values, however, foster creative solutions. They encourage the conversation that says 'What would our values suggest we do?'. That is a three-way discussion involving the situation, the people involved and the values. The number of possible solutions is only constrained by the ability of the people to dream up ideas. Whereas rules constrain solutions, values catalyse them.

Coherence and freedom to act

An organisation is a collection of people sharing a common purpose. In effective organisations, people work together. Coherent action is what differentiates an organisation from a loose collection of people. We join organisations because they contribute to the sense of belonging we all need. They are capable of actions that are beyond the capacity of any individual, but only if they act in concert; only if they are aligned. In the past we have used structures and orders to align people. But this fails the modern world on a number of counts.

First, structures are slow to change; they are designed to create stability. Orders assume the existence of a superhuman who is capable of seeing the need to act, and determine the correct action. This superhuman is determined by their superior position in a hierarchy. Finally, alignment by structure and order leaves little freedom for individual creativity and action. Freedom to act is essential if ideas are to be developed and tested in the market. The world creates many problems and opportunities. For each one, there are many possible answers and responses. But who knows who in the organisation is the person with the idea that will be the next industry leader? The old approach to suggestion schemes, where ideas were put to a management team that would select the ones to pursue, fails. They are slow and often encumbered by the views of people who lack the vision to spot a winner. The heads of the Swiss watch industry turned down the idea of the quartz watch because it did not fit their thoughts about what a watch was and how it worked. Fred Smith's business schoolteacher mocked the idea of an overnight parcel carrier before he went on to build Federal Express. In dynamic organisations, leaders encourage experimentation and teach people how to build a business. They provide support based on how well the idea works. The greater resources go to those ideas that generate the best performance improvements. Winners emerge.

Values provide the vehicle for alignment that provide coherence and allow for freedom. People that share the same values more readily form and act as a community. They recognise the common good and act for it because they see the benefit of scale and social belonging it provides for them. People who really understand the shared values of the organisation know that they should act for the common good when they are able. Indeed it is a duty of belonging to the organisation. The fish in a shoal that triggers a change in direction does not wait to be told to change. It takes personal action at its own initiative knowing that it is acting for the community.

Dialogue: The Primary Process

Dynamic organisations can be designed and built only when people start thinking in terms of organisation as the design of relationships, not structures. For almost 300 years we have been trying to understand the world of organisations by breaking them into pieces. By so doing we have missed the real picture – the way the different pieces are interconnected. Organisation design is about creating conversations that connect people so that they can work to meet the organisation's purpose. Throughout the book, I have focused on the need to develop organisational processes. Underpinning these processes and the associated leadership style are a set of deeper, human processes.

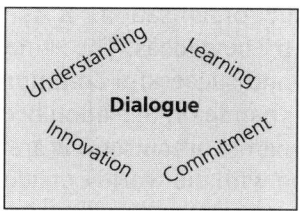

Figure 13.1 Human processes of organisation

These human processes exist whatever the work of the organisation. They are all processes that involve groups of people. At their heart is the simple process of dialogue. Understanding only occurs when people talk to each other about their views of the world. Learning is a process of dialogue between the individual and the people and circumstances surrounding him/her. This interaction builds a greater understanding of the world and causes people to change or reinforce their views of the world. The greater the interactions, the greater the possibility that mental models and reality concur. Innovation is only possible when people cooperate – when they talk to each other. Whilst invention may be the spark of an individual, innovation – the bringing of an idea into being – is a collective act. Commitment too is based on dialogue and is only given when people understand what they are being asked to contribute to. Commitment cannot be demanded, it can only be given.

David Bohm, the modern father of dialogue described it thus.

> In a dialogue, when one person says something, the other person does not in general respond with exactly the same meaning as that seen by the first person. Rather, the meanings are only similar and not identical. Thus when the second person replies, the first person sees the difference between what he meant to say and what the other person understood. On considering this difference, he may be able to see something new, which is relevant to both his own views and to those of the other person. And so it goes, back and forth, with the continual emergence of a new content that is common to both participants.

He goes on to add,

> But of course such communication can lead to the creation of something new only if people are able freely to listen to each other, without prejudice, and without trying to influence each other. Each has to be interested primarily in truth and coherence, so that he is ready to drop his old ideas and intentions and ready to go on to something different when this is called for.[45]

The last sentence of the quotation from Bohm's work is an accurate description of a dynamic organisation. It is interested in truth and coherence and willing to try new ideas. The same basic concept underpins successful organisations and successful communication between people. Dialogue is central to a dynamic organisation because it is a basic process of human interaction. Dynamic organisations are about human interaction of many kinds. Interaction with the world outside to learn about the issues and opportunities that face them. Interaction with other members of the organisations to generate the shared purpose and values that avoid anarchy. This interaction is not just through words, but through actions also. A dynamic organisation communiacts with its environment, using words and deeds to display its intentions and collect feedback.

My whole thesis and a great deal of my experience suggests that organisations can be designed to deal better with change. But to do so requires us to throw away some of our 'accepted wisdom'. The focus of organisation design is bringing values into being. That is a continuing process, not a one-off activity. Organisation design is therefore a continuing activity, not a one off programme of events. The same activities used to build and change an organisation in the first place are required throughout the life of the organisation. Building change capability is a continuous activity. The process of organisational change is therefore the design, not some static vision of where the organisation might be in few years time. What counts in dynamic organisations is not the vision, but the ability to vision, not the teams, but the ability to form teams, not the needs of customers, but the ability to sense customer needs. We need to think of organisation design using verbs, not nouns.

Dynamic organisations can be found in many countries. Global companies like GE and Avis make their cultures work in all parts of the world. There may be slight differences in how the cultures operate, but work they do. National work values will determine how the cultures enact the organisation's values but this is a source of strength to organisations that are willing to learn from any source. The existence of dynamic organisations around the world shows that the things discussed in the book are related to leadership and the development of organisational cultures

Dynamic organisations	Characteristic	Traditional organisations
World's best	*Goal*	Profitable growth
Activity	*Leadership*	Role
Values	*Alignment*	Strategy
World view	*Perspective*	Internal focus
Learning	*Development*	Training
Processes	*Focus*	Outcomes
Broad based performance	*Measures*	Financial
Free access	*Information*	Restricted by hierarchy
Self discipline	*Governance*	Management imposed

Fig. 13.2 Dynamic vs traditional organisations

not on the work values of a particular country. This should not be a surprise. The concepts of organisational design and change discussed here are drawn from the natural world, which works in the same way around the world. Natural laws do not recognise national boundaries. What counts is determined and humanistic leadership.

There is one important trait about dynamic organisations that should be noted, particularly by their competitors. The over-arching goal of these organisations is to be the world's best at everything they do. Their strong external focus means they are constantly looking to identify the new performance leaders and set that standard as their target. This constant improvement makes their performance awesome and everything in their cultures is geared to celebrating that success before recognising that failure is potentially around the next corner. Competitors are going to have to run fast and work hard to catch them, and then run just as fast and hard to keep up with them. Those who are still thinking about getting into the race had better move fast.

The last 100 years of the management of organisations has seen the emphasis shift from the organisation of work, to corporate strategy. The last ten years has seen the emergence of a new understanding that the real work of leaders is to build organisations that can dream up and deliver strategies. I believe the next ten or more years will see the recognition and development of organisation design as the central management responsibility, not a narrow area of expertise.

Appendix Selected Value Statements

I have collected together a series of values statements from leading organisations to show how similar they are. Whilst the words have meaning, what really counts are the actions that reflect them. The similarity of the words is strikingly different to the diverse character of the organisations they are drawn from. This illustrates the creative power that values have. When coupled with different people in different contexts, values can engender significantly different results. It is this characteristic that makes them so powerful for creating alignment in a changing world.

The organisations are presented in alphabetical order.

AES (Energy producer)

Integrity:	the wholeness of the interests of stakeholders' interests, societal needs and ethical concerns.
Fairness:	treating people justly.
Social responsibility:	meeting the needs of society with regard to providing electricity in a safe and cost effective manner.
Fun:	enjoy what we are doing.

Avis Europe (Car rental)

The following statements encapsulate our beliefs and values and our approach to doing business throughout our operating territories.

Business Ethics

We believe it is in the interest of our shareholders, our customers and our employees that we maintain a highly acceptable public image supporting a progressively profitable company. Honesty, integrity and fairness in dealings must and will be absolute and an integral basis of our total philosophy.

Customers

We believe in providing consistently high standards of integrity, service, quality and value in satisfying customer needs. This operating ethos maintains our industry leadership and retains the loyalty and respect of our customers.

Employees

We aim to stimulate duty, mutual loyalty and a sense of pride in working for Avis through employee involvement at all levels, continuous updating of knowledge and skills and attractive and competitive recognition and reward systems. We believe that employees should be actively encouraged to grow and develop their careers with Avis and we always seek to appoint candidates from within the company to fill positions at every level – both nationally and internationally. To this end, we will provide the environment to help employees improve and develop themselves.

Management and Leadership

We believe in local autonomy, working within broad guidelines and underpinned by strong support services at the centre. We are committed to professionalism in leadership; clear direction, clear teamwork development, clear communication, clear and sensibly quick and consistent decisions based on 'what' is right rather than 'who' is right. We recognise that excellence and professionalism amongst Avis management and employees is a key marketing tool. It gives customers confidence and competitors an inferiority complex.

We Try Harder. Ethos

We believe that sustainable competitive advantage comes from out-innovating the competition continuously. In achieving this, we look for continuous improvement in the way we do business. We will never hesitate to adapt to new and more profitable ways of working provided that the integrity and honesty we apply to our business is not compromised. We actively encourage a 'we try harder' and 'can do' mentality and operate a climate of TRUST at all levels. The only mistake is not to try something.

Community

We operate as responsible members of the community and within the laws of the countries within which we do business. We recognise and respect the attitudes, characteristics and customs of local populations.

Environment

We recognise our corporate responsibility to the community at large for public health and safety and environmental protection. We fully comply with all legislation in this respect and actively pursue environmental and safety initiatives on a local, industry wide and global basis.

Suppliers

We ensure integrity and professionalism in all dealings with suppliers and expect the same in return. We seek economic quality and efficiency of service in all supplier relationships and, where possible, 'added value' to the mutual benefit of both. We continuously foster strategic alliances and partnerships with major travel industry organisations who share mutual respect of the customer, a commitment to quality and a desire to maximise and enhance the reputation and value of brand.

Costs

We regard efficiency as central to our whole business philosophy and we continuously search for means to reduce the cost of delivering a better product for the customer.

WE TRY HARDER.

GE (industrial conglomerate)

GE leaders, always with unyielding integrity:

- Have a passion for excellence and hate bureaucracy.
- Are open to ideas from anywhere and committed to Work-Out.
- Live quality and drive cost and speed for competitive advantage.
- Have the self-confidence to involve everyone and behave in a boundaryless fashion.
- Create clear, simple, reality based vision and communicate it to all constituencies.
- Have enormous energy and the ability to energise others.
- Stretch, set aggressive goals, and reward progress, yet understand accountability and commitment.
- See change as an opportunity not a threat.
- Have global brains and build diverse and global teams.

Hewlett Packard (IT)

We have trust and respect for individuals

We approach each situation with the belief that people want to do a good job and will do so, given the proper tools and support. We attract highly capable, diverse, innovative people and recognise their efforts and contributions to the company. HP people contribute enthusiastically and share in the success that they make possible.

We focus on a high level of achievement and contribution

Our customers expect HP products and services to be of the highest quality and to provide lasting value. To achieve this, all HP people, especially managers, must be leaders who generate enthusiasm and respond with extra effort to meet customer needs. Techniques and management practices which are effective today may be outdated in the future. For us to remain at the forefront in all our activities, people should always be looking for new and better ways to do their work.

We conduct our business with uncompromising integrity

We expect HP people to be open and honest in their dealings to earn the trust and loyalty of others. People at every level are expected to adhere to the highest standards of business ethics and must understand that anything less is unacceptable. As a practical matter, ethical conduct cannot be assured by written HP policies and codes; it must be an integral part of the organisation, a deeply ingrained tradition that is passed from one generation to another.

We achieve our common objectives through teamwork

We recognise that it is only through effective cooperation within and among organisations that we can achieve our goals. Our commitment is to work as a worldwide team to fulfil the expectations of our customers, shareholders and others who depend on us. The benefits and obligations of doing business are shared among all HP people.

We encourage flexibility and innovation

We create an inclusive work environment which supports the diversity of our people and stimulates innovation. We strive for overall objectives which are clearly stated and agreed upon, and allow people flexibility in working toward goals in ways that they help determine are best for the organisation. HP people should personally accept responsibility and be encouraged to upgrade their skills and capabilities through ongoing training and development. This is especially important in a technical business where the rate of progress is rapid and people are expected to adapt to change.

Nordstrom (department store chain)

The Nordstrom mission statement expresses the values that support the organisation's first principle – 'At all times use your best judgement'.

> Our goals remain the same. We want to be the best. Our customers want to shop with the best. Our employees want to work for the best. Our communities need us to be at our best. And our shareowners want to own part of the best. Being the best at what we do has always been Nordstrom's goal and always will be. How we become the best is what we must all be willing to question, and moreover, be willing to change.
>
> BILL NORDSTROM

PHH (car fleet services)

The principles that guide our day to day behaviour.

- Moral integrity.
- Openness and trust.
- Dedication to quality.
- Respect for the individual.
- Team spirit.
- Efficiency.
- Initiative.
- Adaptability.

Pizza Hut (restaurant chain)

Be the leader ... Act like the leader

How we work together:

- Customer focus.
- Belief in people.
- Recognition.
- Coaching and support.
- Accountability.
- Excellence.
- Positive energy.
- Teamwork.
- Integrity and openness.
- Fun and enthusiasm.

Proctor & Gamble (consumer goods)

P&G People

We attract and recruit the finest people in the world. we build our organisation from within, promoting and rewarding people without regard to any difference unrelated to performance. We act on the conviction that the men and women of Procter & Gamble will always be our most important asset.

Leadership

We are all leaders in our area of responsibility, with a deep commitment to deliver leadership results. We have a clear vision of where we are going. We focus our resources to achieve leadership objectives and strategies. We develop the capability to deliver our strategies and eliminate organisational barriers.

Ownership

We accept personal accountability to meet the business needs, improve our systems and help others improve their effectiveness. We all act like owners, treating the company's assets as our own and behaving with the company's long-term success in mind.

Integrity

We always try to do the right thing. We are honest and straightforward with each other. We operate within the letter and spirit of the law. We uphold the values and principles of P&G in every action and decision. We are data-based and intellectually honest in advocating proposals, including recognising risks.

Passion for Winning

We are determined to be the best at what matters most. We have a healthy dissatisfaction with the status quo. We have a compelling desire to improve and to win in the marketplace.

Trust

We respect our P&G colleagues, customers, consumers and treat them as we want to be treated. We have confidence in each other's capabilities and intentions. We believe that people work best when there is a foundation of trust.

Shell (oil producer and retailer)

- Belief in people.
- Trustworthiness.
- Excellence.
- Innovation.
- A sense of urgency.

Xerox (document products and services)

Since our inception, we have operated under the guidance of six core values:

- We succeed through satisfied customers.
- We aspire to deliver quality and excellence in all that we do.
- We require premium return on our assets.
- We use technology to deliver market leadership.
- We value our employees.
- We behave responsibly as a corporate citizen.

Notes

1. Source: Royal Institute of International Affairs – Chatham House Forum Web Site.
2. OECD Scientific, Technology and Industry Scoreboard 1999.
3. Figures taken from *Building a Knowledge Economy: Competitiveness White Paper 1998*. UK Department of Trade and Industry.
4. OECD ibid.
5. DTI ibid.
6. For more detail on Avis Europe see the case study included in *Dynamic Organisations*.
7. *What Leaders Really Do*. Harvard Business Review, May–June 1990.
8. Gore's complete set of values are:
   - Fairness: A dedication to maintaining it.
   - Commitment: If you make one, you keep it.
   - Freedom: The company allows individuals the freedom to grow beyond what they are doing, and they are expected to use it.
   - Water Line: A hole above a ship's water line won't sink it, but one below it will. Certain decisions, say like building a new plant demand consultation and agreement. Others, like launching a new product don't. This value substitutes for budgets.

   Quoted in *Fortune*, 21 February 1994.
9. Attributed to Kelly by Tom Peters at the Customer Service Management Conference, December 1998. Reported in *Customer Service Management*, March 1998.
10. The story is about a real company. The author lived through six years with the company during its decline.

11 Richard Schickel, 'The Disney Version' quoted in *Built to Last*, Collins and Porras, Century Business Books.
12 I picked this information up from Peter Pring, then a Director for 3M. Peter was a speaker at a conference I chaired.
13 This story is also told in Arie's book, *The Living Company*, Nichloas Brearley Publishing Ltd.
14 *Losing my Virginity*, Richard Branson, Virgin Publishing Ltd.
15 *The Web of Life*, Fritjof Capra, Harper Collins.
16 'Managers must take the lead' by Nicolas King. *Computing*, 8 April 1999.
17 Olaf Odlind shared the data at a conference in London in 1997.
18 Collins and Porras, ibid.
19 *Dynamic Organisations: The Challenge of Change*, David Jackson, Macmillan 1997. ISBN 0 333 66645 3.
20 *Corporate Culture and Performance*, John Kotter and James Heskett, Free Press
21 'How Hardwired is Human Behaviour', Nigel Nicholson, in *Harvard Business Review* July–August 1998.
22 Taken from notes of a presentation given by Ron Labonte MA Cepid PhD of Communitas Consulting, Canada. I am grateful to Gill Clegg of Bromley Borough Council Environmental Health & Trading Standards unit who provided this insight.
23 Helen Wilkinson. Excerpt from *The Guardian*.
24 This information is extracted from GE Learning Solution's web site – http://www.gelearningsolutions.com
25 In *Dynamic Organisations* I included a self-assessment based on the model described in Chapter 2. This model has been successfully adopted by many UK organisations through the Management Today Service Excellence Awards sponsored and organised by Unisys. The business excellence model developed by the European Foundation for Quality Management (EFQM) and the US Balridge Award are also widely used across Europe and the US respectively as benchmarks. The value of these schemes is not the scores, or for the winners the award itself, but in the learning the assessment process generates. This includes the opportunity to learn from other entrants to the schemes.
26 The DOCSABOX culture toolkit is based on the original research

of Professor Geert Hofstede. Culture profiles (including the ability to benchmark) are developed by examining six characteristics of the organisation.

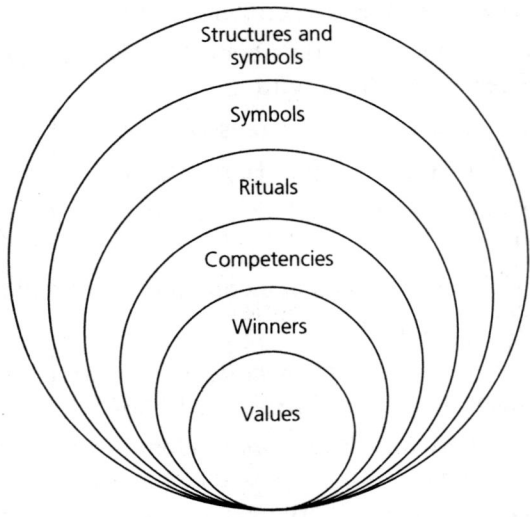

The toolkit can be used as part of an initial diagnosis, to measure the progress of change and can be used by individual teams to help resolve issues and improve performance. Further information can be found at the DOCSA web site: www.docsa.com

27 For more information about the Change Capability Assessment contact Novius Ltd via their web site: www.davjac.demon.co.uk
28 Arie de Geus, ibid
29 'An interview with Jacques Nasser', by Suzy Westlaufer, *Harvard Business Review*, March/April 1999.
30 David Jackson, ibid
31 *Control your own destiny or someone else will*, Tichy & Sherman, Doubleday 1993.
32 Tichy & Sherman, ibid.
33 As quoted in TNT UK's winning submission for the European Quality Prize 1998.
34 Source: Investing in Labor Force Learning Can Boost Bottom Line. American Society for Training and Development, 1998.
35 Business Line 22 December 1998.

36 *Leading Change*, John Kotter, Harvard Business School Press, 1996.
37 I am grateful to Professor Gordon Brown, Professor of Psychology at the University of Warwick for bringing this to my attention.
38 Tichy & Sherman, ibid.
39 This is based on material I picked up from Professor Gordon Brown, Professor of Psychology at Warwick University.

  The graph shows the probability of customers choosing a particular supplier. The effect of the negative change of quality that occurs when T=50 does not have a marked effect on the supplier for some time.
40 The complete model has 30 entities and over 120 relationships. Organisations can adapt the model to their company and then assess the quality of the different parts. Through 'what-if' exercises, they can explore the possible impact of different changes. The tool is not used as a predictor of financial impact but as a way of understanding the possible impact of different change strategies.
41 This technique was first described to me by Richard Pascale who called it the Valentine Day exercise.
42 Charles Savage, author of *Fifth Generation Management*, Digital Press. 1990.
43 *Saving Big Blue*, Robert Slater McGraw Hill 1999.
44 Change Mapping is a proprietary technique of Novius Ltd. It is based on the See Map tool created by Wild Water Ltd.
45 *On Dialogue*, David Bohm, edited by Lee Nichol, Routledge, 1996.

Index

3M 52, 120
Adlington, Anne 35
AES 216
Amalgamated Banks of South Africa 166
American Productivity and Quality Center 151
American Society for Training and Development 132
appraisal systems 132
Atkinson, Chris 36, 134
autpoiesis 60
Avis Europe 20, 22, 32, 85
  beliefs 24
  culture 41
  empowerment 27
  implementing values 180
  leadership 183
  promotion from within 37
  recognition 134
  recognition 183
  statement of beliefs and values 217–18
  strategic appointments 67
  values 66, 120

Bell, Tom 129
benchmarking 33, 153
big picture 68
Birmingham Midshires Building Society 19, 36, 134
  implementing values 180
  blocking behaviour 158
Bohm, David 213–14
bounded change
  navigating 84–86
  process of 87–92
  useful tools for 89, 90, 91, 92
Branson, Richard 57
budgets 138
business
  modelling 168–170

Capra, Fritjof 59
Cathcart, Alun 32, 184
Cendant Membership Services 37, 126, 176
change
  agents 111
  and involvement 200–206
  bounded 83–92
  causes of 108
  creating a framework for 112–45, 195–6
  culture 49
  curriculum 151–2
  dynamic 83, 92–7
  exhibitions 149–50, 201–3

mapping 192
  need for 105
  preparing for 104–11
  processes 136, 192
  projects 153–4
  resistance to 76
  team 109–11
  workshops 110, 204–5
coaching 152, 182
  and resistance 159
Colyer, Lesley 27
communiaction 146
community 77
competencies
  dynamic organisation 16
continuous improvement 85, 101
  and information 153
control
  and creativity 156
  need for 76
Cowieson, Doug 178
culture
  and financial performance 21
  changing 49
  complexity of 79
  of dynamic organisations 210
  profiling 106
  understanding 93–4
curiosity 71, 100
customers
  awareness of 99
  behaviour 165–6
  feedback 164
  information about 31
  listening to 20
  preception of quality 18
  understanding 17

data
  and intuition 168
de Geus, Arie 37, 55, 115

Deming, Edward 95
dialogue 212–14
  and shared vision 156
  and values 42, 67
Disney, Walt 49
DOCSA 106
doing–being link 181
dynamic change 92–7
dynamic mechanisms 100–101
dynamic organisation 210–15
  assessment 191
  characteristics of 98–101
  characteristics of 215
  core competencies 16
  fit of capabilities 40
  roadmap 101–102
economic
  eras 5–7
  growth 3, 9
  shifts 5
employment changes 12
Epstein, Brian 161
evolution
  of brain 53
excellence 39
external focus 99

feedback
  mechanisms 163–7
Firefly Communications 32
First Direct 32, 36
fish
  shoals of 57
Ford 123
fractals 58

GE
  implementing values 180
  leadership 184–5
  management development 152
  performance reviews 129

six sigma 85–6, 121, 131, 153
statement of values 219
values 121, 131
workout 85, 153
Gerstner, Lou 109, 179, 180, 185
Glass, David 34
Gore, Bill 29

Halifax plc 34
Handy, Charles 70
Heskett, James 21, 65
Hewlett Packard 120
statement of values 219–220
hoshin kanri 125
human nature 62–79

IBM 185
industrial era 7
ineraction, need for 77
information
access to 153–4
age 7
and curiosity 71
sharing 33
involvement 178–9
issues management 135

Jackson, Mike 109

Kelly, Kevin 43
knowledge
economy 5, 9
industries 10
Kotter, John 21, 28, 65

Langler, Gerald 28
leadership 13
activities 175–84
activity, not role 94, 174–5
and management 29
and people 42

and power 140
and the CEO 29
and values 61
by teaching 123
extending capability 94–5
feedback 164
implementing values 179
need for 162
staying in touch 136
values based 173–86
learning 139
ability 78–9
and communicating vision 150–53
at cellular level 50
in animals 55
living systems
criteria of 59
Lloyds/TSB 31

Management Today/Unisys
Service Excellence Awards
30, 39, 154
managing
connections 154
Matra BAe 34
meaning, need for 69
measurement
of performance 127
Mitsubishi Heavy Industries 126

Nasser, Jacques 123
National Work/Life Forum 70
Nordstorm 220
Nordstrom, Bill 121

O'Brien, Bill 186
Odlind, Olaf 62
OECD 9, 11
operational planning 125–6

Index

organisation
  and nature 60
  building a winning 43
  design 13–15, 61
  designed for change 43
  redundancy at 3M 52
organisational
  learning 207
  development 161
  processes 61, 95–7, 106, 197
  structure 44, 198
passion 35-38
people
  centred 99
  development 207–8
  development of 182–3
  importance of 6, 14, 62
  processes 130
performance
  and leadership 183–4
  focus on 183–4
  management 131
  measurement 127

Petronius, Gaius 48
PHH 33, 36, 37
principles 221
Pizza Hut 92, 134
  values 221
power
  spread of 158
problem solving skills 129
process
  excellence 21
  of thinking 52
Procter & Gamble 121
  values 221–2
product
  excellence 21
purpose
  and meaning 69

and values 117
developing shared 117
example of 23

recognition 26, 36, 133–5
  at TNT Express Parcels 72–6
  need for 72
recruitment 131
resistance
  dealing with 158–9
  in processes and people 157
  to change 76, 157–9
rewards 133
risk
  aversion to 77

scorecards 128, 206
service based R&D 11
Shell
  statement of values 223
strategic agenda 137
Svenska Handelsbank 138

team
  alignment 171
  change 109
  development 170–1
  feedback 164
  top management 110
technology
  rate of adoption of 8
termite nests 56
thinking 52
TNT Express Parcels 34
  and recognition 36, 72–6, 134
  implementing values 180
  league tables 153
  perfect transaction 37, 41
  values 66
Townsend, John 178

training
  value of 132
Triple A Animal Hotel and Care
  Centre 31, 32, 33, 35, 132
trust 178, 185
Turner, Adair 25
Turner, Chris 210

understanding
  customers 17
  outside world 136–7
Unipart 85
Unisys/Management Today
  Service Excellence Awards
  30, 39, 154
unlearning 50
US Army
  After Action Review 167–8
  and vision 116

values
  and dialogue 67
  and fractals 58
  and learning 53
  and the thinking process 63–5
  as a bais of fit 41
  at PHH 36

developing shared 117
examples of 216–23
personal 65
primacy of 97, 211–12
programming organisations
  with 122
promoting
  179–81
Virgin Group 57
vision
  and resistance 159
  as strategy vs aspiration 115
  Cendant Membership Services
    113–14
  communicating 140–5, 147–9
  shaping the future 176–8
  what is 113–16

Walker, Claire 35
Wal-Mart 34
Welch, Jack 109, 129, 152, 185
Wilkinson, Helen 70
Wilson, Professor Allan 55

Xerox 62, 118
  core values 223